1998

CONTEMPORARY ETHICAL ISSUES

# International
# Ethics

A Reference Handbook

CONTEMPORARY ETHICAL ISSUES

# International
# Ethics

## A Reference Handbook

Gerard Elfstrom

**ABC-CLIO**

Santa Barbara, California
Denver, Colorado
Oxford, England

**Library of Congress Cataloging-in-Publication Data**

Elfstrom, Gerard, 1945–
    International ethics : a reference handbook / Gerard Elfstrom.
        p.   cm.
    Includes bibliographical references and index.
    ISBN 0-87436-864-2 (alk. paper)
    1. International relations. I. Title.
JZ1242.E43     1998
327—dc21                                                97-41076
                                                             CIP

02 01 00 99 98  10 9 8 7 6 5 4 3 2 1

ABC-CLIO, Inc.
130 Cremona Drive, P.O. Box 1911
Santa Barbara, California 93116-1911

This book is printed on acid-free paper ☺ ·
Manufactured in the United States of America

# CONTEMPORARY ETHICAL ISSUES

# Contents

# CONTEMPORARY ETHICAL ISSUES

## Preface

Anthropologists tell us that human beings have existed for some 4 million years and that for the great majority of that period we have lived in small groups, ranging in size from four or five to several dozen individuals. As a species, therefore, we have a long history of dealing with others whom we know intimately, whose pain we can see, and whose joy we can share directly. However, for most of human history, our small groups have had relatively little to do with members of other groups, with the exceptions of trade or war. Hence, we humans have customarily paid little attention to those outside our immediate group. Outsiders were often considered barely human, or not human at all, and their welfare was of little concern. In consequence, human moral thinking developed to guide relations with individuals with whom we have firm personal bonds and whose welfare or anguish we experience directly.

The circumstances of human life have been changing for the past several thousand years, but the pace of change has accelerated at an enormous rate during the past half century. Advances in communication and transportation and the growth of an international economy are important facets of this process of globalization. One greatly significant result is that human beings are forming dense networks of relationships with others in all parts of the world. People are now dependent on others in far corners of the world in ways that would have been inconceivable at the beginning of this century. We never see many of these people, and we are unaware of the existence of many thousands of others, but their actions affect our lives in many ways, and our actions affect them in turn. We are also able to affect the lives of people with whom we have no ties of commerce or friendship. For example, a century ago it would have been nearly impossible for people in the United States to become aware of the suffering of a child in Nepal, and vastly more difficult to do anything about it. Now, we are able to get information about suffering elsewhere, and we are also able to take measures to ease that suffering.

One result of the changes prompted by globalization is that we are facing new issues of ethical responsibility. The common ethical beliefs we carry are based on the assumption that we will have face-to-face contact with those human beings who are morally important to us. Now we must ask whether we have moral obligations to those whom we may never see in person and whose personal ties with us are only fleeting. My aims in writing this book are to introduce readers to these new issues, explain how they have developed, and provide information on some of the people and organizations who have made an important impact in the ethics of international relations.

This book contains a chronology of the major events in the development of international ethics, biographical sketches of major figures in the area, brief discussions of its major topics, lists of useful resource materials in both print and nonprint formats, and a roster of the major organizations active in the area. *International Ethics* can be used in several ways. Some may wish to gain an overview of the subject matter by reading the introduction, then move on to the special topics discussions and lists of resources to gain additional information about particular issues. Others may wish to employ the book in a less structured way, glancing through the various sections and lingering over people or topics as chance or fancy suggest. Others may wish to begin with the biographical sketches, pausing at figures of interest, such as Fred Cuny or Jean-Henri Dunant, then passing along to the organizations or to the special topics sections to discover more about the issues that these individuals addressed. Some, though, may wish to begin by examining the organizations, using postal, web site, or e-mail addresses to discover more about them, then returning to the lists of resources or the special topics treatments to gain additional insights. Yet other readers may approach this book in more traditional fashion, read it through to the lists of resources, then rove through its lists of books, videos, or organizations, occasionally lingering at those that capture their imagination.

# CONTEMPORARY ETHICAL ISSUES

## Chapter 1:
## Introduction

The topics examined in this handbook fall into several main categories. The first includes problems that are of global concern because they affect people the world over; therefore, effective responses to them must be global as well. Pollution control, disease prevention, international crime, and population control all fall into this category. The second broad category includes questions relating to national sovereignty, such as whether immigration and emigration should be closely controlled, whether intervention in the affairs of sovereign states is justified, and whether nations in certain cases should cede portions of their sovereignty to other bodies. The third category includes matters of international trade and global distributive justice: debates about free trade and the activities of multinational corporations, the obligations of wealthy nations to assist the poor, the exploitation of natural resources, and the control of intellectual property. The final category of issues revolves around the development of international governing bodies and legal structures and includes such questions as whether world government is justified and whether international legal standards should be given precedence over those of individual nation-states.

The above categories are clearly interrelated. All hinge on questions of whether human beings have moral responsibility for those in other nations, what relative priority should be given to the nation-state and to national sovereignty in matters of common international concern, and whether and how institutions might be created to adequately address problems that are international in scope and impact.

This chapter provides an overview of international ethics—its definition, its key issues, its history, and its prospects for the future—touching along the way on individual thinkers and schools of thought that exerted a particular influence.

# What Is International Ethics?

## The Study of Ethics

A brief look at ethics in general will help us understand the nature of international ethics. Ethics is the discipline that examines questions of what is morally wrong or right and how we should behave. Ethical considerations generally focus on how we *ought* to treat one another rather than how we actually do (since, obviously, we sometimes treat one another badly).

Most ethical reasoning concerns the ways we should treat other human beings. However, many believe that we also have important ethical responsibilities for animals and the environment. One major criterion of whether we can have ethical responsibilities for something or someone is whether it can be *significantly helped or harmed* by our actions. We cannot have moral obligations to a stone, because we cannot hurt it or benefit it. We can help or harm a frog, a dog, or a cat, though, and we can help or harm our environment; so some people would argue that we have moral obligations to protect these things.

Obviously, humans can be helped or harmed by our behavior in more ways than can a tree. They can suffer in many respects that a tree cannot—by being deprived of social contact, for example. Thus, many people believe that we human beings have special obligations to other humans because they are vulnerable to many types of harm and because our behavior generally affects them more than it does other creatures.

Humans differ from nonhuman creatures in another way that is important in ethical considerations. We hold humans (or, at least, normal adults and mature children) *morally* accountable for their behavior. A tree or a tiger cannot be morally evil. If a tiger kills antelope, we don't say it is morally bad. It is simply acting in accordance with its nature. If we want to stop its killing, we destroy it, pen it up, or move it somewhere else, but we don't discuss its moral responsibility and we wouldn't expect it to follow moral rules. Furthermore, we don't have discussions about ethics with human babies or adults in a coma, and we don't say that their actions are morally right or wrong. Only normal adult (or near adult) humans who are capable of a high level of reasoning, fully aware of their actions, and able to use reason to guide their actions can be judged morally wrong or right. Since most adult humans possess these qualities, we expect them to use their reasoning ability in deciding how to behave, and we hold them responsible for behaving in a morally decent fashion.

The reasoning human beings employ when making ethical judgments is much the same as the deliberative process they use for other sorts of decisions, such as whom to marry or which career to choose. A choice of career, for example, is founded at least in part on a factual assessment of circumstances, including one's abilities (because those poor at math are unlikely to become expert at accounting or engineering, and those with poor eyesight are not well suited to piloting aircraft) and one's personality (because timid people are unlikely to make good policemen or successful sales representatives). Of course, few human choices are based solely on factual data; desires and aspirations must be factored into the equation. For example, an extremely shy person may decide to become a sales representative *because* of the greater challenge that career poses.

Hence, one's choice of career also should take into account one's values, that is, what one believes is important and worthwhile. We must ask how important a large salary is to us, particularly when the hard work and long hours on the job, necessary to achieve the salary, leave little time to raise children or enjoy an active social life. If *both* high income and devotion to children and family are important to us, our values conflict. To resolve the conflict, we must decide which of these values has greatest weight for us. To do so, we must step back from the particular aspects of our lives, such as career, marriage, and social activity, and assess our lives as a whole. We do this by thinking about what sorts of persons we wish to be and what is of fundamental importance to us.

Often when we assess our lives, we seek a fundamental principle or set of principles we can use to give us direction and help weigh our values. For example, we may decide that the basic principle of our life should be helping others, working to improve human life, seeking excellence, or cultivating personal virtue. After this reflection, we use our decisions about the lives we wish to lead and our choice of basic principles to guide our lives and structure our values and desires, so that we can achieve the life we desire.

Ethical reasoning also relies on facts, values, and fundamental principles, and it is often used to resolve conflicts in our values. This balancing of values is difficult and sometimes frustrating because we do not wish to give up any cherished value. Furthermore, thoughtful people disagree on which fundamental principles should guide ethical reasoning. Some argue that we should always try to bring about the greatest amount of good for the greatest number of people. Others argue that we should always perform our duty. Yet others argue that we should seek to cultivate virtue. Notice that these fundamental principles of ethics resemble the fundamental principles we might choose to direct our lives. This is no accident, for ethical thinking about how we should act is really also about how we should live. For example, when considering telling a lie, you are also considering whether you wish to become a liar; and you might therefore ask yourself whether it is important to you to be an honest person.

## International Ethics

International ethics addresses ethical issues and responsibilities that stretch across international boundaries. It begins by examining the assumption that our moral responsibilities to assist other human beings and avoid harming them are not erased if they live far away, reside in a different nation, or have no personal ties to us. Some international ethicists believe that we should accept this assumption. In consequence, these ethicists often believe it is only our ability to cause people harm or give them assistance that is morally important. Others, however, believe that these assumptions are mistaken. They believe that our responsibilities to our neighbors or fellow countrymen greatly outweigh any obligations we have to human beings in general. In fact, many hold the position that we have nearly no obligation to humanity as a whole, and they would argue that the basic assumptions of the practice of international ethics are mistaken.

International ethics differs from other types of ethics in several ways. First, and most obviously, it differs in scope. It is concerned with all human beings, in all parts of the world, rather than only the people in our immediate vicinity or our own nation.

A second way in which international ethics differs from other types of ethics is its complexity. The moral problems we encounter in our daily lives most commonly involve matters that are within our personal control. We can decide whether to cheat on an exam, for example, then easily act in accordance with our decision. However, if we are instead distressed by the suffering of refugees in a war-torn nation, our ability to act and our course of action are not so clear. We may decide that we can best help by donating money to charitable organizations such as the International Red Cross or Oxfam. But some problems are so vast and complex that they can be addressed only by national governments. Private persons or private organizations can do little to halt the suffering in a brutal civil war where civilians on all sides are being killed or starved; at best, private groups can alleviate the pain of, and ward off starvation from, only a fortunate few. Only national governments and international organizations such as the United Nations (U.N.) and North Atlantic Treaty Organization (NATO) are capable of addressing human tragedy of this sort. Many ethicists conclude on this basis that, as private persons, we have no responsibility to alleviate the suffering of innocent civilians. Others argue that we need not accept this conclusion, because even as individuals we can take certain steps toward that goal. One is to inform our elected officials of our concerns and request that they undertake measures to help. These ethicists also assert that we can contribute money or volunteer time and energy to organizations aiding the victims of such warfare.

As the above discussion shows, national governments are vital entities in international ethics. Sometimes national governments are the only institutions capable of addressing problems of international ethics. At other times, they create a problem, as when a government violently represses its citizens. In a case of this sort, attempting to help endangered people requires dealing with their government. Hence, discussions of issues in international ethics often focus on whether governments have moral obligations or whether ways can be found to change their behavior.

International ethics differs from personal ethics in yet another way. When we think about how to treat others around us, we generally have at least some awareness of their values and moral beliefs, and we often share those beliefs. Across the world, though, there are many different human cultures, with widely diverse views of how people should live. In the United States, for example, most people (including some who still practice these types of discrimination) claim to share the conviction that it is morally wrong to discriminate against women and minority groups. In many human cultures, though, women have a distinctly lower status than men. The people in these societies, including many women, might sincerely believe that women should remain subservient to men; that, for example, men but not women should be able to divorce or to own property. Although many in the United States might strongly disagree with these practices, do we have the moral right to impose our ethics, beliefs, or customs on people in other cultures? We must think very carefully about whether to intrude into societies whose cultures and values differ from our own.

Lastly, parents teach individual children about moral values and urge them to follow these values when they become adults, but there is no equivalent to the parental role at the level of international ethics. Some ethicists argue that a consensus on standards of moral conduct is emerging (as encapsulated in the U.N.'s Universal Declaration of Human Rights, for example), and they note that there have been successful efforts to enforce standards of conduct (as when the global community pressured South Africa to end its policies of apartheid). However, many of these theorists would also agree that there are as yet no firm set of moral beliefs of international ethics that all accept and no human institutions capable of enforcing standards of global conduct.

## The Debate about International Ethics

Many thoughtful people believe that talk of international ethics is futile at best and perhaps even foolish. They use several important arguments to support their view. Other groups of ethicists, however, respond with arguments to support their view that international ethics is both feasible and obligatory.

One argument is built on the fact that national governments must often serve as the agents of international ethics. Skeptics point out that national governments frequently serve as the agents of action in international ethics. These skeptics note that national governments are frequently blatantly immoral, both in their treatment of their own citizens and citizens of other nations. Many believe that little can be done to change the ways of despotic governments, and that it is not obvious that the standards of decency and honesty that apply to human individuals also apply to governments. However, if it is senseless to hold governments morally accountable for their actions, then international ethics is senseless as well.

This is an extremely important argument, but those who favor international ethics believe that it overlooks several things. They point out that most people are morally outraged by the actions of the Nazi government of Germany as well as by those of Saddam Hussein, the current leader of Iraq. These ethicists assert that such popular moral outrage is evidence of the widespread belief that Nazi Germany and Hussein's Iraq are morally despicable; but if this is so, then those who react with outrage are applying moral standards to an evaluation of these governments' conduct. Such a reaction provides evidence that, for many, international ethics makes a great deal of sense. Even so, critics of international ethics might conclude that talk of the ethical responsibilities of governments is futile because we cannot expect governments to acknowledge moral obligations or coerce them to reform. Yet supporters of international ethics would contend that this conclusion ignores the instances where governments have acted in ways that bring them moral approval, claiming to do so out of a sense of moral obligation. They note that national governments have aided victims of natural disasters in other nations because they feel obligated to help. Governments also cooperate in disease control and in the disposal of hazardous wastes, at least in part because they feel morally obligated to do so. Furthermore, they note vivid examples of the international community's having exerted pressure on governments to change immoral policies. The most important example cited is the use of economic boycotts and diplomatic pressure to force South Africa to dismantle its policies of apartheid. While there are many reasons why South Africa finally abandoned its policy of apartheid, supporters of international ethics believe that other nations' joint action played an important role.

Skeptics about international ethics employ yet another argument to support their position. They point out that ordinary people have difficulty aiding people in distant parts of the world. In fact, it is difficult for them to become aware of the problems of people in foreign lands. Defenders of international ethics respond that this view is not entirely accurate. Though it is certainly easier for ordinary people to assist their neighbors than to ease suffering in far-off nations, it is still possible to help those in distant parts of the world. Newspapers and television news programs often carry reports of suffering in other lands, so ordinary people do have knowledge of these problems. Also, they assert that donating money and time to organizations such as the International Red Cross or CARE can be as easy as slipping a check in an envelope or calling to volunteer assistance.

However, skeptics also point out that billions live in abject hunger and impoverishment around the world. Ordinary people cannot hope to redress these conditions completely or to greatly ease the sufferings of these billions. Even the U.S. government with all its wealth and power cannot hope to ease the misery of all the anguished people of the world. Advocates of international ethics, while they might concede the truth of these statements, believe that the skeptics are overlooking an important point. The advocates' counterargument can be illustrated by an example. Imagine that you see a burning building with about 25 people trapped inside. You realize that you cannot save all or even most of them from horrible death. Would you then say, Well, I can't help them all, so there is no point in doing anything? It is difficult to imagine that you would. You are more likely to try to save as many as you can, and perhaps enlist the efforts of others as well. Advocates of international ethics argue that the same truth applies to people around the world who are at risk of dying terrible deaths. They assert that although we cannot hope to save all or even most of them, we surely can help a few and can urge others to save more.

Some skeptics take their argument a step further, asking what ties we actually have to people in other nations. Their suffering is lamentable, they say, but surely we are not responsible for it. In fact, we have little to do with them at all. If their problems do not result from our actions and we have no ties to them, then do we truly have an obligation to help them?

Defenders of international ethics are likely to rejoin that this argument depends on several faulty assumptions. One is that we have no moral obligation to help people when we have not caused their suffering and have no direct relationship with them. However, supporters of international ethics point out that years ago, people in the United States were appalled by the Kitty Genovese case (Gansberg 1964). Kitty Genovese was brutally murdered by her boyfriend. He stabbed her many times with a knife as she pleaded for help. The attack lasted more than half an hour, and because it occurred in front of a block of apartment buildings, several dozen people heard her cries, but no one came to her defense. Worse yet, no one even took the trouble to call the police. Kitty Genovese's death caused great turmoil. Many wondered how people could be so callous that they wouldn't even call the police.

Supporters of international ethics ask us to imagine that some of those apartment dwellers had responded that they were not responsible for the attack and that *they* didn't know Kitty Genovese or have any ties to her, so they shouldn't be blamed for not helping her. They ask whether we would be likely to find these responses persuasive. Or is it more likely that we would be disgusted by this attempt to avoid blame? Might we, instead, point out that although the neighbors' claims might be true, they are irrelevant? What is important and relevant is that a human being suffered terribly and many people did nothing to help, even though they could easily have done so. Advocates of international ethics ask what difference it makes if Kitty Genovese is not in New York City and is not being assaulted by her boyfriend, but is instead suffering terribly because she doesn't have food, lacks medical care, or is caught between armies fighting a brutal war. The supporters of international ethics believe that the important point is that she is suffering horribly and that there are things ordinary human beings can do to help.

A second assumption that begs further examination is that we don't have ties to needy people in distant parts of the world. Advocates of international ethics are apt to respond that perhaps a century or two ago this might have been true, but it is not so clearly true today. For one thing, they note, we live amid an emerging global economy. A result is that we have become connected to people in distant parts of the world in many ways. For example, much of the clothing and many ordinary household goods in North America are now imported from Asia. In several cases these goods are produced by workers laboring under miserable conditions in factories that are far from meeting even minimal standards of safety and cleanliness. Moreover, these laborers commonly work for a few pennies or dollars a day, a wage insufficient to provide them and their families a decent livelihood. In addition, even today, child labor is common in some countries. If consumers benefit by saving money thanks to the suffering and mistreatment of laborers elsewhere in the world, supporters of international ethics ask, can one honestly believe that consumers bear no responsibility for the hardships of those laborers? In addition, the market for stocks and bonds has become global. Many Americans invest directly in mutual funds that in turn invest in stocks and bonds in all the markets of the world. Furthermore, many U.S. pension funds have huge sums of money invested around the globe. So, once again, millions of Americans are benefiting from the miserable labor conditions in some parts of the world by trading in the stocks these companies offer and enjoying dividends from their profits.

In addition, advocates of international ethics assert that environmental pollution and disposal of hazardous waste are global problems. The carbon dioxide given off by automobiles in the United States contributes to the ozone depletion of the atmosphere, which in turn may be contributing to global warming, which affects the entire world. Hazardous wastes that can be properly disposed of only at great expense are sometimes simply shipped abroad and deposited in less developed nations that are poorly equipped to deal with them safely.

Advocates of international ethics believe we have an impact on others' lives in yet another way. At times, the U.S. government has decided that its economic or national security interests are best served by supporting governments that brutally oppress their own citizens and menace other nations.

For example, in the years before Iraq invaded Kuwait in 1990, the United States provided it both military and economic assistance, even though Saddam Hussein's record of brutal dictatorship was well known.

Hence, many supporters of international ethics conclude that Americans can no longer say that we lack ties to people in the less developed portions of the world or that we do not benefit from at least some of the suffering they endure. Furthermore, they argue that if we ignore poverty and misery else-where, we are unlikely to escape the consequences. One way in which we are affected is by immigration from impoverished nations. Recent history has shown that it is very difficult to prevent illegal immigration into the United States. Once again, this is partly due to the commercial ties we have with other nations, resulting in a constant flow of ships and air traffic from around the world. People who are impoverished and without hope in their own countries seek an escape route, and many find their way to the United States. If we ignore poverty and misery in people's home nations, we might find that we will have these people here, struggling to achieve the prosperity unavail-able to them in their homelands. Defenders of international ethics argue that pollution, like poverty and misery, flows in all directions. If we in the United States are irresponsible in managing our pollutants, then other nations are unlikely to be sympathetic to our pleas that they control theirs—particularly when their pollutants are partly created by the factories that produce the cheap T-shirts and sneakers we like to buy. So, these ethicists claim that we are contributing to pollution both by failing to control our own wastes and by supporting polluting industries when we buy their products.

Furthermore, advocates of international ethics believe that we in the United States have an even more general ethical responsibility for the well-being of people in other nations. The United States was one of the founding members of the United Nations, and as such, it agreed to the provisions of the organization's charter and, more directly, to the U.N.'s Universal Declaration of Human Rights. In fact, Eleanor Roosevelt, wife of Franklin Delano Roosevelt, was instrumental in fashioning the Universal Declaration of Human Rights. This document established the principles that all human beings everywhere are morally entitled to certain basic requirements of human life and that their rights of freedom of speech and political associa-tion must be respected. Hence, supporters of international ethics claim that by endorsing the Universal Declaration, the U.S. government conveyed its acceptance of these principles. In addition, the United States has signed sev-eral other treaties that commit it to respecting human rights and supporting human needs.

However, there remains another argument against international ethics that goes beyond the skeptical arguments examined above. The argument is that it is foolish and self-defeating to attempt to assist the impoverished and miserable people of the world. This argument was stated in memorable fash-ion in the 1970s by biologist Garrett Hardin (Hardin 1974). It is often called "lifeboat ethics" because it is based on a comparison of the earth with a lifeboat. A lifeboat has limited space and limited supplies. Hence, it can hold and sustain a fixed number of people. If a lifeboat is already filled to capacity, the decision to allow more people aboard is both foolish and futile. It is foolish because exceeding the capacity of the boat increases the risk that it will capsize, dooming all aboard. It is also futile, because the limited supplies aboard will not sustain the newcomers for long.

Hardin's argument is based on a number of claims, such as that the planet earth is indeed like a lifeboat, that the people of the wealthy nations of the world are like those who have scrambled into the lifeboat first, and that the impoverished people of the world are like those who are still thrashing around in the water. To the extent that these claims of fact are false or questionable, Hardin's argument is weakened. Supporters of international ethics assert that claims that the earth is nearing the limit of its capacity to sustain human life are false. On the contrary, they argue, vast stretches of the world, and of the United States in particular, remain unsettled by human beings. Furthermore, the most densely populated portions of the earth are not necessarily the poorest and most miserable. Japan, for example, has about half the population of the United States, but it is crammed onto several islands that, taken together, are slightly smaller than California. Making matters worse, most of that land is mountainous, and only about 13 percent can be used for food production (CIA 1994: 202–204). Worse yet, Japan has practically no natural resources. Most raw materials for the goods its factories produce must be imported. Yet Japan is certainly not poor and miserable. Also, Singapore, Hong Kong, and the Netherlands are also among the most densely populated areas of the globe, yet they are also quite prosperous. Moreover, in the United States, economists, local chambers of commerce, and local governments frequently extol the value of larger populations: Towns and cities where population is increasing are considered healthy and vibrant, while those that are losing population feel threatened. Hence, in our ordinary lives, we generally view more people as desirable.

Secondly, as supporters of international ethics argue, while a lifeboat has strictly limited resources, humans are busily increasing crop yields and discovering new resources. Furthermore, computers, which are among the most potent generators of wealth and power in the present age, require extremely small quantities of natural resources. At present, for example, computer chips are commonly smaller than a human fingernail, and they will soon become smaller and more powerful still. They are powerful because of the intelligence of their design and manufacture, not because they require vast quantities of raw materials. Hence, it is human intelligence and ingenuity that make computers powerful and valuable, not the ordinary materials of which they are made. Computers employed in industrial planning and control might also help us make better and more efficient use of natural resources.

Advocates of international ethics also claim that the earth's circumstances differ in another important way from Hardin's lifeboat. In Hardin's example, those in the lifeboat are not the cause of the plight of all and they are not making everyone's circumstances worse. However, the looming threat to human life on earth is not that the earth's resources will be exhausted. It is that environmental pollution will endanger life and make the earth's resources unusable. The difficulty is that the wealthy people of the earth generate the lion's share of pollution and use the great bulk of its resources. Poor and miserable people use few resources, and in comparison to the wealthy, generate little pollution. Hence, supporters of international ethics argue that those in the lifeboat and those struggling alongside are not all equally innocent victims. Rather, those who are wealthy and comfortable are largely contributing to the problem.

But then why do we hear so much talk of overpopulation in the less developed parts of the world, skeptics might respond. Proponents of international ethics are prone to answer that the problem with population is not absolute size, as many of the impoverished portions of the world are relatively sparsely populated. The problem is that population growth is outpacing their societies' ability to sustain new lives. Thus, the rate of population increase, rather than total population, is the problem. However, defenders of international ethics believe that the cure is not, as Hardin would have us believe, standing aside to let poverty and disease winnow out the weak and inferior. Rather, Hardin's opponents argue, there is ample statistical evidence that the rate of population growth declines as prosperity increases. Thus, the solution is to assist the economic development of the impoverished nations of the world.

# The Development and Study of International Ethics

## A Brief History of International Ethics

International ethics evolved slowly, over a lengthy stretch of human history. Though it is now developing rapidly, a significant number of people, ideas, events, and movements paved the way. Among the first was the emergence of the early Christian church and St. Paul's decision to encourage gentiles as well as Jews to join. This apparently simple idea was a momentous change in ideology, for it meant that *all* human beings are fit to become Christians. Before Christianity, most of the world's peoples believed they were the only genuine human beings. All other tribes or groups were semihuman at best. International ethics is grounded on the belief that all human beings, wherever they are found in the world, are equally human and equally deserving of our concern, and St. Paul's decision to preach to the gentiles tacitly introduced this principle to human thought. Hence, his choice was a first step toward international ethics.

The next stage in the development of international ethics was inaugurated by Stoic philosophy, which reached full flower during the period of the Roman Empire. The Stoics accepted the idea that all human beings are equally deserving of concern but added the conception of natural law. Natural law is the set of universal principles that should govern the conduct of all human beings and that explicitly postulates that all human beings are morally important. The Roman Empire contributed to this evolution by making use of the notion of natural law to formulate statutes for its domains.

The medieval Christian church continued the movement began by the early church and Stoicism. It recast the idea of natural law as a set of divine commands and made God their ultimate enforcer. It added the beliefs that the various feudal kingdoms scattered across Europe were part of a larger unity, the Christian church, and that political leaders gained their moral title to rule only from the church. Jurists and theologians also formulated a doctrine of justified revolution in the Middle Ages, arguing that citizens were entitled to rebel against rulers whose actions violated natural law.

The next important period in the emergence of international ethics was the Enlightenment in eighteenth-century Europe. The Enlightenment was an intellectual movement exemplified by figures such as Voltaire in France and Immanuel Kant in Germany. The philosophy of the Enlightenment was based on the premises that humanity would continue to prosper through the use of reason and that all human beings in all parts of the world possess reason equally. Furthermore, Enlightenment thinkers taught, reason should be used to discover principles of moral conduct. The principles they believed were revealed by reason greatly resembled those of Stoic and medieval natural law. Enlightenment thinkers were also an important counterpoise to the nationalistic movements of their day, movements dedicated to the idea that national unity and national interests should take precedence over ties of universal humanity.

Enlightenment thought also played a significant role in the founding of the United States. In fact, the beginning of the Declaration of Independence encapsulates Enlightenment thought beautifully: "We hold these truths to be self-evident, that all men are created equal, that they are endowed by their Creator with certain unalienable rights, that among these are Life, Liberty and the pursuit of Happiness." Note that the Declaration asserts that these basic principles are discovered by reason and that the fundamental rights it finds are enjoyed by *all* human beings, not only American citizens.

The influence of Enlightenment philosophy continued through the nineteenth century in political and diplomatic efforts to establish a basis for international law. Foremost among these were the several Geneva Conventions, the first of which was drafted in 1864. The conventions codified the rules of warfare and began to establish a means to adjudicate disputes about international laws and rudimentary methods of enforcing those laws. Since then, the Geneva Conventions have been modified several times, but they remain in force today as the body of international law governing the conduct of war. The early twentieth century brought more ambitious efforts to codify international law and to establish international governing bodies. The first attempt to create a form of international government occurred after World

War I. Spearheaded by the enthusiastic U.S. President Woodrow Wilson, the effort resulted in the League of Nations—an organization that was never very successful, in part because the United States did not join. Although Woodrow Wilson was its spiritual father, the U.S. Congress refused to approve U.S. membership. The League withered away as World War II boiled across Europe and Asia. Amid the ashes left by the war, a universal determination emerged to prevent its like from ever plaguing humanity again, and the United Nations was born. Early on, the United Nations formulated its Universal Declaration of Human Rights, a codification of the moral entitlements of all human beings. Though an imperfect document, it nonetheless confirmed a set of universal moral principles, among them the principle that all human beings are worthy of moral concern.

At present, the circumstances of human life are hastening the development of international ethics. These include the emergence of a global economy and the multiplication of problems of common concern, including environmental pollution, crime, disease, and population control, as well as stunning technological advances in communication and transportation that allow easy travel to all parts of the world and nearly instantaneous communication across the globe. A consequence of these developments is that they are throwing human beings closer together. Places that were once exotic and inaccessible are now only a few hours away by jet, and they are often joined to us by an ever expanding web of economic ties. Hence, Americans' activity has a greater and more immediate effect on others than in the past, and the actions of others have a similar impact on us. In addition, the common problems now shared by all humanity require that we cooperate and show concern for one another to a far greater extent than in the past.

## Contemporary Scholars and Activists

At present, scholars in several academic disciplines are contributing important work on the ethics of international relations. Richard Falk is prominent in the area of international law, as is Charles Beitz in political science. Among theologians, Michael Walzer of Harvard University has been highly influential. Several philosophers also have devoted careful thought to these matters, among them Henry Shue of Cornell University and Brian Barry of the London School of Economics. Natural scientists also have been actively addressing moral problems associated with pollution, overpopulation, and disease control.

The major activists of international ethics are generally found in international organizations. Boutros Boutros-Ghali, the Egyptian statesman who was recently U.N. secretary-general, is foremost among them, as is his successor, Kofi Annan. However, officials of bodies within the United Nations, such as UNESCO, are also doing important work. Also, many officials of national governments are actively addressing matters of international ethics.

Within the U.S. government, for example, one such official is Mark Gearan, the director of the Peace Corps. In addition, major international financial organizations such as the World Bank and the International Monetary Fund are playing central roles in international ethics by providing funding and guidance for economic development in less developed nations. Finally, and in some ways most importantly, nongovernmental organizations such as Amnesty International are working to protect the rights of political prisoners throughout the world. Other groups, such as the Worldwatch Institute, play an important role by gathering information on the violation of human rights in many nations. In addition, the international relief organizations, such as CARE, the International Red Cross, the French group Médecins sans Frontières (Doctors without Borders), and Oxfam International, are directly attempting to meet the needs of people whose lives have been disrupted by war, famine, or natural disaster.

## Analyzing the Issues of International Ethics

### Basic Concepts

National sovereignty is foremost among the concepts of international ethics. It is the idea that national governments have supreme legal authority within their boundaries, that citizens owe obedience to them, that these governments are not subject to any higher authority, and that outsiders are not entitled to intrude in their affairs. Jean Bodin, a sixteenth-century French philosopher, was among the first to discuss national sovereignty. The idea would have seemed nonsensical a few centuries earlier, with the medieval church insisting that political authority was dependent on theological authority. In the twentieth century, however, it gained fresh attention following gross violations of national sovereignty in the two world wars. In consequence, respect for national sovereignty, as an essential element for the preservation of the peace, was made a basic principle of the U.N. charter. In recent decades, however, the international community has determined that sovereignty must be overridden when a national government, like that of South Africa or that of Cambodia under the Khmer Rouge, brutally abuses its citizenry and violates their human rights.

Nationalism is a second fundamental idea that shapes international ethics, and it is closely related to the concept of sovereignty. It is the doctrine that a distinct people, defined as a group sharing a language, culture, history, and ideology, is entitled to its own sovereign state. The concept of nationalism is considerably newer than that of sovereignty, having first emerged early in the nineteenth century. It played an important role in efforts to unify the domains of Germany and Italy, which before unification had been hodgepodges of small fiefdoms and principalities. Because most European nations at the time had already evolved from monarchies to democracies, and thus a monarch could no longer serve as the focus of allegiance and unity, another conceptual basis for the goal of unification was needed. It was found in the idea of nationhood. Also at this time, massive conscripted armies replaced small professional armies as the dominant military forces of Europe. Where sheer coercion was inadequate to entice vast numbers of ordinary citizens to join these armies, an appealing ideology was needed, and nationalism became useful toward this end also. Later in the century, it formed part of the ideological basis for colonies' struggles against foreign rule. At present nationalism is a focus of considerable turmoil, as the remnants of the former Soviet Union and its European satellite nations have discovered that the political boundaries established for them during the Soviet era were often arbitrary and did not fit the political allegiances of the people and ethnic groups within them.

A major shortcoming of nationalism as an ideology in support of sovereign statehood is that few of the world's nation-states are nations in the purest definition of the term. Only Japan, Iceland, and Nepal come close to having the ethnic homogeneity that stems from a lengthy, shared history. Even these genuine nations are tightly bound to other parts of the world by ties that are vital to their existence. The great wealth of Japan, for example, has come largely from its many commercial links to the rest of the world. Iceland plays a key role in NATO's military structure, and its major industry, cod fishing, depends on global markets. If few genuine nations exist, and none that are entirely self-sufficient, then the moral basis of the appeal to nationalism is greatly diluted.

Distributive justice is another primary concern of international ethics. Distributive justice addresses the principles by which the world's goods (including wealth and natural resources, of course, but also other desirable things such as education, health care, prestige, or power) are allocated to people and institutions. The Greek philosopher Aristotle was the first to discuss the topic in detail, and since then, many philosophers and theoreticians, particularly in the twentieth century, have given it rigorous analysis. To see how controversies regarding distributive justice arise, consider education: Most individuals seek satisfying careers and comfortable salaries, and their access to higher education is often crucial in helping them meet these goals. We can ask, therefore, whether it should be available only for those able to pay for it or whether is should be available to all people with ability and ambition. When we ask this question, we are asking what principle of distribution we should use to determine who should have the opportunity to gain an education. In the context of global ethics, considerations of distributive justice play a central role in discussions of the ownership and exploitation of natural resources and intellectual property as well as in questions of aid from wealthy nations to poorer ones.

The concept of rights, which is also important to questions of international ethics, points to human entitlements. If rights are codified as law (as in the U.S. Bill of Rights), then they are referred to as legal rights. If they are grounded in appeals to moral principle, then they are referred to as moral rights. Human rights, the array of entitlements each person enjoys simply by virtue of being human, is a particularly important category of moral rights. There is much controversy over the question of whether human rights exist, and if they do, which moral entitlements they include. There is also vigorous discussion of the nature of human rights. Some argue that human rights exist only as negative constraints on the action of others. Hence, if we have the right to life in the negative sense, then others may not kill us. Another view is that human rights are positive rights, meaning that if we have these rights, then others are obliged to help us secure them if we cannot do so on our own power. So if we have the right to life in the positive sense, then others are obliged to assist us when, for instance, our lives are threatened by famine, or if we are ill and cannot afford medical care.

Discussion of human rights dates from the time of Thomas Hobbes and John Locke, two English philosophers of the seventeenth century, but has become especially vigorous since the atrocities of World War II. General revulsion over the treatment of human beings by other human beings during that war prompted many to turn to the concept of human rights in hopes that it would offer one way to avoid such calamity in the future. The attraction of rights is that they are strong moral entitlements, and human rights are the entitlements all human beings enjoy simply by virtue of being human. Hence, appeal to human rights seemed a good way to provide a moral basis for the universal protection of human beings. Many of these rights are encapsulated in the U.N.'s Universal Declaration of Human Rights, where they are defined both negatively and positively. However, there is still much controversy over exactly which rights human beings should have, whether these should be interpreted in the positive as well as the negative sense, and exactly what obligations these rights place on human beings and on their governments.

## Methodology

The methodology of international ethics is at the bottom much the same as that of other domains of ethics. It involves seeking out relevant facts, making assessments of pertinent values, making decisions about fundamental moral principles, weighing competing claims to moral entitlement, and making decisions about responsibility and obligation. In addition, ethical thinking generally involves estimating the consequences of various actions available to us, considering who will be helped and who harmed by one course of action rather than another, and determining whether some consequences are more important than others. (For example, is it more important that I save a child from drowning or that I get to work on time?) However, most people also believe that some actions are morally wrong in themselves, no matter how beneficial their consequences might be. (For example, would we be justified in killing an innocent person so that we could use that person's organs to save the lives of four other people, one of whom might need a heart, another lungs, and two others kidneys?) Most of us, most of the time, weigh some or all of these factors in making moral decisions.

Let's consider another example: Imagine that you are a forklift operator at a chemical company near the small town where you live. Your supervisor tells you to pick up several barrels of waste and dump them in a nearby creek. You notice that the barrels have signs stating that they hold hazardous materials. You also know that the creek feeds into a reservoir that is the source of your town's water supply. These are important facts, and they (along with some other facts about the effects of harmful chemicals on human health and ways in which they can contaminate water supplies) support the conclusion that following your supervisor's orders will endanger the health or lives of those in your community. You then draw a further conclusion that dumping the barrels in the creek would be morally wrong because of the harm it might cause others.

However, when you mention this to your boss, he answers that those few barrels of chemicals won't hurt anybody; there are thousands of gallons of water in the town reservoir and only a few gallons of chemicals in those barrels. Besides, your company can't afford the cost of disposing of these chemicals in any other way. Waste disposal companies charge huge fees for getting rid of such chemicals. "So follow orders, or you're fired!"

Notice what has happened: Your boss is denying your beliefs about the facts. You believe the chemicals will cause harm to your community, and he denies this. So in this case, a portion of your moral investigation involves checking the facts. If your boss is correct, no harm will result from dumping the chemicals, and you will have done nothing wrong if you follow his orders. However, if your beliefs about the facts are correct, then dumping the chemicals is morally wrong because of the harm it will cause.

If after investigation you decide the facts do support your beliefs, but your boss continues to maintain his position, you face several conflicts of *values*. One results from his claim that the company can't afford to dispose of the chemicals in any other manner. In other words, there appears to be a conflict between your company's financial health and its helping to maintain a clean environment. So you must balance the company's welfare against that of the environment. In addition, if you are right in your belief that dumping these chemicals will cause harm to your community, then there is a conflict also between your company's finances and the health of those in your community.

You also face another, more immediately personal conflict of values—a conflict between protecting your family and neighbors and keeping your job. Jobs are clearly important for the money they offer, money needed to sustain life. Furthermore, being fired from this job could make it more difficult for you to get other jobs; so it is not simply *this* job that is at risk but also future jobs. You must therefore ask yourself whether you are willing to accept these sacrifices to protect others, and you must consider the possibility that your refusal will be futile, since your boss will likely order someone else to dump the waste if you refuse. As a result, you could make a considerable personal sacrifice but still fail to protect your community.

When you consider these difficulties and try to sort them out, you will have to think about your life as a whole, about what sort of person you want to be and how you want others to view you. You might also wonder how you would respond if others in your community found out about the dumping and asked whether you knew about it and what you did to prevent it.

In sum, factual knowledge is extremely important for ethical decision making, but facts cannot make decisions for us. We must also consider our values, and weigh them when they conflict with one another. The difficulties of gathering accurate factual information (particularly on matters as complex as ecology) and the anxiety of weighing values show why ethical judgments can be maddeningly difficult and why many people try to avoid them. The problem, as the above example demonstrates, is that we often *can't avoid* ethical decision making, frightening and perplexing though it may be. You must either dump the chemicals or not. The claim that you were only following orders does not excuse you, because *choosing to follow orders is also your decision.*

The elements of ethical decision making used at the level of international relations are essentially the same as those employed in interpersonal and community relations. Once again, an example may help to clarify the decision-making process. You might look at a newspaper one day and notice an account of a particularly vicious and bloody civil war. You read that several ethnic groups are fighting for control of a nation where they had previously lived in peace. There are well-documented accounts of mass slaughter, eviction of thousands of people from their homes, and use of rape and torture as means of intimidation. The fighting has created thousands of refugees with no means of earning a living and has destroyed the government and economy of a once self-sufficient nation. You are appalled by these reports but are soon distracted by your own nation's problems and controversies over taxes, education policy, pollution control, and the like. However, as the days pass, you read more accounts of this war and are horrified by TV newscasts that show pictures of starving children, mass graves, homes destroyed, and masses of dazed refugees. You decide you cannot ignore their suffering any longer. Though you have many problems, you come to believe that they are minor in comparison to what these people are facing. You decide that their misery demands that you help.

Now, however, you are struck by the complexity of the problem. There are war crimes being committed, refugees needing aid, people being forced from their homes, and so on. There are *many* needs and *many* things to be done. Then you wonder what you can do to help and whether your efforts will accomplish any good. Obviously you can't stop a war, and you can't restore order to an anguished nation. Neither can you track down war criminals, or even begin to feed and house masses of refugees. But clearly *all* these things need to be done. You are aware that if only a small portion of this suffering were occurring in your own nation, you, your neighbors, and many governments would rush to help. You also recognize that this is not simply your problem but a problem for all the people and governments of the world. So once again, you wonder what you can or should do.

As with ethical thinking of other sorts, you must first get the facts about the civil war. You will want to discover more about the conflict, who is suffering, and in what ways. You must also seek factual information about what measures can be taken to ease their suffering and end the war, and you must also find out what groups are able to be of assistance and what they are doing. Then you must learn what you can do. Perhaps you discover that you can donate money to the groups helping war victims. You might also find that you can volunteer to work with these groups. But you might also recognize that only national governments have the resources to end the civil war and restore order; so you might decide that you should urge your elected officials to take action, as well as call other people's attention to the problem and urge them to lobby their governments.

You might also be deterred from action by disagreements of fact among reports of the suffering or by the distance between you and the source of the problem. You might then give greater weight to the arguments skeptics make against the practice of international ethics. For example, you might agree that these suffering people should be able to take care of themselves, and if they can't, it's their own fault. You might also think about the many other demands on your time, energy, and money. You have many things to worry about, so why should you concern yourself with the problems of people you have never met in a nation you have never seen? Notice that you're now faced with a conflict of values: You must ask whether the problems of these distant others should matter to you, particularly when your efforts to help them might interfere with your other priorities and goals. You must, in other words, weigh the arguments and values that counter international moral obligations against those that favor such obligations.

As with other sorts of ethical thinking, you therefore must pause to think about your life and the sort of person you wish to be. You must also ask what basic principles you wish to use to guide your life and decisions. You might believe you are a good and decent person, that is, you are honest, show concern for others, and help them whenever you can. You might decide that it is very important that you be able to think of yourself in this way and that helping others is a very important principle of your life. But then you might wonder how you can continue to think of yourself in this way if you ignore the very great suffering of many human beings. So, as with ethical decision making in other spheres of your life, you will be embroiled in a difficult and complex process. But you must also recognize that it is a decision that you cannot avoid. Either you help the war victims or you don't. You must weigh the skeptical arguments against those of the advocates of international ethics, and you cannot avoid responsibility for your decision.

# The Major Issues Today

One obvious domain of vigorous controversy is whether the world community is either justified in, or obligated to, intervene in the world's troubled nations to protect human life or restore order. Questions about the ethics of intervention in Bosnia, Rwanda, Somalia, and Haiti have been hotly debated. Oddly, the world community has given Liberia scant attention, although conditions there have been as bloody and as chaotic as in Rwanda and Bosnia.

A second issue, and one that has received less attention in the United States than in Europe, is whether nations are justified in yielding portions of their sovereignty in order to address problems, such as global pollution, that require a coordinated response from the world community. Sovereignty is currently a focus of controversy in Europe because the European states are attempting to create an international community with a considerable degree of economic and political unity, while many are still reluctant to relinquish national sovereignty over certain policy areas. Loss of sovereignty recently has been a sore point also in the United States, where several critics of the North American Free Trade Agreement have claimed that in signing the treaty the United States unjustifiably ceded its sovereignty over national environmental and labor safety standards.

Concerns about distributive justice also have ignited significant controversy. Some years ago, during the so-called North-South debates, the poorer nations of the world were insisting that the wealthier nations had an obligation to help them advance economically. The issue emerged again in a more subdued fashion during the 1995 Group of Seven meetings in Halifax, Nova Scotia, where the leading nations of the world approved plans to prevent the world's financially struggling nations from falling into financial crisis. The issue also surfaced in arguments over the Law of the Sea Bed Treaty, which establishes rules for exploiting riches beneath the world's oceans and thus beyond the boundaries of any particular nation-state. Poorer nations have vigorously asserted that the benefits of these riches should be made available to all, while representatives of wealthy nations have countered that private enterprise cannot be expected to take the financial and technological risks needed to exploit these resources if they cannot expect to retain most of the profits.

Ecology is a fourth area of controversy. Many of the world's nations agree that global standards for pollution must be established and enforced if environmental disaster is to be averted. However, the poorer nations of the world insist that they should not be required to bear the financial burden of upholding these standards and that the wealthier nations, which have greatly contributed to pollution and are in a better position to reverse it, should bear the costs of cleanup.

Another topic of considerable debate is immigration and emigration. As the wealthier nations of the world are being flooded by legal and illegal immigrants from poorer nations, they protest that these immigrant populations are placing a strain on social services and are creating or exacerbating social problems. In addition, many poorer citizens of the wealthier nations believe that immigrant laborers are taking jobs away from them.

There is also heated disagreement regarding the status and treatment of women. Women across the globe are uniting to seek worldwide improvement of their circumstances, but many people in traditional societies where women have been relegated to subservience are resisting these movements on the grounds that they are unwarranted intrusions into their lives and cultures.

Other matters about which international concern is mounting include disease and crime. Recently citizens of the advanced nations of the world have become uncomfortably aware of the possibility of a global epidemic that might challenge even the wealthiest nations' resources. Outbreaks of pneumonic plague in India in autumn 1994 and of the virus *Ebola* in Africa the following year have demonstrated that global cooperation is needed to prevent catastrophe.

The global reach of organized crime has also gained notice recently. The director of the U.S. Federal Bureau of Investigation is opening offices abroad on the grounds that, because crime is increasingly international, efforts to combat it must be international as well. Fears have been kindled by the discovery of plans to smuggle arms and nuclear materials from the former Soviet Union. As in the case of disease, it is clear that only a global effort is capable of addressing the problem of international crime.

The above categories are clearly interrelated. They all hinge on questions of whether human beings have moral responsibility for those in other nations, the importance of the nation-state and national sovereignty, and problems surrounding efforts to create institutions capable of addressing problems that are international in scope and impact.

**References:** Central Intelligence Agency. 1994. *The World Factbook, 1994.* Washington, DC: Central Intelligence Agency, Superintendent of Documents.

Gansberg, Martin. 1964. "Thirty-eight Who Saw Murder Didn't Call Police." *New York Times* (27 March).

Hardin, Garrett. 1974. "Living in a Lifeboat." *BioScience* 24: 561–568.

# CONTEMPORARY ETHICAL ISSUES

## Chapter 2:
## Chronology

International ethics has evolved over a long period of time, its growth fueled both by human ideas and by developments in human history. This chronology includes the dates of intellectual and historical developments that exerted a particular influence. The ideas and circumstances that nurture international ethics have multiplied in the twentieth century, particularly since World War II.

**300 B.C.**    The Greek philosopher Zeno founds Stoicism. The Stoics teach that the universe is rational, that all human beings share the capacity to reason, and that the rational order of the universe should guide human behavior. These ideas are the foundation of the Stoic conception of natural law as a universal guide for all human beings as well as of the view that all human beings are equally worthy of concern.

**ca. 43 B.C.**    Cicero's *De legibus* transforms the Stoic conception of natural law

| | |
|---|---|
| **ca. 43 B.C.** *cont.* | from a guide for individual conduct to a guide for legislation. Cicero was a lawyer and statesman of the Roman Empire and also a Stoic. The date of writing of *De legibus* is uncertain, but it is likely that it appeared near the end of Cicero's life (he died in 43 B.C.). |
| **50** | At the Council of the Apostles in Jerusalem, St. Paul successfully argues that Christianity should not be a Jewish sect but should be open to all people. He particularly emphasizes the unity and equality of Jews and Gentiles within Christianity. His insistence lays the foundation for the idea that all human beings, whether or not they are members of the same ethnic group, are equally worthy of respect and concern. |
| **1631** | The definitive edition of the Dutch jurist Hugo Grotius's *Law of War and Peace* appears. Completed in 1625, it is considered the first definitive text of international law regulating the conduct of war. Grotius's work was inspired by his desire to make wars more humane for combatants and ordinary citizens alike. |
| **1789** | The Declaration of the Rights of Man and of the Citizen is approved by the French National Assembly. Along with the U.S. Bill of Rights, this document also provides support for the ideas that all human beings are equal and enjoy human rights by virtue of their humanity. |
| **1791** | The United States' Bill of Rights (the first ten amendments to the Constitution) is ratified. The Bill of Rights is important both in subsequent U.S. history and political thought in the next two centuries. It gives support for the idea that all humans are equal and that all have human rights. |
| **1863** | The Red Cross is founded by Jean-Henri Dunant, a Swiss citizen, whose original purpose was to create an organization devoted to assisting victims of war. It would later become a global organization, expanding its activities to aiding refugees and victims of natural disaster. |
| **1885** | The Berlin Conference results in the first important international agreement to ban international trade in slaves. |
| **1899** | The International Peace Conference of 1899 is held at The Hague, The Netherlands. Called at the behest of Russia, |

| | |
|---|---|
| **1899**<br>*cont.* | the conference is intended to reduce armaments in the world. It fails in this effort but results in a number of declarations regarding the laws of war, including the protection of noncombatants and the neutrality of shipping. These declarations are subsequently accepted by a number of nations and become the foundation of contemporary international laws of war. |
| **1907** | The Second International Peace Conference, also held at The Hague, continues the efforts of the first conference, helping to lay the foundation for new international laws of war. |
| **1919** | The League of Nations is established to promote international peace and security. U.S. President Woodrow Wilson is instrumental in founding the League, but ironically, the United States never becomes a member. The League dissolves itself in 1946 to make way for the newly created United Nations. |
| **1945** | The United Nations is founded. An international organization composed of most of the world's nations, the United Nations adopts a charter for the International Court of Justice, its principal judicial body.<br><br>The International War Crimes Tribunal convenes in Nuremberg, Germany, to conduct trials of Nazis charged with war crimes. The trials continue into 1946. |
| **1947** | In a speech at Harvard University on 5 June, U.S. Secretary of State George C. Marshall announces the establishment of the most ambitious program of foreign assistance in history. Known as the Marshall Plan, it lays the foundation for economic reconstruction of the war-ravaged nations of Europe. |
| **1948** | The U.N. Universal Declaration of Human Rights is ratified. This document delineates the major moral entitlements of all human beings. |
| **1949** | The U.N. Convention on the Prevention and Punishment of Genocide is approved by the General Assembly. This document gives a detailed definition of the crime of genocide and authorizes punishment for the crime either by competent national courts in the nation where the crime |

**1949**
*cont.*

was committed or by a suitable international court. The document enters into force in 1951 but is not ratified by the United States until 1988.

**1950**

The U.N. Security Council votes to dispatch a U.N. army to Korea, in response to the invasion of South Korea by North Korea. The occasion marks the creation of the U.N. army and also the broadest collective security action in history.

The European Convention on Human Rights is ratified by the members of the Council of Europe in Rome on 4 November. Five additional protocols to this convention are also ratified in subsequent years, the last on 20 January 1966 in Strasbourg, France.

**1959**

The European Court of Human Rights is established in Strasbourg as one of the obligations undertaken by the parties that ratified the European Convention on Human Rights. The Court's function is to hear and resolve complaints of human rights violations in the nations that have bound themselves to the European Convention on Human Rights.

**1961**

The U.S. Peace Corps is established by an executive order of President John F. Kennedy and approved by Congress. Its purpose is to provide a way for U.S. citizens to obtain training and experience in international service, in nations that have requested U.S. developmental assistance.

**1963**

On 5 August, the United States, United Kingdom, and Union of Soviet Socialist Republics ratify the Treaty Banning Nuclear Weapons Tests in the Atmosphere, in Outer Space and Under Water.

**1968**

The U.N. International Conference on Human Rights meets in Teheran, Iran, from 22 April through 13 May, to review world progress in enhancing human rights since the adoption of the U.N. Universal Declaration of Human Rights and to propose further measures for protecting human rights.

The United States and the Soviet Union draft a nuclear nonproliferation treaty that is later approved by the U.N. General Assembly.

| | |
|---|---|
| **1972** | The United States and the Soviet Union agree to the first treaty to limit antiballistic missiles. |
| **1975** | Representatives of 35 nations gather in Helsinki, Finland, at a conference on security and cooperation in Europe. The final act of the conference, on 1 August, is to ratify the Helsinki Accords, which enumerate a number of human rights. The accords are of special significance because they are signed by representatives of a number of eastern bloc nations. Human rights activists within the eastern bloc rely on this commitment to seek increased respect for human rights within their nations. |
| **1976** | The International Covenant on Civil and Political Rights enters into force on 23 March, after being ratified by a sufficient number of nation-states. The covenant is adopted by the U.N. General Assembly on 16 December 1976. The Covenants are designed to give legal force to the moral imperatives embodied in the U.N. Universal Declaration of Human Rights. The states that ratify the Covenants formally commit themselves to protecting and preserving fundamental human rights and freedoms. Whereas the Universal Declaration of Human Rights has moral force for all nations and all people, the Covenants are legally binding only on those states that formally ratify them. |
| **1993** | The International Criminal Tribunal for the Former Yugoslavia is created by the U.N. Security Council on 25 May. This is the first international war crimes tribunal held since those at Tokyo and Nuremberg after World War II. |
| | The World Conference on Human Rights is held from 14 June through 25 June in Vienna, Austria. It convenes to assess the state of global human rights systems and the machinery for protecting human rights and to endorse measures designed to further enhance the protection of human rights. This conference results in the Vienna Declaration and Programme of Action, which is adopted by the delegates on 25 June. |
| **1994** | The U.N. International Conference on Population and Development is held in Cairo, Egypt, from 5 September through 13 September. On 13 September, 179 states adopt a 20-year Programme of Action, which embodies a new approach to population management, which emphasizes the |

**1994**
*cont.*

interrelation between population and development, the empowerment of women, and the needs of individual men and women. A key element is the commitment to work to empower women by expanding their access to education, health care, and employment.

The International Criminal Tribunal for Rwanda is instituted by the U.N. Security Council on 8 November. Its purpose is to prosecute individuals responsible for violations of international humanitarian law, the crime of genocide, in particular. The Tribunal has begun hearings in Arusha, Tanzania, and has confirmed indictments against a number of individuals accused of crimes against humanity. It began holding trials on 30 May 1996 and continues to receive indictments and conduct trials of those accused.

**1995**

The U.N. Summit for Social Development meets in Copenhagen, Denmark, from 6 March to 12 March. The meeting is devoted to discussing ways of attacking poverty across the globe. Its main result is the Copenhagen Declaration and Programme of Action, which embodies a program of action designed to achieve the goals of eradicating poverty, promoting useful employment for all persons, and eliminating social discrimination and exclusion.

The Fourth World Conference on Women is held in Beijing, China, in September. This conference results in adoption of the Beijing Declaration and Platform for Action, which establishes a comprehensive plan to improve the status of the world's women, particularly by combating such issues as domestic violence and sexual abuse and by working to achieve equal political and social status for women.

**1996**

The U.N. Conference on Human Settlement (Habitat II) meets in Istanbul, Turkey, from 3 June to 14 June. Its purpose is to examine ways of achieving adequate shelter and sustainable development for all human beings. The conference results in adoption of the Istanbul Declaration on Human Standards. It commits the world's political leaders to working to improve the housing standards of the world's people and establishes a plan of action to achieve this goal.

**1997**

The Chemical Warfare Convention, undertaken to ban the development, production, and possession of chemical and

**1997**
*cont.*

biological weapons, enters into force on 29 April after being ratified by 97 nations.

The Earth Summit+5 is held from 23 June to 27 June. This special session of the U.N. General Assembly is devoted to reviewing and appraising the implementation of the agenda established at the U.N. Conference on Environment and Development held in 1992 in Rio de Janeiro, Brazil.

# CONTEMPORARY ETHICAL ISSUES

## Chapter 3: Biographical Sketches of Issue Makers and Ethicists

The following are brief biographies of the people who have played significant roles in the development of global ethics. They includes people who are leaders of national, international, or nongovernmental organizations; individual activists who have made significant contributions; and those who have broadened and deepened our understanding of global ethics.

### Kofi Annan (b. 1938)

A native of Ghana, Kofi Annan became the seventh secretary-general of the United Nations on 1 January 1997. He received his undergraduate degree from Macalester College in St. Paul, Minnesota, in 1961, and pursued graduate studies in Geneva, Switzerland, in 1961 and 1962. He has some 30 years of experience working in the United Nations and has held posts dealing with peacekeeping, refugee issues, administration, and personnel. He served as U.N. undersecretary for peacekeeping operations prior to becoming secretary-general. He negotiated the release of Western hostages and U.N. staff held in Iraq following its invasion of Kuwait in 1990, and after the war ended, participated personally in the oil-for-food negotiations with Iraq. More recently, he has overseen the activities and placement of U.N. peacekeeping forces in the former Yugoslavia. As secretary-general he has pledged to seek social justice and nurture economic development around the world.

## Marcus Aurelius Antoninus (121–180)

Marcus Aurelius was born to an aristocratic Roman family and became Roman emperor in 161. His reign was turbulent, and he spent much time and energy suppressing rebellions by Germans, Britons, and Parthians along the boundaries of the empire. He was trained in rhetoric but was more interested in philosophy, particularly that of the Stoic philosopher Epictetus. Marcus Aurelius's thought echoed the Stoics' views that human life is futile and transitory and that what matters most is the individual's command over his or her own state of mind. It was also reminiscent of the Stoics' pursuit of calmness and tranquillity; their appreciation of beauty and order in the natural universe; and—most important for international ethics—their insistence on kindness, justice, and forbearance toward all human beings, based on the belief that all are members of a single community governed by a single set of moral standards (the law of nature). The usual historical judgment is that Marcus Aurelius governed his empire in a manner consistent with these philosophical beliefs. He attended to his duty, did not abuse his powers, lowered taxes, and tried to reduce the brutality of gladiatorial contests. He did, however, persecute Christians, because he believed them a serious threat to the integrity of the Roman Empire. He died at the headquarters of the Roman army encamped on the Danube.

## Boutros Boutros-Ghali (b. 1922)

Boutros Boutros-Ghali served as secretary-general of the United Nations from 1992 through 1996. Born in Cairo, Egypt, he received a bachelor's degree in law from the University of Cairo in 1946 and a Ph.D. in international law from the University of Paris in 1949. Between 1949 and 1977, he was a professor of law at the University of Cairo, and from 1954 to 1955, a Fulbright research scholar at Columbia University. In 1977, he became Egypt's minister of state for foreign affairs, a post he held until 1991, when he was appointed deputy prime minister for foreign affairs. After his election as secretary-general of the United Nations in 1992, his stated goals were to strengthen the organization of the United Nations, to work to meet the challenges and opportunities offered by the end of the cold war, and to strive to realize the ideals embodied in the U.N. charter. He was particularly active in encouraging U.N. peacekeeping and peacemaking missions. The United Nations dispatched more peacekeeping missions during his tenure in office than during its previous 40 years of existence, with missions sent to El Salvador, Cambodia, Angola, Mozambique, and many other countries. He also was committed to nurturing the development of poor nations and to helping the nations of the world establish democratic institutions. While he was secretary-general, the United Nations sent missions to over 70 nations to aid them in achieving democratic elections.

## Lester Brown (b. 1934)

Lester Brown is the founder and president of the Worldwatch Institute, a nonprofit research organization focusing on global issues. Brown spent his early years as a farmer, growing tomatoes in southern New Jersey. He received a degree in agricultural economics from Rutgers University in 1955. He also has an M.S. in agricultural economics from the University of Maryland and an M.P.A. from Harvard University. In 1959, he became an analyst for the U.S. Department of Agriculture's Foreign Agricultural Service and subsequently served as an adviser to Orville Freeman, U.S. secretary of agriculture. Brown founded the Worldwatch Institute in 1974 with a grant from the Rockefeller Brothers Foundation, and he remains president of the institute. In 1984, he began publication of the *State of the World* reports. These reports, which are translated into all the world's major languages, provide an annual review of global environmental trends. Brown, who was named a MacArthur Fellow in 1986, has published many books and articles on global environmental and population trends.

## Michel Camdessus (b. 1933)

Managing director and chair of the executive board of the International Monetary Fund, Michel Camdessus was born in Bayonne, France. He was educated at the University of Paris and received postgraduate training at the Institute of Political Studies and the National School of Administration. Camdessus held various posts in the French government and in international bodies, and was named governor of the Bank of France in 1984. In 1987, he was appointed managing director and chair of the executive board of the International Monetary Fund, and he began his third term as managing director there in 1997. He is noteworthy for his insistence that the fund's resources increasingly be used to assist the economic development of poor nations.

## Jimmy Carter (b. 1924)

The thirty-ninth president of the United States, James Earl Carter, Jr., was born in Plains, Georgia, and received his B.S. degree from the U.S. Naval Academy in 1946. He later took graduate courses in nuclear physics at

Union College. While in the Navy, Carter worked with Admiral Hyman Rickover on developing the nuclear submarine for U.S. forces. After his father died in 1953, Carter returned to Plains to manage the family business, Carter's Warehouse. In 1971, he was elected governor of Georgia, and in 1976, president of the United States. During his term in office, from 1977 to 1981, he successfully negotiated the return of control over the Panama Canal to the citizens of Panama; concluded the Camp David Accords, which achieved peace between Egypt and Israel; and completed the SALT II nuclear disarmament treaty with the Soviet Union. He also placed considerable emphasis on human rights during his presidency and attempted to promote them throughout the world. After his term ended, he and his wife Rosalynn founded the Carter Center in Atlanta. The center is a nonprofit organization dedicated to assembling people and resources to "promote peace and human rights, resolve conflict, foster democracy and development, and fight poverty, hunger, and disease throughout the world." Carter has monitored elections in many nations around the world, including Panama, Nicaragua, Haiti, and Guyana. He also leads an effort to eradicate guinea worm disease, which cripples or disfigures 2 million people in Africa each year. He is coordinating an effort to increase worldwide immunization of children from 20 percent to 80 percent. He has also personally worked to mediate conflicts in Sudan and Ethiopia, Haiti, North Korea, and Bosnia. He is the author of 12 books and spends a week of each year working for Habitat for Humanity, building homes for needy people.

## Marcus Tullius Cicero (106–43 B.C.)

A famed Roman orator, Cicero was also renowned as a philosopher and politician. He studied law and philosophy in Rome, Athens, and Rhodes and held a number of official positions in the Roman government. His philosophical writing generally followed the Stoic tradition. His work *De officiis (Obligations)* was highly influential, particularly in Europe in later centuries. It developed the idea that there is a natural order of the universe that provides moral guidance for all human actions independently of social customs or traditions. Hence, it helped establish the idea that a single moral law binds all human beings and that all human beings have moral claims on all others.

## Fred Cuny (b. 1944; missing and presumed dead, 1995)

A colorful freelance global aid worker, Fred Cuny had a practical genius for getting things done. Cuny was born in Texas and attended several colleges. At one of them, Texas Animal and Industrial College in Kingsville, he became involved with migrant farm laborers and developed an appreciation of their difficulties. He later studied urban planning at the University of Houston. He worked as a city planner some time thereafter. In the late 1960s, he traveled to Biafra, Africa, to serve as an aid worker. Biafra was the scene of a murderous and ruinous civil war, and was the first case where the international community became involved in large-scale humanitarian relief efforts. The relief effort in Biafra became a model for other international humanitarian missions that followed in the 1970s, 1980s, and 1990s. As a result of his experiences, and dismayed by the lack of preparation and expertise the international relief agencies displayed, Cuny became interested in the practical problems of supplying food aid in emergency situations. He returned to the United States and founded a company, the International Relief and Reconstruction Corporation, a consulting firm that provided expertise and training in disaster relief to international agencies. Cuny later worked in Cambodia, Guatemala, Thailand, and other countries. He gained national attention for his efforts in Kuwait following the Gulf War. There he worked closely with American and international groups to provide humanitarian relief and to resettle refugees. Cuny then moved on to Somalia and, following his activities in Somalia, began work in the former Yugoslavia. His most notable achievement in the Balkans was his creation of a means of supplying water to Sarajevo during the siege. His work in Sarajevo brought him to the attention of George Soros, head of the Soros Foundations. When war broke out in Chechnya, Cuny traveled there to provide emergency aid to the Chechens. He was last seen in Chechnya on 31 March 1995, when he set off with a small group to meet with the Chechen guerrilla leader, in hopes of negotiating a cease-fire between Chechen and Russian troops. He is believed dead.

## Lynn E. Davis (b. 1943)

Lynn E. Davis has been U.S. undersecretary of state for arms control and international security affairs since 1993. She received her B.A. from Duke University and her Ph.D. from Columbia University. She has held several staff positions on the Senate Select Committee on Intelligence and the National Security Council. Davis has taught national security policy at the National War College and political science at Columbia University. She also served as Director of Studies at London's International Institute of Strategic Studies. During the Carter administration, she worked four years as deputy assistant secretary of defense for policy plans. Before accepting her present position, Davis was vice president of the RAND Corporation in Santa Monica, California.

## Elizabeth Dole (b. 1936)

Born in Salisbury, North Carolina, Elizabeth Dole is a graduate of Duke University and received her law degree as well as a master's degree in education and government from Harvard University. She has held several high offices in the U.S. government, including those of secretary of transportation and secretary of labor. She has been president of the American Red Cross since 1991. As president, she oversees the activities of some 30,000 staff members and more than 1.5 million volunteers. She also initiated an ambitious disaster relief campaign, which resulted in $350 million to aid victims of such natural disasters as floods, hurricanes, and earthquakes. In 1994, she received the Maxwell Finland Award from the National Foundation for Infectious Diseases in recognition of her efforts to assure the safety of blood supplies.

## Jean-Henri Dunant (1828–1910)

A Swiss businessman and philanthropist, Jean-Henri Dunant founded the International Committee of the Red Cross. On a business trip in 1859, he happened upon the scene of the Battle of Solferino, an encounter between the French and Austrian armies in the town of Solferino in northern Italy. The battlefield held some 40,000 dead or wounded, and Dunant was horrified by the sight, since the armies were unprepared to assist their own men. Dunant organized the villagers to provide what aid they could. As a result of this experience, Dunant was determined to create societies to provide relief to the wounded in battle. He also sought an international convention that would establish principles concerning the just conduct of war and treatment of wounded, prisoners, and noncombatants. In 1863, Dunant and a small group of citizens of Geneva, Switzerland, established the International Committee for the Relief of the Wounded in Warfare. This organization eventually became the International Committee of the Red Cross. In that same year, the group also invited representatives of 16 nations to Geneva for a conference to reach agreement on a set of rules of war. This resulted in the first Geneva Convention, adopted in 1864, and the foundation of the international law that continues to evolve in the present time, the most recent development being the adoption, in April 1996, of the Chemical Warfare Convention, outlawing the possession, development, and use of chemical and biological weapons.

## Mark Gearan (b. 1957)

B orn in Gardner, Massachusetts, Mark Gearan was named the fourteenth director of the U.S. Peace Corps in 1995. Prior to his appointment, he held offices on the staffs of a number of prominent politicians, including President Bill Clinton and Vice President Al Gore. Since becoming director, he has visited Peace Corps volunteers in several nations and has opened programs in Haiti and South Africa. Among other things, he has refocused Peace Corps activities to give greater emphasis to economics and development. To that end, he has worked to recruit more volunteers with backgrounds in business. Gearan has also instituted a program that allows volunteers and returned

Peace Corps veterans to provide short-term assistance to communities during humanitarian crises or natural disasters.

## Hugo Grotius (1583–1645)

A Dutch jurist, Hugo Grotius is viewed as the father of international law. Grotius studied law at the University of Leiden and became a lawyer at age 15. He later became involved in politics, and when his political faction lost power, he was tried and condemned to death. He succeeded in escaping from prison and took refuge in Paris, where he wrote the book for which he is most noted, *De jure belli ac pacis (The Law of War and Peace)*. This book is generally considered the first definitive text on international law and the ancestor of present-day international and humanitarian law. Grotius's fundamental idea, taken from the Bible and from classical history, is that there is a natural law, a fundamental order of the universe, that establishes norms of conduct for human beings. The principle that Grotius believes grounds this law is the universal right of rational self-preservation, which he asserts that all people desire for themselves and are bound to respect for others as well. He further asserts that this natural law provides rules to constrain the conduct of nations as well as individual human beings. As far as nations are concerned, his most important application of natural law theory is to the rules governing war. Grotius did not believe that all wars are morally wrong, but he did argue that wars fought for the wrong reasons and for the wrong ends are prohibited by natural law. He also believed that natural law offers direction for the ways in which all wars should be conducted. One of his primary goals was to make war more humane by encouraging respect for private persons (i.e., noncombatants) and their property.

## Dag Hammarskjöld (1905–1961)

A skilled diplomat, Dag Hammarskjöld served as secretary-general of the United Nations from 1953 until his death in 1961. Hammarskjöld was a Swedish citizen, the son of a former prime minister of Sweden. He was educated at the Universities of Uppsala and Stockholm and received a Ph.D. in 1934. Hammarskjöld entered governmental service in 1930 and held a number of posts. In 1951, he was named a member of Sweden's delegation to the United Nations. In 1953, he was elected secretary-general of the United Nations, succeeding Trygve Lie in that post, and was reelected to the position in 1957. He died in a plane crash in the Congo while on a U.N. mission. Hammarskjöld greatly extended the influence and activities of the United Nations during his tenure as secretary-general and enhanced the prestige of the office. He led several delegations to attempt to reduce tensions in troubled areas of the world and was instrumental in using U.N. forces for peace-keeping and observation missions.

## Trygve Lie (1896–1968)

A Norwegian statesman and diplomat, Lie served as head of the Norwegian Labor Party and held several posts in the government of Norway. He was elected the first secretary-general of the United Nations in 1946. Lie's tenure as secretary-general was notable for his active endorsement of the United Nations' role in the Korean War. Following his career in the United Nations, Lie returned to service in the Norwegian government.

## Aryeh Neier (b. 1937)

Since 1993, Aryeh Neier has been president of the Soros Foundations and the Open Society Institute, a privately funded, nonprofit organization dedicated to promoting freedom of expression and democratic processes around the world. Neier was born in Berlin, Germany, came to the United States in 1947, and has since become a naturalized citizen. He received his B.S. from Cornell University in 1958. Prior to his appointment to the Soros Foundations and the Open Society Institute, Neier was executive director of Human Rights Watch and national director of the American Civil Liberties Union (ACLU). He also has served as an adjunct professor of law at New York University and is an internationally recognized expert and activist in the domain of human rights. Neier has conducted investigations of human rights abuses in 40 nations and has played a major role in establishing an international tribunal to prosecute those responsible for war crimes and crimes against humanity in the former Yugoslavia. He has written four books on human rights abuses and also contributed articles to *The Nation*, the *New York Review of Books*, the *New York Times Magazine*, and the *New York Times Book Review*.

## Phyllis E. Oakley (b. 1934)

Phyllis Oakley has been U.S. assistant secretary of state for population, refugees, and migration since 1993. In this position she heads the State Department's Bureau for Population, Refugees, and Migration. The primary responsibilities of this bureau are to formulate U.S. policies on population, refugees, and migration and to administer U.S. refugee assistance and admissions programs. Oakley received her undergraduate degree from Northwestern University and is a graduate of the Fletcher School of International Law and Diplomacy at Tufts University. She is a career member of the Foreign Service Office, having first joined the Department of State in 1957, later retiring to raise a family, then rejoining in 1974. She has held a variety of posts in the State Department. She worked in the State Department's Afghanistan office from 1982 to 1985, and from 1989 through 1991 she was on loan to the U.S. Agency for International Development, working in its Afghanistan Cross-Border Humanitarian Assistance Program. She also has taught American history at Centenary College in Shreveport, Louisiana, and has served as consultant on international affairs for the YWCA. Among other responsibilities, Oakley oversees U.S. contributions to U.N. refugee relief activities. She also directs U.S. assistance to the International Red Cross. In fact, the U.S. government is the largest single contributor to this group. In additional to financial assistance, Oakley works closely with U.N. agencies and international nongovernmental organizations to coordinate refugee assistance programs in various parts of the world. In recent years, the greatest needs have been in the former Yugoslavia and the war-ravaged nations of sub-Sahara Africa. Oakley is also responsible for helping formulate and direct U.S. policies guiding admission of refugees. The United States resettles more refugees within its borders than any other nation. In past years, the majority of those the U.S. admitted were refugees from Communist nations. At present, fewer refugees come from communist nations and many more are escaping religious or ethnic strife or the oppression of totalitarian governments.

## Sadako Ogata (b. 1927)

Born in Tokyo, Sadako Ogata became the U.N. High Commissioner for Refugees in 1991, and she was reappointed to that office in 1993. Prior to her appointment, she held several posts within the United Nations, including that of the Japanese representative to the U.N. Commission on Human Rights, and worked with UNESCO. She has been a professor of diplomatic history and international relations at Sophia University in Tokyo and the University of the Sacred Heart in Tokyo. In her present position, she oversaw the program to aid over 2 million persons displaced by the conflicts in the former Yugoslavia. She also supervised postwar resettlement efforts in Cambodia, Ethiopia, and Vietnam. In addition, she has worked to improve policies to protect refugees seeking asylum.

## St. Paul the Apostle (ca. 5–67)

Paul is among those who were instrumental in nurturing the idea that all human beings in all cultures have equal moral stature and are equally deserving of moral concern. Born to a Jewish family in Tarsus in Cilicia, Paul became a strict Pharisee and studied in Jerusalem with the Sahara Gamaliel. Paul initially was a persecutor of Christians, but he later radically changed his views and became a Christian. He then became a roving missionary and was particularly insistent on bringing the Christian message to Gentiles. His primary literary legacy is in the form of letters he wrote to churches. He employed concepts found in Hellenic Jewish teachings to rebut those who condemned his mission of preaching to Gentiles. Paul was particularly insistent on the essential unity of Jew and Gentile and asserted that Jews and Gentiles should retain their distinctive identities but treat one another as brothers.

## Mary Robinson (b. 1944)

In June 1997, Mary Robinson was appointed U.N. High Commissioner for Human Rights by U.N. Secretary-General Kofi Annan. She holds primary responsibility for overseeing U.N. human rights activities, including supervising the U.N. Centre for Human Rights in Geneva, Switzerland, and the streamlining of human rights oversight activities throughout the U.N. system. Robinson became a member of the English bar in 1973 and has special expertise in constitutional and European human rights law. She was also a member of the International Commission of Jurists from 1987 to 1990 and a member of the Commission of Inter-Rights from 1984 to 1990. Before accepting her present post, Robinson served as president of Ireland, an office she held from 1990 to 1997. As the Irish president, she was the first head of state to visit Rwanda following its episode of genocide, and she returned there several times. She was also the first head of state to visit the international tribunal for the former Yugoslavia and the first to visit Somalia. During her tenure as president, Robinson placed special emphasis on serving the needs of developing and needy nations, in part because of Ireland's tremendous suffering during the great famine of the nineteenth century.

## Eleanor Roosevelt (1884–1962)

Born in New York City, Eleanor Roosevelt was an enthusiastic supporter of social causes during her youth. She married Franklin Delano Roosevelt in 1905. After her husband was elected president of the United States in 1932, Eleanor Roosevelt became active in governmental affairs. She held several offices, including that of assistant director of the Office of Civilian Defense during World War II. She was U.S. delegate to the United Nations from 1945 to 1953 and was named to that position again in 1961. In 1946, she served as chairwoman of the U.N. Commission on Human Rights, a subsidiary of the Economic and Social Council. In this post she played a vital role in formulating the U.N. Universal Declaration of Human Rights. While working on the committee to formulate the U.N. Universal Declaration of Human Rights, she was instrumental in breaking a deadlock between the United States and the Soviet Union on the matter of what sorts of rights should be included. The United States believed that only rights of the sort encapsulated in the U.S. Bill of Rights should be included, while the Soviets insisted that the declaration should instead include what they termed social and economic rights, that is, rights to decent working conditions, minimum wages, decent health care, adequate education, and the like. Roosevelt saw no reason why both sorts of rights couldn't be included, and her suggestion ended the impasse. She hoped that the U.N. Universal Declaration of Human Rights would serve as a sort of Magna Carta for all mankind. That is, it would be the inspiration and foundation for laws that would benefit all human beings. She also believed that the document needed to be supplemented by concrete measures to ensure that the rights it contained were actually implemented and respected. Finally, she played an important role in gaining U.S. support for the U.N. declaration at a time when there was growing hostility to the United Nations and all associated with it in the United States.

## Bertrand Russell (1872–1970)

Among the most colorful and rambunctious figures of the twentieth century, Bertrand Russell was a renowned British philosopher, mathematician, and public figure. He made important intellectual contributions to the philosophy of science, the foundations of logic and mathematics, and several other branches of philosophy. He was among the most influential intellectual figures of this century, and some assert that he is the most influential figure since Voltaire. Born in Wales, Russell was a member of a distinguished English family. His grandfather was a noted statesman and twice prime minister. Russell was educated at Trinity College, Cambridge, and later taught there intermittently. He became a committed and active pacifist during World War I, and his activities resulted in a prison term and loss of his position at Cambridge. For the next several decades he supported himself largely through writing and speaking. He renounced his pacifism before World War II, in the face of the Nazi threat, because, he asserted, he was not unalterably opposed to any and all wars, only those that were unjust. He returned to pacifism after the war and became a committed activist, working for world peace and nuclear disarmament. With Jean-Paul Sartre, he organized the War Crimes Tribunal held in Stockholm, Sweden, in 1967, which condemned U.S. conduct in the Vietnam War.

## Albert Schweitzer (1875–1965)

Albert Schweitzer had several careers—theologian, musician, and philosopher—but that for which he is best known is medical missionary. Born in northeastern France, Schweitzer received his doctorate of medicine in 1913, and soon thereafter established a hospital in Lambaréné, in today's Gabon, which was then part of French Equatorial Africa. Apart from his fund-raising trips abroad, Schweitzer spent the rest of his life there, building an extensive medical complex. However, his influence lay as much in his moral vision as in his actions. Schweitzer's thinking borrowed elements from German, Indian, and Christian thought. His basic concept was that of civilization, which he contrasted with culture. For Schweitzer, civilization was universal and binding on all human beings, whereas cultures were distinctive and particular to their regions and historical eras. Schweitzer viewed civilization as a value that human beings should strive to achieve. Allied to this view, he held a Buddhist attitude toward life in all its forms. Believing that all forms of life were sacred, he even refused to kill the flies that roamed his hospital.

Among his many other awards and honors, Schweitzer received the Nobel Peace Prize in 1952.

## Amartya Sen (b. 1933)

A ctive in behalf of women's rights, famine prevention, population control, and economic development, Amartya Sen has made significant contributions to economics and philosophy. He has held a professorship in both subjects at Harvard University since 1988. Sen was born in Santiniketan, India, in 1933. He was educated at Presidency College in Calcutta, where he received his B.A. in 1953, and in Cambridge, England. He is a graduate of Trinity College, Cambridge, where he received a B.A. in 1955 and a Ph.D. in 1959. He taught at Oxford University, Cambridge University, the London School of Economics, Cornell University, and Delhi University before accepting the posts at Harvard. He has been president of a number of professional organizations, including the American Economic Association and the Indian Economic Association. His interests are broad and varied, and include social choice theory, welfare economics, the theory of measurement, moral and political philosophy, and the rationality of choice and behavior. He has written and spoken widely, and has been particularly influential on issues of global population, the status and rights of women, and economic development. Specialists assert that Sen has changed the way the world's governments think about poverty and famine. He argues that famine is not simply a consequence of nature but also results from political and economic conditions. Hence, governments should put less emphasis on handing out food and more on putting money into the pockets of needy people. Sen also has written important work on the social, economic, and personal consequences of inequality between men and women. His work is unusual among economists in being founded on the belief that individual human rights deserve higher priority than the pursuit of material well-being as well as for arguing passionately that the protection and nurturing of individual rights result in enhanced economic well-being for impoverished people.

## John Shattuck (b. 1943)

S ince 1993, John Shattuck has been assistant secretary of state for democracy, human rights, and labor in the U.S. State Department. The State Department Bureau for Democracy, Human Rights, and Labor has broad and varied responsibilities, which include promoting democracy across the globe, formulating U.S. human rights policies, and coordinating U.S. policies for human rights–related labor issues. Among the bureau's most important responsibilities is formulating the Annual Country Reports on Human Rights, which monitor human rights observance in nations across the globe and provide a factual basis for U.S. policy decisions. It also serves as a useful resource for human rights activists and organizations in the United States and overseas. Shattuck received his B.A. from Yale University in 1965. In 1967, he received an M.A. in international law and jurisprudence from Cambridge University, and in 1970 he received an LL.B. from Yale Law School. He was executive director of the American Civil Liberties Union's Washington Office from 1976 to 1984 and served on the ACLU's National Council. He was vice chairman of Amnesty International's U.S. section. From 1984 to 1993, he was vice president of Harvard University and taught human rights and civil liberties law at the Harvard Law School. He has received several awards for his work, including, in 1989, the Free Press Association's H. L. Mencken Award.

## George Soros (b. 1930)

George Soros is the founder of the Open Society Foundations and of the Soros Foundations, which oversee the various Open Society Foundations. This group of organizations is dedicated to the task of creating and sustaining the infrastructure required for an open society, one in which freedom of expression, tolerance, and democratic processes are of fundamental importance. Soros was born in Budapest, Hungary, and migrated to England in 1947. In England he attended the London School of Economics and became familiar with the work of Sir Karl Popper, a distinguished philosopher who argued strongly in favor of the principles that characterize Soros's open society. Many of Soros's later activities show the influence of these ideas. Soros emigrated to the United States in 1956, and in time, became wealthy as a result of the success of his international investment fund. He established his first Open Society Fund in 1976 and now has a network of Open Society Foundations in 30 nations, ranging from Haiti to the states of the former Soviet Union. Soros has donated more than $300 million in each of the past several years to support the work of these foundations.

## Voltaire (1694–1778)

Voltaire was a renowned French philosopher, author, historian, and wit. He was born in Paris and studied at a Jesuit school, where he received a rigorous classical education. Voltaire, who was famous for his sharp tongue, was imprisoned several times in the infamous Bastille for offending powerful public figures. He visited England in 1726 and was enormously impressed by British thought and Newtonian science. On his return to France, he did much to popularize both. He also spent several years at the court of Frederick II, King of Prussia. Voltaire believed that all human beings have a natural sense of benevolence toward others and a sense of justice. In his famous satiric novel *Candide*, Voltaire lampooned the belief that European civilization is superior to all others, particularly those deemed primitive by Europeans. He simultaneously conveyed the belief that human beings of all races and cultures are capable of achieving high standards of moral integrity, and he endorsed the values of toleration and justice.

## Raoul Wallenberg
### (b. 1912; missing since 1945 and now believed dead)

Raoul Wallenberg is believed to have saved some 20,000 lives during World War II. Wallenberg was born into an extremely wealthy Swedish family and eventually entered the family enterprise of banking. His business activities frequently took him abroad, and he mastered several foreign languages. At the request of Franklin Delano Roosevelt, Wallenberg joined the U.S. War Refugees Board and was sent to Hungary to help Hungarian Jews escape. He employed many irregular strategies, including bribery and extortion, to prevent the Jews from being sent to the Nazi gas chambers. He also had thousands of fake documents printed that proclaimed the bearers to be Swedish citizens. When the Russian army occupied Budapest, Wallenberg ventured to meet with its commanding general, and thereafter disappeared. Russian sources now assert that Wallenberg died in prison in Moscow in 1947. However, recent reports from concentration camp inmates claim that he was seen alive after 1947. He was declared an honorary citizen of the United States by the U.S. Congress in 1981.

## William B. Walsh (1920–1996)

Dismayed at the poor health of people in the South Seas islands he visited as a medical officer during World War II, William Walsh founded Project HOPE in 1958 . His project soon took the shape of a floating civilian hospital ship, the USS *HOPE*, which sailed among the South Seas islands, dispensing surgical and medical care and health information and training. The USS *HOPE* sailed from 1960 through 1974, when it was retired from service. Project HOPE continues today as a land-based medical and humanitarian assistance organization. It presently has 45 health education and humanitarian assistance programs in 20 nations and serves approximately 1 million people each year. Walsh was born in Brooklyn, New York, and received his undergraduate training at St. John's University and his medical training at the Georgetown University School of Medicine, where he received his M.D. in 1943. He was among the first American physicians to treat Japanese civilians in Hiroshima after the atomic bomb was dropped. Following his war service, Walsh practiced as a heart specialist in Washington, D.C. He is author of three books on Project HOPE and has received numerous awards, including the U.S. Medal of Freedom (the highest civilian award in the United States) in 1987.

## Woodrow Wilson (1856–1924)

The twenty-eighth president of the United States, Woodrow Wilson served two terms, from 1913 to 1921. Wilson was born in Staunton, Virginia, and received his B.A. from Princeton University in 1879. He studied law at the University of Virginia and was admitted to the bar in 1882. He practiced law briefly before enrolling at Johns Hopkins University, where he received his Ph.D. in political science and jurisprudence in 1886. Wilson then taught at Bryn Mawr, Wesleyan University, and Princeton University. In 1902, he was elected president of Princeton, the first noncleric to hold the position. After a time, he moved into politics, and in 1910 he was elected governor of New Jersey, where he instituted several reforms that brought him nationwide fame. Elected president of the United States in 1912, Wilson instituted a number of reforms under the rubric "New Freedom." In 1918, he announced his Fourteen Points program to the U.S. Congress, outlining the basic principles that he believed would lead to a just and lasting peace following World War I. Among other things, Wilson believed the peace agreement should establish a new world order, to be governed in accordance with the principle of the self-determination of peoples, free of secret diplomacy and war, and possessing an association of nations to preserve international justice. The peace treaty that eventually ended World War I fell short of Wilson's hopes, but it did contain a provision creating the League of Nations. Unfortunately, reservations in the United States concerning the potential loss of U.S. sovereignty that joining the League might entail, along with Wilson's failing health, prevented the United States from joining. Without U.S. participation, the League of Nations was crippled and never functioned as Wilson had hoped. However, it did pave the way for the United Nations, which has proven vastly more successful than the League of Nations and has at least partially fulfilled Wilson's aspirations for a new world order.

## James D. Wolfensohn (b. 1933)

As president of the World Bank since 1995, James D. Wolfensohn has dedicated himself to understanding the challenges and issues facing his organization by traveling to its programs across the world and discussing the bank's activities with World Bank staff as well as local citizens and groups. As president, Wolfensohn has given his support to a number of World Bank initiatives. For one, he wishes to give the World Bank a greater role as a source of knowledge and expertise regarding economic development. In addition, he wishes to give nations and local communities receiving World Bank assistance a greater voice in developing and executing projects. He also participated in an effort with Michel Camdessus, president of the International Monetary Fund, to reduce the level of debt of the most heavily indebted poor nations of the world. In addition, he has committed the World Bank to assist in the global fight against corruption by reducing financial assistance to nations that fail to make serious efforts to combat corruption. Lastly, he has directed the World Bank to join forces with environmental groups to support sustainable development, that is, economic development that does not deplete the world's store of natural resources.

Born in Australia, Wolfensohn is now a U.S. citizen. He received his B.A. and LL.B. degrees from the University of Sydney and an M.B.A. from Harvard University. He is currently chairman of the Institute for Advanced Study at Princeton University and has been an active supporter of the arts for many years. Wolfensohn was previously an international investment banker, serving as president and chief executive officer of James D. Wolfensohn, Inc. Founded in 1981, the organization operates in the Americas, Asia, and Europe, offering financial and strategic advice to 30 major corporations.

# CONTEMPORARY ETHICAL ISSUES

## Chapter 4:
## Key Issues
## in International
## Ethics

The entries in this chapter outline key issues and questions within the domain of international ethics. Each entry provides a synopsis of the issue or question, the complexities and difficulties they pose, and an account of the prevailing positions and arguments on that issue or question.

## Crime

For the past several years, the Federal Bureau of Investigation (FBI) has been opening offices in many foreign nations. It is pursuing this policy because crime has increasingly become international in scope, and the FBI reasons that efforts to fight crime must therefore become international. The Russians, who have welcomed the FBI to Moscow, obviously agree.

It might be surprising that crime fighting has become a major international activity, but international crime has grown alongside the global economy. In some cases, criminal activity such as the international drug trade is the first contact some areas of the world have with the international economy. Human nature being what it is, crime intrudes into every domain. Certainly, the same conditions that have made global economic activity possible—that is, the advances in transportation and communication and the political commitment to free markets and opening national borders—also support criminal endeavor.

The most important and lucrative of these criminal activities is the international drug trade. The insatiable appetite of many for illicit drugs has spawned elaborate and often highly sophisticated manufacturing and distribution networks that now operate across the world. These drug rings are sufficiently agile and inventive to survive in face of determined governmental efforts to eliminate them, and when one or another network is dismantled, others soon sprout up in its place.

Many other, less spectacular modes of crime also parasitically thrive on conditions designed to enhance economic trade. Some of these activities are ancient, such as the time-honored practice of smuggling, which has taken on new forms under the conditions of global commerce. For example, there are thriving networks for stealing and transporting goods (automobiles, in particular) across national boundaries. However, some types of criminal activity are unique to the international domain. Examples include criminal rings that smuggle laborers into prosperous nations to seek work as well as industries that customarily flout international copyright conventions and patent agreements.

Nations that are lax in enforcing international patent and copyright agreements and laws often find themselves hosts to industries that are devoted to producing copies of films, music, books, and patented products without paying royalties or obtaining legal permission. Poor people in poor nations have great incentive to skirt copyright and patent laws, since the goods produced under these conditions can be sold for far less than the originals, and they can thus turn a good profit in their locales. Because of the great financial benefits from this activity, many governments, particularly those of developing nations, are disposed to turn a blind eye to copyright violations. In addition, today's global financial markets have created opportunities for other types of swindling, double-dealing, and fraud on a global scale.

International criminal activity raises several knotty moral issues. One difficulty is that international crime might bring considerable benefits to one nation while causing vexing problems for other nations. Drugs such as cocaine create great difficulties for many wealthier countries and regions—the United States and Europe in particular—but are often the most reliable source of income for the poor farmers who grow coca plants in the mountains of Colombia. Colombia's highly profitable drug trade provides a significant portion of its national income, and many segments of the economy, from the construction industry to automobile sales, are supported to a significant extent by the drug trade. If Colombia were to succeed in eliminating its homegrown drug industry, its economy and the livelihood of many of its citizens would be erased.

Of course, Colombia suffers from the violence and corruption caused by the drug industry and from the diversion of so much money, human energy, and intelligence to the cocaine trade, which is distorting its economy and preventing other sorts of economic development from emerging. Nonetheless, Colombia and many of its citizens would be seriously harmed by the eradication of the drug cartels. Hence, one might well question whether other countries, such as the United States, are justified in pressuring Colombia to eliminate its drug trade.

Removing Colombia's cocaine from the world market might aid the United States in its battle against drugs, but it will certainly result in considerable hardship for many of Colombia's ordinary citizens. In essence, a wealthy and powerful nation, the United States, is pressing a poor nation to serve its goals of combating the drug trade. Some argue that it would be better to have a common set of international laws regarding criminal activity, so that different nations would not have varying standards of what counts as crime and there would be a single agency equipped and authorized to investigate crimes and enforce laws. This arrangement would go a long way toward removing the awkward situation that exists between the United States and Colombia.

However, if it is true that international crime requires international law enforcement, then perhaps there should be an international criminal code that is binding on all nations and an international law enforcement agency that would have jurisdiction in all nations. Another very considerable problem is that differing nations have vastly different types of courtroom and trial proceedings and wildly different standards of punishment. In those Islamic nations that function in accordance with Islamic law, *shar'ia*, the penalty for theft is amputation of a limb and the penalty for adultery is death. In many other parts of the world, these penalties would be considered grossly cruel and unusual punishment. But if crime is spread worldwide, some would ask whether courtroom procedures and punishments should be global as well.

Another difficulty that accompanies the emergence of global crime is that many nations' codes of law and investigative machinery are ill suited to deal with certain sorts of crimes. With the development of global financial markets, the possibility of global financial swindles has become a significant problem. However, some nations do not have laws that regulate these sorts of crimes and lack investigative agencies with the expertise to uncover and investigate such crimes.

The measures discussed above would require that nations surrender some of their sovereignty, and many would consider this an ominous step along the way to world government. Understandably, measures of this sort are vigorously debated. Some assert that there is no need for an international legal code and international enforcement agencies, and furthermore, that these institutions would be undesirable. They assert that there is no need for such international machinery because the police bureaus of the world's nations are already accustomed to cooperating and can be expected to cooperate more fully and smoothly in years to come. Improving legal systems and investigative machinery, as well as coordinating the inclusion of legal statutes, can be accomplished by the same mechanism of the cooperation of individual governments with one another. Hence, multinational legal codes and law enforcement bureaus are not needed. Only the expansion and refinement of the present system of national cooperation is needed. Furthermore, they argue, there is little reason to ask individual nations to abandon their systems of courtroom procedure or traditions of punishment for the sake of international standards. Once again, if any modifications are necessary, opponents of international law enforcement agencies argue that they can be achieved by the cooperation of individual nations, who will modify their legal systems as needed. However, beyond modifications that individual governments agree are necessary, there is no need to attempt to move governments away from the systems of law and punishment that the people of each individual nation find congenial and that fit smoothly with their culture and values. Even systems of punishment such as those contained within the *shar'ia*, which may appear cruel and outmoded to people in Western nations, fit well with the cultures in which they are found, and there is no need to insist that people abandon a system that reflects their values.

Many peoples and governments would vigorously resist pressure to conform to systems of legal standards that they believe are alien and unsuited to their nations. An attempt to impose conformity with a global system would probably fail, particularly because of the large number of nations and wide variety of legal systems in the world. The result of such an attempt would be chaos, with less effectual legal control than exists in the present system of international cooperation. Furthermore, it is argued that these systems would be undesirable because they would necessarily infringe on the sovereignty of the nations of the world and would disrupt the cultural practices of many of its peoples. Because national governments are obligated to represent the interests of their people, a violation of national sovereignty is a failure to observe the autonomy of the world's peoples. In extreme cases, the violation of national sovereignty might be justified, but when there are less extreme measures available for achieving global law enforcement, it would be morally unjustified. A similar argument applies to global systems of law that impinge on national legal cultures.

Those in favor of a global system of law and a global agency of law enforcement respond vigorously to the arguments presented above. They assert that the very diversity and complexity of the world's cultures and legal systems will prevent international legal cooperation and agreements from evolving into an effective global legal system. Moreover, such agreements are apt to favor the wealthier and more powerful nations, which can bend the less wealthy and powerful to their wills (as in the case of Colombia and the United States). Only a unified system will allow the flexibility and provide the resources to deal effectively with the increasingly sophisticated, powerful, and wealthy criminal rings. In the case of Colombia, the nation is in thrall to the drug cartels. Hence, it is unlikely that Colombia, relying only on its resources, would be able to respond effectively to the problem of coping with its drug manufacturers and traders. Outside assistance, and perhaps even goading, are needed.

Proponents of global law argue that in a closely interdependent world, with dense international ties of trade and communication, a standardized system of law and trial procedure is needed to provide the rule of law to all people. The legal systems of many nations and regions are already changing to accommodate the needs of global commerce and global interconnectedness. For example, nations have changed copyright and intellectual property laws, as well as worker safety and environmental protection regulations as a result of international trade agreements. In other cases, Russia, Japan, and China, in particular, governments have found that the pressures of the global financial markets are forcing them to alter their regulation of financial institutions and stock and bond markets.

Since it is reasonable to expect that the global economy will continue to expand and that the nations will continue to become more closely interconnected, the problem of international crime is likely to loom ever larger in the years to come. Effective international measures will have to be devised to cope with it. At the very least, an effective response will require greater standardization of laws and of legal processes. In addition, the law enforcement agencies of the world will be forced into ever closer cooperation if they are to be effective in carrying out their duties. However, at this point, it must be noted that it is not obvious whether a unified system of law and law enforcement bureaus is necessary to get the job done, or whether the challenge of international crime can be met by less ambitious measures.

**For further reading:** Bossard, Andrâe. 1990. *Transnational Crime and Criminal Law.* Chicago: University of Illinois, Office of International Criminal Justice.

Clark, Roger Stenson. 1994. *The United Nations Crime Prevention and Criminal Justice Program: Formulation of Standards and Efforts at Their Implementation.* Philadelphia: University of Pennsylvania Press.

Fooner, Michael. 1989. *Interpol: Issues in World Crime and International Criminal Justice.* New York: Plenum Press.

Nadelmann, Ethan Avram. 1993. *Cops across Borders: The Internationalization of U.S. Criminal Law Enforcement.* University Park: Pennsylvania State University Press.

Raine, Linnea, and Frank Cillufo, eds. 1994. *Global Organized Crime: The New Empire of Evil.* Washington, DC: Center for Strategic and International Studies.

United States Congress, House Committee on Banking and Financial Services. 1996. *Organized Crime and Banking.* Washington, DC: U.S. Government Printing Office.

United States Congress, House Committee on the Judiciary. Subcommittee on Crime. 1996. *The Growing Threat of International Organized Crime.* Washington, DC: U.S. Government Printing Office.

United States Congress, Senate Committee on Foreign Relations. 1993. *International Criminal Courts.* Washington, DC: U.S. Government Printing Office.

# Disease Prevention and Control

No problem is more genuinely international than that of disease prevention and control. The same astounding advances in transportation and communications that have sparked the emergence of a global economy have also created the conditions that have made disease prevention and control a global issue.

In fall 1995, one corner of India suffered an outbreak of pneumonic plague. The international community was immediately concerned, fearing that infected individuals would quickly spread the disease via jet travel to other parts of the world. What would have been strictly a local problem a century or even a half century ago became a matter of global concern as a result of convenient and relatively inexpensive air travel.

The outbreak in India reveals yet another problem. Shortly after the flare-up of pneumonic plague, the world community became aware that India's medical laboratories were ill equipped to cope with problems of that sort. They lacked the equipment, trained personnel, and effective public health laws that would have assisted them to isolate the cause of the disease, determine its nature, determine the scope of the outbreak, and establish controls on population movements to prevent the disease from spreading. Had the disease been more virulent, the entire world might have suffered as a result. Thus, the problems of insufficient laboratory equipment, technical expertise, and public health measures posed a risk not only to the citizens of India but to all of humanity.

Related to this is the problem that people in many parts of the world have not yet been immunized against a number of potentially deadly, easily prevented diseases. Once again, the difficulty is that many nations lack the finances and the institutions to undertake immunization programs. However, should these diseases recur in any part of the world as a result of inadequate programs of inoculation, they will become a problem and a danger to all of humanity due to vastly increased human mobility.

The global economy also creates several difficulties for disease control and prevention in more direct fashion. For much of 1996, the United Kingdom's relations with the other nations of Europe were strained due to the outbreak of bovine spongiform encephalopathy, or mad cow disease, in Great Britain. This is a disease with no known cure that results in degeneration of the nervous system and eventual death. The disease was first discovered in cows, but later the British government discovered that it could be transmitted to humans who ate food products made from diseased cows. Many European nations immediately halted the import of beef products from Britain. Because beef exports are an important source of revenue for the British, particularly for cattle farmers, they immediately undertook measures that would allow the ban to be lifted. Concern immediately spread to other parts of the world, including the United States, for fear that infected beef products from Britain might result in disease there. Once again, what would have been a local problem a few decades ago immediately became an issue of global concern as a result of the existence of transglobal trade.

The burgeoning international trade in drugs, medical equipment, and genetically engineered products has also resulted in problems of international disease control. For example, in the United States, there are very strict regulations controlling the development and sale of drugs. All drugs must be approved for sale by the Food and Drug Administration and must pass lengthy and expensive batteries of tests before approval is given. This results in several problems. One is that drugs that are not certified as safe and effective in the United States might be put on sale in parts of the world where regulation is looser or nonexistent. Some argue that it is morally wrong for U.S. corporations to sell drugs elsewhere in the world before they have been deemed safe for American citizens. The claim is that allowing such a practice in effect puts less value on the lives and well-being of people in other parts of the world than on those of U.S. citizens. Furthermore, some argue that the U.S. government has an obligation to the citizens of other nations to prevent this practice.

However, the question of government drug regulation cuts in several directions. Several medications, it is claimed by some, are helping patients and saving lives in other parts of the world but are unavailable in the United States because of the latter's strict and elaborate testing requirements. Some argue that U.S. standards are overly strict and cumbersome and are preventing Americans from gaining timely access to medications that might save their lives. Such arguments were made recently by AIDS activists in the United States who were concerned because drugs available to AIDS patients elsewhere in the world were not available in the United States because of strict drug regulation. In their view, the problem was not lack of concern for citizens abroad but overzealous efforts at home to ensure the absolute safety of medications, which were preventing useful medications from reaching people who needed them in a timely way.

Yet another difficulty results from furious activity in the field of genetic engineering. This area has shown enormous promise as an avenue for creating new modes of treating disease, new medications, and new methods of testing for diseases. Genetic engineering is tremendously important, but it is also the source of two significant problems. One is the prospect of creating entirely new organisms, completely unlike any beings that have existed on earth before. Some of these organisms might cause new diseases, which because they are unknown in the natural world, might be untreatable. If such flawed organisms escape into the environment, the result could be a catastrophic epidemic. A second, related problem is that these new products may react with the natural environment in unexpected ways that will not have been apparent in laboratory testing. Once again, the result could be catastrophe for humanity. Following nearly 20 years of vigorous activity in this area, no problems of the kind have yet occurred as the result of genetic engineering. However, complacency might allow disaster to creep in. Once again, the problem is twofold. On the one hand, some techniques of genetic manipulation are quite simple, available even to high school science laboratories. On the other hand, the means required to test genetically engineered products for safety and impact on the environment are costly and difficult. Although genetic engineering is scrupulously monitored in some parts of the world, others have placed no controls on it. Thus, humanity is vulnerable to mishaps resulting from genetic engineering on several fronts. Irresponsible experimentation in unregulated areas of the world could place humanity at risk. Moreover, the processes are sufficiently complex that unexpected problems might arise even in carefully regulated societies.

Thus, the problems of international disease prevention and control are complex and difficult. They include issues of whether international institutions are needed to monitor outbreaks of disease and to devise responsive measures. An obvious difficulty here is whether these institutions should have authority over national governments, and if so, how this authority should be exerted. A related problem for all nations is the provision of adequate laboratory facilities, properly trained technicians, and effective public health laws. Exacerbating this problem is the fact that the countries where massive public health crises are most likely to occur are also those least likely to have laboratories and technicians capable of responding to such crises, or governmental institutions capable of devising and enforcing effective public health legislation. Given variable economic and cultural conditions among nations, any effort to establish global standards for drug regulation and testing, medical procedures, and the control of genetic engineering would face these kinds of obstacles.

A different and even more complex set of problems arises in areas where matters of disease control and prevention overlap with global commerce, as in the case of the outbreak of mad cow disease in Great Britain. In such matters, issues of disease prevention and control are entangled with concerns of commerce, national sovereignty, and conflicting national interests, as well as simple politics. Once again, there is the question of whether international machinery is needed to address these matters and what sort of authority this machinery would have over nations and business concerns.

In every case mentioned above, whatever its complexity, several major issues arise: Firstly, are international institutions needed to affect international disease control and prevention, and what sort of authority over nations should such institutions have? Secondly, what resources should be made available to the impoverished and less developed nations of the world to assist them in responding to outbreaks of disease? Because any effective prevention of or response to disease requires appropriate legislation and enforcement, such assistance might be construed as including support for the creation and enforcement of laws in these nations. Thirdly, we are confronted by the apparent need to devise globally applicable standards of safety and effectiveness for medications, medical procedures, and medical research, particularly that involving genetic engineering. Today, different areas of the world have quite diverse standards governing these matters, but given the realities of international trade, we must decide whether some countries' standards are too lax and therefore a threat to humankind (as might be the case with genetic engineering) or whether such standards should be accepted as valid because of differing cultural valuations of human life and well-being in different parts of the world. We must decide whether there should be minimal standards that apply to all nations and what those standards should be.

In view of the above difficulties, some argue that the only response that might effectively safeguard human life around the world is effective international machinery for responding to and controlling outbreaks of disease. International measures are necessary for disease prevention because the incidence of disease anywhere in the world is no longer a local problem that can be expected to remain confined to a single area but a global problem. To be effective in protecting human life and fighting disease, these institutions would have to exercise authority over the national governments of the world and have access to all people in need of their services.

Standards of safety and effectiveness for medical products and techniques as well as controls of medical experimentation are another domain where many argue that protection of the lives of all people requires an international response that will be binding on all governments. Any other response would be futile because, once again, outbreak of disease anywhere in the world is a danger to the world as a whole, and because any other approach would in effect assign a lesser value to the lives and welfare of people in poor areas of the world than to people in wealthy domains.

Finally, many of those who favor a vigorous global response to matters of disease control and prevention also argue that there must be international machinery for responding to disputes among nations, or among nations and corporations, that have implications for public health. Other attempts at a response are likely to be ineffective and to become embroiled in politics or narrow self-interest. Once again, there must be a common set of standards providing all people at least a minimum level of protection, with provision for stricter standards for those who desire them and who are able to implement them.

However, others argue in response that the above approach is futile because nations are unlikely to yield sufficient authority to multinational institutions to allow the latter to function effectively. Even if nations did formally agree to allow such institutions to be created, it is unlikely that they would actually allow them to function effectively. Furthermore, it is morally unjustified to usurp people's capacity to decide their own responses to matters of public health and disease control.

Hence, opponents of international public health institutions and legislation argue that the present system of allowing individual nations to cooperate with others in solving problems of public health is preferable to more ambitious global responses, not only because it is more likely to be effective but also because it will respect people's autonomy and local control. They make the same sort of argument with regard to standards of safety and effectiveness of medication and regulation of medical research. They claim that the various peoples of the world should be allowed to set varying standards to meet their own needs and preferences. For example, some nations might wish to have very strict standards, since they may place the greatest value on safety. Other nations, however, might place a greater value on making new and potentially helpful medications available to patients who need them, even if these new medications are not tested as rigorously as people in some countries might desire. Lastly, they argue that the present system of bilateral agreements among nations is the best response to the difficulties that arise when international commerce and medical concerns clash. International attempts at control are unlikely to be effective, and nations will wish to remain free to work out their own problems in ways best suited to their own situations.

Like the other ethical issues examined in this book, international disease control and prevention is likely to continue to gain importance in future years. Recently, some medical authorities and researchers have warned of a possible future "global pandemic" resulting in enormous loss of human life and in considerable disruption of social institutions. The conditions of cheap and convenient global travel and the thickening network of global commercial ties will make the problems of international health more immediate. There is little disagreement about the existence of urgent problems in global disease prevention and control. Disputes are focused on the questions of what the most effective response is likely to be and the degree to which the sovereignty of national governments can or should be overridden to address these problems.

Several important institutions operate internationally in the service of human health, the most prominent among them being the U.N. World Health Organization. The U.S. Centers for Disease Control, although a branch of the federal government, also is routinely called into service to deal with outbreaks of disease around the world. It is likely that such organizations will play an ever larger role in matters of world health and that they will have an increasing impact on people's lives. Whether these organizations will evolve into genuine global health care agencies with authority over national governments and power to coerce recalcitrant governments into cooperation is a matter that is not yet clear.

For further reading: Collins, Charles. 1994. *Management and Organization of Developing Health Systems*. Oxford and New York: Oxford University Press.
Garrett, Laurie. 1994. *The Coming Plague*. New York: Farrar, Straus & Giroux.
Horton, Richard. 1995. "Infection: The Global Threat." *New York Review of Books* 42 (6 April): 24–28.
Hurrelmann, Klaus, and Ulrich Laaser. 1996. *International Handbook of Public Health*. Westport, CT: Greenwood Press.
Mann, Jonathan, et al. 1992. *AIDS in the World*. Cambridge, MA: Harvard University Press.
Preston, Richard. 1994. *The Hot Zone*. New York: Random House.
Richardson, Sarah. 1995. "The Return of the Plague." *Discover* 16 (January): 69–70.
Siddiqi, Javed. 1995. *World Health and World Politics: The World Health Organization and the UN System*. Columbia: University of South Carolina Press.
World Health Organization. 1988. "Health for All—All for Health." *World Health* (January/February): 3–29.

# Distributive Justice

Issues of distributive justice include questions of how the world's goods (such as financial wealth and natural resources, but also other resources that are important to human beings, including education, health care, prestige, or power) are to be allocated to people and institutions. On the international level, the main cluster of issues centers on the question of whether wealthy nations have a moral obligation to help poorer nations prosper.

At present, few concerns are more pressing than the vast gap in wealth, power, and influence that separates the prosperous from the impoverished nations of the world. In the United States, for example, the economy produces approximately $20,000 a year for each individual. Figures for Japan, Germany, and other wealthy nations are comparable. On the other hand, the economies of nations such as Mali and Mozambique produce barely several hundred dollars of wealth each year per individual.

Many nations are scrambling to join the most prosperous. These rising nations include South Korea, China, Thailand, and Taiwan. It seems likely that these nations, all located on the Pacific Rim, will soon join the ranks of the wealthy. In fact, some argue that the nations on the Pacific Rim will become economically dominant in the coming century.

What is dismaying, however, is that despite some brilliant success stories, the gap between the very wealthy and the very poor nations of the world has been increasing and appears destined to continue to widen for the foreseeable future. The reasons for this trend are complex, and scholars and diplomats are not in full agreement about them. However, all agree that at least part of the explanation is found in the impact of the global economy on people and nations. At present, nations and individuals must become active participants in the global economy if they are to have any chance of economic success and gain the power and influence that attend prosperity. The successful nations are all active participants in the global economy, and the nations that are gaining increased wealth and influence, such as South Korea and China, are also laboring energetically and nimbly in the global economy. The economic success stories of the past several decades all have come from nations that learned how to take advantage of the opportunities global commerce offers.

To be able to take advantage of the global economy, a nation must have expertise in navigating in the global free market; a command of technology in general and computers in particular; and a sound infrastructure consisting of a competent government, a sophisticated judicial system, and an efficient communications system as well as roads, ports, financial institutions, and so on. The nation possessing these attributes also will have a citizenry that is predominantly well educated, disciplined, highly motivated, and skilled in communication and business practices. Without both types of resources, no nation can succeed in the world market.

At present, the greatly impoverished nations of the world have few of these human or institutional resources, often due to protracted political and social instability. Some are plagued by incompetent and corrupt governments that have been subject to frequent change by military coup; others are fractured by ethnic rivalries that prevent the creation of stable governmental and economic institutions. In some cases, the state is dominated by a small economic and political elite that seeks to maximize its own benefit and to that end has established barriers preventing other members of the population from gaining access to economic and political power. In others, the people and the economy remain under the sway of traditional tribal cultures that are not conducive to forming the skills and institutions they need in order to join the world economy. These factors, singly or in combination, conspire to prevent impoverished nations from making economic headway.

The main issue of distributive justice, therefore, is whether the wealthy nations of the world are obliged to assist the impoverished nations of the world, and if so, in what ways. There are many various reasons why nations might be unable to gain wealth and influence in the present age, but there are few means for political leaders to bring prosperity to their peoples unless their nations become functioning elements of the global economic system. The difficulty is that these nations must develop the cultures and institutions as well as the human characteristics needed to compete effectively in the twenty-first century. One implication is that they will be required to import other nations' business and social cultures, with all their attendant difficulties, and that traditional cultures and traditions will be jeopardized. National groups such as Islamic militants in the Middle East are responding, at least in part, to precisely such an encroachment of contemporary global values and institutions. Because the global market is dominated by European and American cultural and economic practices, Islamic militants are combating what they perceive as Western values and Western corporate activity. These same issues are being publicly debated also in nations such as Japan, South Korea, or Taiwan, which have enjoyed brilliant success in the latter twentieth century but which are also concerned that their traditional values and cultures are imperiled both by their efforts to compete and by the success of those efforts.

It is important to note, however, that the question of distributive justice can be posed at two levels. One is to question what wealthy and comfortable nations are obliged periodically to offer impoverished nations facing crises such as mass starvation, epidemics, natural disasters, or social upheavals. This is the less controversial of the two facets of distributive justice, since most people agree that the privileged nations should offer at least minimal assistance to nations in grave crisis. However, this sense of obligation is not directed only toward impoverished nations, since many nations felt obligated to send aid to Japan when it was struck by a massive earthquake several years ago. Japan is enormously wealthy and competent, but its resources were stretched thin by the magnitude of the disaster that befell it. The obligations of nations to assist a nation whose problems are due to social or military upheaval are more complex, because an effective response to these problems might require the use of military force and is unlikely to be welcomed by the participants battling with one another, as was the case in the recent conflict in the Balkans or the disastrous U.N. intervention in Somalia a few years ago. (For a discussion of these issues, see the section titled Intervention, later in this chapter.)

The more difficult question is whether wealthier nations are morally obliged to help impoverished ones achieve the standards of living and work that the wealthier enjoy. In other words, the question is whether the wealthy nations are obliged to help the impoverished embark on programs of economic development. This is a more difficult problem than giving aid to nations experiencing a temporary crisis, because economic development requires long-term assistance. It will require the commitment of vast sums of money, and it will require that people in poorer nations cast aside traditional patterns of living and traditional relationships to gain the personal and educational skills needed to compete in the global economy. It also will necessitate that nations alter their basic social institutions, such as those of government, law, and finance, to cope with the demands of the global economy. Hence, a program of long-term assistance requires far more money, a much greater investment in planning and education, and a deeper intrusion into the lives and institutions of a nation than does a one-time response to crisis.

Some argue that wealthy and successful nations have no obligation to help impoverished nations raise their standards of living. They claim that the vast gap in wealth and influence is not due to the actions of the wealthy nations; in other words, the basic problems are not imperialism or the exploitation of weaker nations. Rather, some nations simply are not equipped to compete in the global economy. Just as individuals cannot be held responsible for dealing with all the ills and suffering in the world, neither can wealthy nations, which for all their wealth still have finite resources. Furthermore, they argue that the kinds of programs that would be required to bring prosperity to these nations would require massive intrusion into their lives, cultures, and institutions. It would amount, in other words, to a sort of colonialism, albeit benevolent in intent, carrying the implicit message that the wealthy nations of the world must manage the impoverished for the latter's benefit and self-improvement. Finally, they argue that the programs necessary to bring full development would necessarily alter native cultures and traditional patterns of life. These are of great value to the people living in poorer nations, often of greater value than economic success. Furthermore, many argue that there is great intrinsic value in having many different modes of life in the world, and that humanity as a whole would be impoverished if any traditional modes of life were eliminated for the sake of economic development.

However, others argue vigorously that wealthy and successful nations do have a strong moral obligation to assist impoverished ones. They assert that it is commonly agreed that all people have certain minimal human rights (*see* Human Rights) and that these rights can be honored in many cases only by vigorous programs of outside assistance. Thus, regardless of whether the wealthy nations of the world are responsible for the ills of the impoverished, they have a strong obligation, based on the human rights of all people, to help them.

Furthermore, those who favor assistance to the poorer nations argue that it is not always the case that the wealthy are guiltless in causing the problems of the impoverished. Often the governments of wealthy nations conspire to keep tyrannical or greedy ruling classes in power in poor nations when doing so will serve the wealthy nations' military, economic, or political ends. Multinational corporations from wealthy nations also have often been guilty of exploiting natural resources, exporting hazardous wastes, or displacing peasants from the land to suit their purposes. Also, many assert that the wealthy and influential are often able to arrange international treaties and international law and government so that these institutions operate to serve their ends and undermine the interests of the impoverished nations. Hence, the wealthy have an obligation to help where they previously have caused harm.

Those favoring assistance also argue that national development is not necessarily an all-or-nothing affair, nor is it necessary that people who do not wish to cooperate be forced to. They argue that many very simple additions to a nation's life, such as improved schooling, provision of elementary medical care, improved water and roads, and perhaps improved population control methods, would be of great help to many nations and could be provided at minimal cost. They point out that many have attempted to get the wealthy nations of the world to commit a mere 1 percent of their gross national product to assist the impoverished nations. However, the wealthy have for the most part been unwilling to commit to even this modest goal, although the money that would become available could relieve an enormous amount of suffering in the world and could address many of the long-term problems of impoverished nations. Also, making treaties and rules to prevent poor nations from being exploited and offering them guidance and expertise in dealing with the problems of competing in a global economy would be enormously helpful and would cost little. In addition, they argue that competing successfully in the global economy need not require sacrifice of all traditional values, as the success of South Korea and Japan attest. People will make accommodations, as they have before, to allow their cultures to develop. Cultures are not static and should not be turned into museum pieces. Rather, they are parts of human life and must change as human life changes.

Lastly, those favoring assistance argue that since power and influence accompany wealth in the contemporary world, nations must become part of the global system simply to avoid being exploited or overrun by those who are successful. In other words, if nations are to avoid the fate of being perennial adolescents, they must actively join the global economy in order to be able to look after their own affairs, even if they must sacrifice elements of their traditional cultures and ways of life. Life must change, and so must human culture.

For the foreseeable future, it is likely that the widening gap between wealthy and impoverished nations, and wealthy and impoverished groups within wealthy nations, will continue to focus attention on distributive justice. It is likely that debate on this subject will become more intense. However, some very powerful institutions are currently working to assist the development of impoverished nations. The International Monetary Fund and the World Bank are now led by individuals who have committed themselves to these goals. Moreover, with the end of the cold war, the United Nations has lost some of the lethargy into which it had plunged, has placed more emphasis on functioning competently and efficiently, and has given great emphasis to addressing the problems of impoverished nations. Finally, some of the leaders of the wealthy nations have committed themselves, at least in principle, to improving the lives of the underprivileged of the world. A recent president of France has been a strong proponent of these goals and has sought the cooperation of other wealthy nations in pursuing increased economic development for impoverished nations.

For further reading: Chichilnisky, Graciela. 1982. *Basic Needs and the North/South Debate*. New York: World Order Models Project.

Hout, Wil. 1993. *Capitalism and the Third World: Development, Dependence, and the World System*. Aldershot, Hants, England: E. Elgon.

Shue, Henry. 1996. *Basic Rights: Subsistence, Affluence, and U.S. Foreign Policy*. 2d ed. Princeton, NJ: Princeton University Press.

Van Liemt, Gijsbert. 1988. *Bridging the Gap: Four Newly Industrializing Countries and the Changing International Division of Labor*. Geneva, Switzerland: International Labor Organization.

Weisband, Edward, ed. 1989. *Poverty amidst Plenty: World Political Economy and Distributive Justice*. Boulder, CO: Westview Press.

World Bank. 1996. *World Bank Annual Report 1996*. Washington, DC: World Bank.

# Emigration and Immigration

Article 13, Paragraph 2, of the U.N. Universal Declaration of Human Rights reads, "Everyone has the right to leave any country, including his own, and to return to his country." This statement reflects the common belief that all human beings should have freedom of movement, including the freedom to leave a nation if they wish, and perhaps as important, to return if they wish. However, all the inhabitable land masses of the earth are currently under the dominion of one national government or another. Hence, if people are to be able to leave a nation, they must have access to some other nation. The right of exit is hollow if nations are unwilling to receive emigrants and exiles, but the U.N. declaration does not stipulate that *nations* are obligated to give haven. The difficulty is poignantly illustrated by the plight of Palestinian workers in Libya. In September 1995, Libya attempted to evict its Palestinian workers and their families. However, since no other nation was willing to grant them entry, the Palestinians languished in dismal camps and buses in the deserts abutting Libya's borders. Several other nations agreed to receive them only after several weeks of complicated negotiations.

Article 15 also states that "everyone has the right to a nationality" and "no one shall be arbitrarily deprived of his nationality nor denied the right to change his nationality." Once again, this right means little if nations have no obligation to grant citizenship to those who request it. However, no nations automatically grant citizenship to all who seek it. All nations grant citizenship to some groups but attempt to exclude others, and some have such exacting standards that it is essentially impossible for those who are not natives to obtain citizenship.

The arguments favoring and opposing the rights of freedom of movement and transfer of citizenship and national governments' corresponding obligations are frequently as heated as they are complex. Furthermore, the arguments regarding the rights to freedom of movement differ from those concerning rights to citizenship.

The foundation of arguments in favor of the right to freedom of movement rests on an important feature of human nature: The freedom to be where one wishes is an important component of human well-being. Persons forced to remain where they reside, or forced to leave their homes when they wish to stay, are likely to be unhappy and may find it difficult to live as they desire. Their lives may be miserable if they cannot visit other people to create new ties or renew old ones, but they may also be dismayed if they are forced to abandon ties created over a lifetime. They might wish to travel to satisfy curiosity, or to obtain further education or economic advancement. They might also wish to travel to escape difficulties such as political oppression, lack of economic opportunity, or a confining native culture. Often, though, when people live in economically depressed or less developed nations, they must migrate across national borders in search of jobs. Because freedom of travel is so closely linked to the requirements for human happiness and unhappiness, many are convinced that all persons are entitled to this freedom, as the U.N. Declaration states.

Another, quite different argument in favor of freedom of travel holds that it is much easier for governments to oppress and exploit their citizens if national borders are closed. People enjoying freedom of movement can leave a nation whose government abuses them or adopts policies they find objectionable. It is partly for this reason that the Soviet Union long prevented any but the most loyal Communist Party cadres from traveling beyond its borders. Conversely, governments, whether democratic or not, will have greater incentive to be more sensitive to their citizens' desires if disgruntled individuals have the freedom to leave.

Nonetheless, both governments and individual citizens present important arguments opposing unlimited freedom of movement across national boundaries. States commonly devote significant resources of time and money to rearing and educating their people. Nations need the skills and knowledge their citizens possess and are harmed when people take their talents elsewhere. Those most likely to leave poorer nations are the young and highly educated—the very individuals whose energy and skills are most needed for their nations' economic advancement. Moreover, many citizens have sensitive information, whether about technology or placement of military forces. If allowed to leave, they might make this information available to others. For these reasons, some governments and some people assert that their citizens have a duty to remain in place and that their governments are justified in preventing them from leaving.

In addition, citizens and governments of nations that aliens seek to enter are often disturbed by the influx of outsiders. Since many come seeking work, ordinary citizens and officials of host nations are concerned that they will take jobs away from native citizens. Natives argue that individuals born and raised in a nation should have first access to its jobs and opportunities. In addition, those who enter a nation to seek work often remain there for years or decades and might eventually wish to bring their families. They are likely, as a result, to use the social services, such as medical care, education, or welfare benefits, that their host nation offers. Since national funds for such programs are limited, aliens' demands on them may stretch them to their limits and result in fewer services available for native citizens.

Resident aliens also have been blamed for numerous social problems that beset their host nations. The maladies range from increased crime and drug abuse to social decay, higher unemployment, and economic distress. In recent years, these claims have been voiced most frequently and loudly in European nations, which have become hosts to large numbers of aliens from the decaying Soviet empire, Africa, and as far abroad as India and Sri Lanka.

In more general terms, those opposed to free movement across national borders argue that nations unable to control their borders will have difficulty controlling crime, the transmission of disease, or business operations. A nation's ability to control the movement of people across its borders is a central feature of national security and well-being.

Furthermore, opponents of free international movement assert that aliens who remain in a nation for significant periods of time and in large numbers are likely to have an impact on the culture. They might introduce different foods, languages, values, and ways of life that will alter or threaten the culture of their host nation. National culture and a sense of national identification are often precious to individuals and to nations. Some have gone to great lengths to preserve their culture and protect it from outside influences. Iceland, for example, with a small and intensely homogeneous culture, forbade the transmission of foreign television programs in order to protect its native language and way of life. Nepal is taking similar measures to preserve its distinctive, ancient culture.

However, people able to reside where they wish are still considerably burdened if they cannot enjoy the rights of citizenship where they live or if they cannot gain the citizenship they desire. A resident alien might enjoy many benefits of citizenship and fulfill many of its obligations, such as paying taxes and obeying local laws; however, the lack of citizenship is still a serious obstacle to full participation in social and political life. Aliens are less able to protect their rights than are citizens and are more vulnerable to oppression by governments or other citizens. Also, nations do not commonly guarantee aliens permanent residence or access to social services and protections. As a result, resident aliens are often forced into exile at times of economic or social unrest. Furthermore, a person without citizenship in *some* nation will have difficulty traveling across national borders and generally will lack the support provided by a government committed to protecting his or her interests abroad.

Citizenship is important to individuals in yet another way. Citizenship and national identification are closely intertwined. A citizen is generally considered a member of a nation and thought to share in that nation's culture and identity. Citizenship gives official warrant to an individual's claims to membership in a nation. Since national identification is commonly of great importance to persons, citizenship is equally important for providing official certification of this tie.

Because citizenship is important to the lives and well-being of individuals, many claim it is the right of all, as asserted by the U.N. Declaration. However, national governments and their citizens often claim the right, rooted in the perquisites of sovereignty, to strictly regulate the award of citizenship and sometimes to refuse it. Many argue that a nation unable to control membership in its political institutions or determine who enjoys the rights and protections of citizenship cannot be fully sovereign. Also, they assert that no nation can afford to give free entry to any and all applicants for citizenship. The wealthy and well-ordered nations of the world would soon be swamped with applicants, and as a result, would lose the qualities that made them desirable and successful. Moreover, those opposed to free rights of citizenship point out that many nations that are not politically stable or economically sound are magnets for aliens because these unfortunate nations are nonetheless marginally better off than their neighbors. Certainly these nations would be quickly overwhelmed by masses of outsiders seeking citizenship.

The global economy and advances in transportation are likely to continue to motivate people to leave their home nations in search of better lives or greater opportunity elsewhere. Communications technology has made it far easier for people in oppressive or economically depressed nations to learn of better conditions abroad. Also, most experts predict that human population will continue to grow at a dramatic rate for the next few generations. Moreover, most of this population growth will occur in economically less developed nations. Young people in these nations, finding few opportunities and much misery at home, will likely seek better conditions and greater opportunity elsewhere.

Hence, greater masses of people will seek residence and citizenship in other nations in coming years. However, the pressures of immigration have recently prompted many nations traditionally hospitable to immigrants, such as the United States and several nations of Europe, to restrict the number of immigrants they will accommodate. However, it is possible that these restrictions will eventually be removed or eased. For example, many of the wealthy nations are experiencing declining population growth. As their populations age, fewer people will become available to keep their economies vibrant and prosperous. Hence, despite their reluctance to allow aliens entry, they might be forced to open their borders to sustain their economic success. Furthermore, national prosperity now depends on a workforce of highly trained, technically proficient people. But a large proportion of the U.S. scientists and engineers were born abroad, and it appears unlikely that the

United States can afford to suffer the consequences of losing them. In addition, many of the privileged people of the world are seeking residence abroad. Many, for example, are employees of multinational corporations and spend years working in other nations. In fact, career advancement now often requires work experience abroad. Also, many wealthy retirees are moving elsewhere, seeking lower costs of living and more tranquillity.

Thus, over the long range, it appears likely that restrictions on emigration, immigration, and citizenship will loosen. In fact, as the global economy continues to develop, it is quite possible that control of national borders and of residency within a nation will lose importance. After all, many people in the United States now routinely move from state to state, changing state citizenship each time they do. The nations of Europe are taking hesitant steps toward greater economic and political unity, making travel and relocation far easier than in the past. Hence, in years to come, moving from nation to nation within Europe may be of no greater consequence than moving from New Jersey to Florida is in the United States. Patterns like these could spread over time to characterize the world as a whole.

**For further reading:** Borders, William. 1979. "Icelanders Only Want to Be Left Alone." *New York Times* (15 December): 3.

Castles, Stephen. 1993. *The Age of Migration: International Population Movements in the Modern World.* New York: Guilford Press.

Crossette, Barbara. 1995. *So Close to Heaven: The Vanishing Buddhist Kingdoms of the Himalayas.* New York: Knopf.

Harris, Nigel. 1995. *The New Untouchables: Immigration and the New World Order.* London: I. B. Tauris.

International Conference on Migration. 1993. *The Changing Course of International Migration.* Paris: Organization for Economic Cooperation and Development.

Jacobson, David. 1996. *Rights across Borders: Immigration and the Decline of Citizenship.* Baltimore, MD: Johns Hopkins University Press.

Jehl, Douglas. 1995. "To Palestinian Deportees, Peace Accord Brings Little Joy." *New York Times* (30 September): 4.

Sassen, Saskia. 1996. *Losing Control? Sovereignty in an Age of Globalization.* New York: Columbia University Press.

Shiller, Nina Glick, et al. 1992. *Towards a Transnational Perspective on Migration: Race, Class, Ethnicity, and Nationalism Reconsidered.* New York: New York Academy of Sciences.

# Free Trade Agreements

Free trade agreements are treaties designed to eliminate or reduce barriers to the flow of goods or services across international boundaries. Most commonly, trade barriers are removed by paring down tariffs on goods imported from the other parties to the agreement and by altering laws governing standards of quality for goods.

Business enterprises, particularly large, multinational corporations, generally favor free trade agreements. The managers of large corporations commonly believe that free trade agreements will provide new markets for their products and services and lower their costs in those foreign markets. Consumers and consumer groups also tend to favor these agreements because the flood of goods from nations with lower wages and harsher working conditions will lower the prices of the products they desire. Political leaders, too, are generally in favor of free trade agreements. Heads of national governments commonly accept the argument that all nations benefit from the efficiency and competition that free trade zones encourage. Furthermore, most political leaders now believe that their nations must become part of the global economy in order to achieve prosperity and influence in the world, and they are convinced that allowing free trade in goods and services across their borders is part of the price they must pay for being allowed to join the global economy.

However, ordinary workers are more likely to be deeply concerned about free trade agreements than any other facet of the global economy. There is no mystery to this, since they are acutely aware that free trade agreements can directly affect their livelihoods. This can occur in two ways. On the one hand, large corporations may use free trade agreements to take advantage of lower labor costs in other nations. Because tree trade agreements allow large corporations to easily and cheaply import goods into their home nation from other nations where costs may be lower, these agreements might give corporations the incentive to move parts of their operations to those other nations. They may move manufacturing, distribution, and even clerical functions, thus eliminating jobs in their home nations. Hence, laborers are vitally concerned that free trade agreements may allow their jobs to be taken away from them and moved out of the country. However, free trade can affect workers' livelihoods and working conditions even when their jobs are not immediately at risk. That is, corporations may use the threat of relocating operations to prod workers into accepting reduced wages or less desirable working conditions. Employers might claim that competition from corporations based overseas will put them out of business if they fail to reduce wages, shed jobs, and change the rules of labor.

Many laborers and others who are opposed to free trade agreements often base their arguments on the assertion that the first obligation of a nation and of the business enterprises within a nation is to provide jobs and a decent livelihood for their laboring people. They may also argue that domestic industries should be protected from foreign competition on the grounds that these industries are more likely to bring jobs and prosperity to their home nations.

Those opposed to free trade agreements are prone to argue that such treaties are simply instruments that will allow huge corporations to exploit labor and other national resources. They often believe that those political leaders who favor free trade agreements have fallen under the influence of multinational corporations, and as a result, have drifted away from their primary obligation of looking after the people and enterprises of their own nation.

Opponents of free trade agreements argue that the citizens and the governments of a nation have a far stronger obligation to look after the people of their own nation than they do to benefit people elsewhere. The primary obligation of the political leaders of a nation should be to secure the wellbeing of that nation's citizens. Their view is fundamentally opposed to the central premise of the ethics of international relations. They offer several arguments to support this point of view: First, they point out that the political leaders of a nation are elected to office with the explicit understanding that they are responsible for the welfare and prosperity of their citizens. It is their obligation to protect citizens from harm and to work diligently to improve their lives. Because support of free trade agreements violates these obligations, political leaders who support them are morally remiss, in the opponents' view.

Furthermore, opponents of free trade agreements commonly believe that the business enterprises of a nation also have an obligation to look after the welfare of their nations and their laborers before all else. They point out that the businesses of a nation were given charters by their home nation and that the businesses' initial success generally is gained within its boundaries. Hence, because their home nation makes their very existence and their commercial success possible, these enterprises have an obligation to repay their nation by remaining loyal to native workers and by placing the economic prosperity of their nation above all other concerns, including opportunities for greater profit. Any other course of action is irresponsible and immoral.

Opponents of free trade also point out that the people and the institutions of a nation have many ties and obligations to one another. They pay taxes, for example, with the understanding that the revenue will be used to benefit the nation. They have made business agreements, received education and health care, and enjoyed the opportunities a nation has to offer. These benefits are the result of the efforts of other citizens and the government of their nation. Hence, because individuals and corporations have benefited hugely by taking advantage of national resources, they are obligated to repay some of this debt by working primarily for the benefit of their home nation.

However, opponents of free trade agreements make other arguments as well. For example, they often assert that corporations that move operations to other nations to gain the benefit of lower wages and less stringent working conditions are simply exploiting the laborers in the nation where they move, since they will be paying them far less and will have far less commitment to their welfare than to the laborers of their home nation. Furthermore, corporations are apt to simply move their operations to yet other nations after a few years, if they discover that they can take advantage of still lower wages and less stringent rules governing working conditions elsewhere. Corporations with no strong moral commitment to their home nation are unlikely to develop any vigorous sense of responsibility to the other nations they may enter. Once they determine that their only compelling goal is to seek profits, they will exploit and manipulate laborers and nations whenever and wherever they can to serve that goal.

Thus, opponents of free trade agreements conclude that these arrangements simply allow multinational corporations to exploit workers and nations whenever and wherever they please. Rather than allowing this exploitation, they assert that national political leaders should work vigorously to assure that corporations fulfill their primary obligation of benefiting the workers and institutions of their home nation.

Those favoring free trade agreements argue that rather than exploiting nations or laborers, these treaties benefit all by ensuring stiff competition among corporations seeking to enter markets and by making the most efficient uses of resources, whether natural resources, human resources, or financial resources, wherever they may be found. They argue that only unfettered global competition is likely to bring prosperity and decent laboring conditions to people around the world.

Proponents of free trade may agree that free trade agreements will allow some of a nation's jobs to move to other nations. However, they claim that this outcome is often the best result for all, even including laborers, since the labor that can be performed more efficiently in less developed nations should be performed there. Moreover, the jobs that are most likely to be moved to other nations involve unskilled, undesirable labor. Moving jobs of this sort to other nations will provide motivation to create better, more skilled jobs to replace them. In support of this claim, proponents of free trade agreements point to the global experience of a nation's unskilled labor moving from one nation to another to be replaced by labor and industry demanding more skill and more investment. The "Four Tigers of Asia"—South Korea, Taiwan, Singapore, and Thailand—were impoverished nations a few decades ago. They started on the road to their present prosperity by concentrating on products that required only unskilled labor and low technology. Later, with more capital, business expertise, and increasingly skilled labor, they moved on to more sophisticated products that required a more skilled and more highly paid workforce. The Four Tigers have advanced by moving successively to manufacturing more sophisticated goods and offering their workers increasingly higher wages. This example gives credibility to the claim that the short-term loss of jobs is actually a long-term benefit, making way for better jobs.

Furthermore, although some workers may be harmed when their jobs are moved elsewhere, many others in an economy will benefit from lower costs for the goods that are produced under the new conditions. Proponents of free trade point to the chastening experience of nations that have attempted to protect their own jobs and industries by preventing free trade across their borders. The native industries of these nations, insulated from global competitive pressures, become inefficient and have little incentive to seek innovation or improve their products. Hence, their economies stagnate because they are saddled with inefficient and uninnovative industries, high costs, and low quality. Proponents of free trade like to point out that nations that at one time erected protectionist barriers, such as Chile and Argentina, have suffered with spluttering economies and have now recast their policies to encourage free trade across national borders. Their economies have become much stronger as a result, and their citizens enjoy the benefits of lower prices and more desirable goods.

In addition, proponents of free trade claim that workers in low-wage nations are not necessarily being exploited by the multinational corporations that hire them. Often the foreign businesses pay higher wages and offer better working conditions than native industries, so workers are glad for the jobs they offer and seek them eagerly. In 1996, many in the United States were stunned to learn that some popular American consumer goods were produced at factories in Indonesia, where wages and working conditions were far inferior to those in the United States. However, many were shocked again to learn that Indonesians eagerly sought jobs in those plants because wages and opportunities were greater there than elsewhere. Also, the leaders of host nations often view the presence of the types of jobs and industries that multinational corporations bring as first steps in the process of advancing economic development. Further, the multinational corporations are generally sources of badly needed investment capital for impoverished nations. Many developing nations are unable to gain loans from commercial banks and can receive only minimal support from international aid agencies. As a result, developing nations now are disposed to avidly court multinational corporations in order to gain the benefits of their wealth and expertise.

Furthermore, supporters of free trade point out that elimination of trade barriers forces nations to compete in the global economy, that is, they are required to compete for the presence of multinational corporations and for other investments. Hence, the same benefits of efficiency, innovation, and competence that competition brings to corporations also accrue to nations and their citizens. These benefits contrast starkly with the effects of insisting on a national right to the activities of certain corporations and of closing national borders to the attentions of others. Therefore, they conclude, rather than exploiting people or nations, free trade brings great benefits to both.

At present, it appears that pressures to expand the range of free trade among nations will continue to be felt, with the result that the domains of trade uninhibited by national boundaries will continue to grow. This being the case, the sharp moral disagreements over the nature and justification of free trade also will continue. However, at present, most national leaders appear convinced that the benefits of free trade considerably outweigh any potential harm, so they are likely to continue to support the expansion of free trade and open national borders. Two probable results are a greater appreciation of the moral stature and claims of people and governments across the world, regardless of the nation where they reside, and a dilution of the belief that nations, people, and corporations should place greatest emphasis on the interests of their home nations.

**For further reading:** Baer, M. Delal, and Sidney Weintraub, eds. 1994. *The NAFTA Debate: Grappling with Unconventional Trade Issues.* Boulder, CO: Lynne Rienner Publishers.

Golden, Ian. 1993. *Trade Liberalization: Global Economic Implications.* Paris: Organization for Economic Cooperation and Development.

Lusztig, Michael. 1996. *Risking Free Trade: The Politics of Trade in Britain, Canada, Mexico, and the United States.* Pittsburgh, PA: University of Pittsburgh Press.

Miller, Henri. 1996. *Free Trade versus Protectionism.* New York: H. W. Wilson.

Nader, Ralph, ed. 1993. *The Case against Free Trade: GATT, NAFTA, and the Globalization of Corporate Power.* San Francisco: Earth Island Press.

Orme, William. 1993. *Continental Shift: Free Trade & the New North America.* Washington, DC: Washington Post Co.

Tussie, Diana, and David Glover. 1993. *The Developing Countries in World Trade: Policies and Bargaining Strategies.* Boulder, CO: Lynne Rienner Publishers.

Weintraub, Sidney. 1997. *NAFTA at Three: A Progress Report.* Washington, DC: Center for Strategic and International Studies.

# Human Rights

World War II was a period of nearly unimaginable cruelty and barbarism. The Nazi government of Germany attempted to eradicate its Jewish population, as well as the Jews living in the nations it conquered. In addition, it killed vast numbers of Poles, Russians, gypsies, and others. Nazis also performed barbarous medical experiments on the inmates of concentration camps, starved many to death, and destroyed the lives of millions of people.

Following World War II, the international community, aghast at the criminal conduct of the war, resolved to prevent such outrages from recurring. One result was the emergence of a conception of international human rights. These rights were deemed sufficiently important that the newly created United Nations adopted its Universal Declaration of Human Rights in 1948. This roster of basic human rights has been accepted by the members of the United Nations (this includes the majority of nations) and has served as the basis for many of the world community's activities aimed at improving the lot of human beings.

However, the concept of human rights and its use to establish basic standards of treatment for all human beings have been the focus of heated controversy. This discussion is extremely important, because a fundamental conception of human rights may play a crucial role in establishing an international moral order and providing a foundation for the way in which people, governments, and corporations treat one another as global ties draw them ever closer.

Part of the controversy over human rights is focused on the basic nature of rights. All agree that talk of *human* rights refers to the idea that there are certain moral claims to which all human beings have recourse simply because they are human. For example, citizens of the United States like to point out that they have the basic rights listed in the Bill of Rights of the U.S. Constitution. What this means is that citizens of the United States have certain entitlements that are honored and protected by the fundamental law of the land. If any of the rights protected by the Constitution are violated, people may go to the courts to seek redress. These, however, are legal rights, in the sense that they are established and preserved by the law of a particular nation. Thus, the rights enumerated in the U.S. Constitution pertain only to citizens of the United States. A conception of human rights, however, is broader than that of legal rights, because it refers to rights that should be enjoyed by all human beings, no matter what governmental system rules over them or what their life circumstances may be.

The controversy over rights, however, partly concerns the question of what it is to have a right. Nations in the Western European tradition of political thought are committed to the view of rights as fundamental moral entitlements. By this they mean that a person possessing a right may claim that others have a very weighty moral obligation to ensure that he or she is able to enjoy the exercise of that right. For example, a common right that many believe has great importance is that of freedom of speech. To say that an individual has the right of freedom of speech means that a person can claim that other human beings and human governments have a strong moral obligation to allow him or her to express opinions freely, even if they are offensive to others.

Differing strands of political thought, particularly that of the nations of the former Soviet Union and also some of the less developed nations of the world, argue that rights should instead be viewed as goals that all human beings and all governments should commit themselves to attempting to achieve. Thus, the right of freedom of speech, from this perspective, would be viewed as an ideal that people and societies should strive to create, rather than a present entitlement that people can claim to enjoy.

This difference of opinion regarding rights is reflected in the content of the U.N. Universal Declaration of Human Rights. Many of the rights listed in the first portion of the document are familiar to readers in Western European nations. They include freedom of speech, freedom of political association, and freedom of religious practice, among other rights. The rights listed in the latter portion of the document, however, appear quite different. They include rights to education, sufficient leisure time, good health, and so on. It would be odd to claim that rights of this latter sort are moral entitlements, because many nations lack the material or human resources to fulfill such expectations and are not likely to at any time in the near future. However, it would seem that the rights of the first portion of the document can easily be honored even by nations with few resources. Few resources are required, for example, to provide legal mechanisms to protect freedom of speech or to avoid arbitrary detention and punishment of citizens.

The controversy about human rights, therefore, encompasses two discussions. One is the argument about whether it makes sense to talk about universal moral standards that apply to all human beings in all cultures. The second is the question of exactly how human rights should be considered, with the debate between those who believe that human rights should be viewed as present, very weighty moral claims or whether they should be, instead, viewed as important goals that people and governments should work toward.

Those opposed to a conception of universal human rights offer several strong arguments. They point out that there is a wide array of governments and cultures in the world, with a wide array of values, religions, and cultural practices. Many cultures have no conception of rights. Some of these cultures emphasize duty rather than right, and do not have the conception that people could demand things as rights. Some cultures assign a higher priority to the society as a whole than to the welfare of the individual. In addition, in some cultures, such as traditional Islamic societies, there is no space for freedom of religious practice, freedom of speech, or democratic government. For example, in 1979, when Ayatollah Khomeini came to power in Iran with a popular mandate to establish an Islamic state, he said explicitly that his aim was not to establish a democracy, which he viewed as a creation of Western European cultures. Rather, he intended to create an Islamic republic, a theocracy ruled by religious leaders who would place the greatest emphasis on nurturing the Islamic religion in Iran.

In consequence, opponents of human rights are apt to claim that individual rights are an invention of Western European cultures that has no application to many other cultures. Furthermore, they claim that the diversity of cultures, values, and governmental structures in the world is so great that it is impossible to come to any meaningful agreement on fundamental standards of life that all people should enjoy. Although they acknowledge that the U.N. Universal Declaration of Human Rights has great prestige, they argue that its provisions are so general that they do not effectively guarantee any substantive rights to any people. Furthermore, they claim that there has never been any serious attempt to enforce the rights contained in the declaration against errant governments or to use the United Nations to establish an effective global legal system.

Those who endorse the conception of international human rights concede to several claims made by their opponents. They agree, for example, that there is a wide diversity of cultures and values in the world and that some cultures hold values and have practices that are opposed to the rights listed in the declaration. Nonetheless, they claim that the document, and the conception of human rights in general, have an important role to play, and that there are very good reasons to believe that there should be some rights that all human beings enjoy simply by virtue of being human. They claim that, despite the diversity of the world, there are some things that all human beings would wish to claim as their right. For example, no one could seriously wish to be subject to arbitrary or capricious arrest, trial without guarantees of fairness, or cruel punishment. No one could seriously desire to be prevented from speaking out on issues of importance or from engaging in political activity. They note the irony in the fact that some political or ideological movements enjoy freedom of political association even while they propose to create societies in which the right of freedom of association would be extinguished. Hence, they claim there are sufficient grounds, found in values and desires shared by all human beings, to allow the creation of a basic roster of rights that all should enjoy, and they believe there is reason to believe that all humans would accept such a roster.

Furthermore, those who favor international human rights argue that much of the opposition to the concept of those rights comes from tyrannical governments anxious to preserve tight control over their populations. Many citizens of these authoritarian nations desire and speak out in favor of many of the rights that their governmental leaders claim are irrelevant to their society. Hence, although the Communist government of mainland China asserts that concepts of political freedom and civil rights are alien to Chinese culture and traditions, many Chinese citizens heartily endorse these very ideals. Many of these citizens vigorously supported these ideas in Tiananmen Square in the spring of 1989 but had their aspirations crushed by the Chinese government.

The incident in Tiananmen Square began as a demonstration by students, primarily from Beijing University, favoring greater democracy in China. The demonstration progressed to a sit-in, then a hunger strike. The students' actions received wide support from ordinary citizens in Beijing and prompted similar demonstrations in other Chinese cities. After several weeks of dithering, the Chinese leadership determined that the students' activities constituted a dire threat to the order and unity of China and that the demonstration would have to be crushed by force. On 3–4 June, tanks and armed troops were dispatched to the area to remove the students and their supporters. In the ensuing battle, many Chinese were killed and many others wounded.

Proponents of a universal conception of human rights also concede that the Universal Declaration of Human Rights has not been as effective in improving the lot of human beings as many had hoped. However, this does not imply that it has had no effect at all or that it has no importance for human life. For example, an International War Crimes Tribunal is currently in session in The Hague, The Netherlands, which is trying several people charged with war crimes committed during the civil war in Bosnia. Among other important charges against the defendants is that of having violated human rights. Hence, although the Universal Declaration of Human Rights still does not guarantee global rights in the way that the U.S. Constitution guarantees the rights of its citizens, it has played an important role in helping to construct a system of international law that will be more effective in protecting people's rights and taking action when these rights are abused. In addition, they point out that people fighting against tyrannical regimes, those active in groups working for international human rights, and governmental treaties often cite the Universal Declaration to support their arguments against oppressive governments.

The debate regarding the nature of rights is more complex. However, an important clue to resolving the debate is to notice that some rights seem best described as present entitlements, while others seem best described as important goals that humans and governments should strive for. Guarantees of good health and adequate education, for example, are beyond the resources of most nations at present. Nonetheless, we can agree that these are highly important goals toward which governments and social institutions should pledge their efforts. On the other hand, rights such as freedom of speech or freedom of religion do not depend heavily on wealth or social resources, and therefore they can easily be treated as present entitlements that all governments and all peoples are strongly morally obligated to honor. Furthermore, it has been argued that these latter rights—so-called civil rights—are fundamental in the sense that they guarantee individuals legal protection in living as they wish, allowing them to struggle to improve their circumstances as well as to fight abuse by other individuals or governments.

Although the record of the Universal Declaration of Human Rights has been uneven in the first half century of its existence, the concept of universal human rights seems destined to play a larger role in human life in the future. This is because human beings across the world are becoming increasingly entangled in one another's affairs and have increasingly thicker nets of relationship to one another. If these relations are to continue in fruitful fashion, with mutual trust and respect for all parties, then some common foundation of human moral standards will be needed. Though the conception of human rights is of western European origin, this need not disqualify it from useful service. After all, modern medical care is also of Western European origin, yet it is proving extremely valuable for all nations and peoples. Furthermore, there is a tradition of some 50 years of relying on the Universal Declaration of Human Rights as a guidepost for human relations. It is improbable that another guidepost can be found to better serve humanity's needs and aspirations.

**For further reading:** Beitz, Charles. 1979. *Political Theory and International Relations.* Princeton, NJ: Princeton University Press.

Bozeman, Adda. 1971. *The Future of Law in a Multicultural World.* Princeton, NJ: Princeton University Press.

Claude, Richard Pierre, and Burns Weston. 1992. *Human Rights and the World Community: Issues and Action.* 2d ed. Philadelphia: University of Pennsylvania Press.

Crawford, James. 1994. *Democracy in International Law.* Cambridge, England: Cambridge University Press.

Donnelly, Jack. 1993. *International Human Rights.* Boulder, CO: Westview Press.

Kommers, Donald, and Gilbert Loescher, eds. 1979. *Human Rights and American Foreign Policy.* Notre Dame, IN: University of Notre Dame Press.

Shue, Henry. 1996. *Basic Rights: Subsistence, Affluence, and U.S. Foreign Policy.* 2d ed. Princeton, NJ: Princeton University Press.

# Indigenous Peoples

Although most nations are rapidly joining the global economy—and as a result, are gaining many elements of common culture spread by international trade and consumption—a number of indigenous peoples remain whose cultures are largely intact, often because they are isolated from the major political and economic currents. These indigenous or aboriginal peoples are so called because they embody ways of life once pursued in societies consisting of small tribes, common before the development of modern, industrial economies. However, these remaining unscathed cultures are now being subjected to a variety of forces that may eliminate them.

Generally, indigenous peoples are most endangered by the pressures of economic development and the population explosions of the nations where they are found. Sometimes, the land where they reside is desired for agricultural or industrial use. At other times, their cultures are more indirectly threatened by the proximity of development, because these economic projects offer jobs and sometimes easier lives than those afforded by native ways of life.

The problem is twofold. Some traditional human societies require vast quantities of land for their hunting and gathering or herding modes of life, while the same land may be in demand for purposes of national economic development. The question that commonly arises in such cases is whether one group of people should be allowed to exploit or coerce another, or whether every group should be entitled to live the sort of life it desires, without intrusion by more powerful or wealthier outsiders.

A second, related question is whether the native cultures of indigenous peoples are valuable in and of themselves. Many people believe that a variety of cultures is important for human life, but this variety of ways of life and values is being eroded by the global economy, which is bringing a common, global consumer culture along in its train. Hence, apart from the question of whether people should be protected from manipulation by outsiders, there is the question of whether their ways of life are important for all of humanity and thus deserve protection for their own sake.

These problems are of concern to international ethics for several reasons. First, if the native cultures of indigenous peoples have value in themselves and are important sources of insight into human nature and the human condition, then they are a resource for all humanity and deserve the united efforts of the human community to give them protection. Second, to the extent that members of native cultures are being coerced and exploited by others, their human rights are being violated. Those who accept the view that human rights exist that are the common entitlement of all humanity are often led to the conclusion that the human community is obligated to respond to the violation of human rights wherever it occurs. Furthermore, individuals who are members of vulnerable indigenous peoples may not consider themselves citizens of the nations within whose boundaries they reside. Their cultures may contain no concept of nations or national boundaries, and people within these groups are likely to identify only with their indigenous group. But if they are not genuine members of the nation in which they reside, then it may be argued that their problems are the concern of all humanity, since they cannot rely on the nation where they reside to protect them.

A particularly poignant example of this problem involves the native Indian tribes living along the Amazon River in Brazil. These people are hunter-gatherers; they gain their livelihood from the rain forests, using their intimate knowledge of plant and animal life in these regions and their detailed grasp of the local terrain. Because the hunter-gatherer's way of life requires large amounts of land to support relatively small populations, these Indians often regard vast tracts of forest as their homeland. They may have roved across vast stretches of terrain for many generations. Although they have obviously had many occasions for contact with outsiders, their native cultures are largely intact, and they have generally been able to live as they have for centuries. However, these tribes currently face threats from several sources. In many areas, they are facing difficult, sometimes violent, encounters with gold hunters who are mining many parts of the Brazilian forests. Also, cattle ranchers and farmers desire to burn the forests to gain extra land for their activities. From another direction, the indigenous tribes are facing pressure from refugees from Brazil's crowded coasts, who are seeking to clear land to farm and gain a subsistence of their own. In many ways, therefore, the interests of these Indians are at odds with those of the nation of Brazil, which seeks their land for space to accommodate its exploding population as well as for the extraction of resources (including gold and other mineral wealth and the valuable hardwood forests) to support the national economy. (Of course, the destruction of the rain forests is associated with global warming, which is also a problem for the entire world. *See* Pollution Control.)

In light of these concerns, many argue that the international community has the obligation to make a concerted effort to preserve the cultural and social integrity of indigenous peoples wherever they are found. They offer several arguments to support their views. One is that the interests of native cultures are often at variance with those of the nation in which indigenous peoples reside. Hence, the global community cannot rely on the national governments to preserve and protect natives from exploitation by outsiders, particularly since the members of the native cultures may not consider themselves members of the larger nation. In this case as in others, the global community might be required to intrude if the national government cannot be relied upon to protect all who live in its domain. In the same fashion, the international community has a clear obligation embodied in international law to protect refugees living in nations other than their homelands. Once again, the interests of refugees may conflict with those of the nation where they reside. Also, refugees generally will not consider themselves part of the nation where they reside, and the natives of the nation will view them as aliens. Hence, some argue that the obligation of the world community to preserve and protect indigenous peoples is similar to its obligation to protect refugees.

In addition, those who argue for an international obligation to preserve indigenous peoples may argue that exploitation, violations of autonomy, and physical abuse of human beings are legitimate areas of concern for the international community in whatever guise they appear. Even citizens within a nation who are treated in such fashion by their government or by other residents of a nation are legitimately the subjects of international concern when their governments fail to take effective action to protect their rights. They also argue that native cultures are valuable in themselves, a significant part of the heritage of all humanity. Therefore, it is the legitimate concern of all humanity to prevent their elimination. The diversity of human ways of life is valuable in itself and can be highly important even to the vast majority of humanity that does not share the culture.

Several modern, advanced nations are currently wrestling with the problem of preserving indigenous cultures. The Japanese and the South Koreans, for example, are enthusiastic participants in the global economy and have proven highly adept at mastering the technology and business practices necessary to prosper in the contemporary world. However, many citizens of both nations are concerned that their commercial and political success is endangering their distinctive native cultures. Hence, the people and governments of both nations are taking measures to protect and nurture traditional ways of life. Few who have experienced these cultures fail to be convinced that they make valuable contributions to humanity. However, because these nations are economically successful and politically self-confident, they are well equipped to protect their own cultures. Indigenous peoples, in contrast, are generally very poor and highly vulnerable to external pressures. Hence, they cannot be expected to effectively protect their cultural and social integrity. Because of this, many people are convinced that the world community has the obligation to do so.

A number of people are opposed to these arguments. They point out that it is the responsibility of the sovereign government of a nation to look after the welfare of its citizenry. In the instance of indigenous peoples inhabiting large tracts of land within a nation, there may be good reason to be more concerned about the welfare of the vast majority than the needs of a small minority of citizens. This is particularly the case where the members of the minority are not being killed or abused. So long as provision is made to secure other means of gaining a livelihood for them, there is no reason to believe that attempts to use the land inhabited by native societies to support the interests of the larger nation are inevitably unjust. After all, under the governmental right of eminent domain, property is commonly taken from other citizens to serve the common welfare. This commonly happens when roads or public buildings are constructed, for example. In other cases, the use of land by its owners is restricted or channeled in order to serve broader public interests, as occurs when environmental protection regulations are put into force. Furthermore, it is the obligation of national governments to protect their citizens from abuse by others. Hence, if members of indigenous peoples are being exploited, it is the responsibility of national governments to intervene. Outside groups have neither the authority nor the coercive ability to effectively intrude on behalf of abused citizens.

Finally, those who oppose international intervention argue that it is the nature of cultures to change. It would be absurd to attempt to preserve a human culture in the same way as an artifact in a museum. Artifacts in museums are removed from the cultures in which they played significant roles; now they serve only for display and for examination. Cultures are embodied in human beings and can therefore be preserved only by isolating the human beings that hold them. Most of the world's native cultures have died out.

Most of the people who wish to preserve the native cultures of the world have no desire to live the sorts of lives they wish to protect. If the members of these cultures find other ways of living, then they should be allowed to take up these ways of life, just as any member of another society is free to take up differing modes of life. Hence, attempts to preserve the cultures of indigenous peoples are grotesque and absurd. These cultures should be studied carefully and understood by scientists, of course, but it would be wrong to coerce people into maintaining a culture when they desire lives of different sorts.

Not many indigenous peoples remain in the world. Few people are members of these cultures. The pressures of vastly increased population and economic development will fall more heavily on these cultures in the years to come. Even with efforts to protect the members of these cultures from abuse and coercion, they are likely to drift off to other societies in search of greater opportunities and easier lives. The indigenous peoples who remain will continue to be at the mercy of extremely powerful forces arrayed around them and will have few resources available to protect their own interests—unless they adopt at least a few characteristics of the surrounding cultures.

**For further reading:** Burger, Julian. 1990. *The Gia Atlas of First Peoples: A Future for the Indigenous World.* New York: Doubleday.

Kemf, Elizabeth, ed. 1993. *The Law of the Mother: Protecting Indigenous Peoples in Protected Areas.* San Francisco: Sierra Club Books.

Levin, Michael David, ed. 1993. *Ethnicity and Aboriginality: Case Studies in Ethnonationalism.* Toronto: University of Toronto Press.

Miller, Marc. 1993. *State of the Peoples: A Global Human Rights Report on Societies in Danger.* Boston: Beacon Press.

United States Congress, House Committee on Foreign Affairs. Subcommittee on the Western Hemisphere. 1994. *Indigenous Peoples and the Natural Environment of Brazil.* Washington, DC: U.S. Government Printing Office.

Weatherford, J. McIver. 1994. *Savages and Civilizations: Who Will Survive?* New York: Crown.

Werther, Guntram F. A. 1992. *Self-Determination in Western Democracies: Aboriginal Politics in a Comparative Perspective.* Westport, CT: Greenwood Press.

# Intellectual Property

We usually think of property as physical objects, whether land, the houses built on it, the furnishings in the houses, or the raw materials and factories that produce these furnishings. However, ideas, works of art, books, or knowledge can also become property if legal means exist to grant particular people or organizations control over access to them or the ways in which they are used. The legal instruments that allow books, ideas, etc., to become property include patents and copyright laws. Because patents and copyrights are presently issued by nation-states, controversies have arisen when the patents or copyrights of one nation are not respected by other nations. This would occur, for example, when a book copyrighted in one nation is printed and sold in another nation without seeking a licensing agreement or paying royalty fees. However, ideas and knowledge protected by the patent or copyright laws have become increasingly important.

Access to and control of technology and information are among the keys to the world's wealth and power, and there is every reason to believe this will remain the case for the foreseeable future. In centuries past, control of natural resources or military power were the primary keys to power and wealth. However, these factors are no longer of central importance, or, to the extent that they are important, they rely on technology and information. For example, vast pools of petroleum have existed under the sands of the Middle East for billions of years, but they have only become valuable and important with the development of internal combustion engines and use of these engines as major sources of power. Lacking this technology, the Middle East's oil would be no more valuable than the sand under which it is buried.

Nations and people able to control technology and information will likely continue to dominate those unable to do so. Lack of access to information and technology will effectively prevent any nation from developing economically and from gaining influence in the world. Patents and copyright laws are instruments that nations, corporations, and individuals now employ to preserve control over these vital resources. The problem is that although wealthy and powerful nations and individuals recognize that they must preserve control over these resources to maintain their comfortable status, poorer and less developed nations and individuals also recognize that they must gain access to these resources to improve their lot in the world. Individuals from modest backgrounds can often gain access to education, sometimes at the world's elite universities, but they are unlikely to be able to take copyrighted or patented material home with them once they receive their degrees. Hence, the struggle to gain control over information and technology is the struggle over patents and copyrights.

However, intellectual property includes more than technology and scientific data. It includes television programs, movies, or books for mass audiences, which are commercially valuable and vitally important for disseminating ideas and cultural trends but which do not directly affect human technological prowess or the ability to control others. Nonetheless, many of the great battles concerning copyright laws have been fought over materials of these sorts because they are commercially valuable, often worth millions of dollars to those able to control their dissemination.

However, the same circumstances that make information and technology important also undermine efforts to control access to them. Unlike gold or silver, information and technology are valuable only when they are put to use. If they are not employed in service of human ends, they are of little benefit. This is most particularly the case in the domain of the global economy. Multinational corporations wish to enter new markets, make alliances with other corporations, or exploit new technology. They can accomplish these ends only by putting their intellectual resources to work, and this often can occur only by making them available to others through licensing agreements or joint manufacturing ventures, or by creating products that embody new technology and making them available to ordinary people or to corporate partners. For example, several years ago, the United States was anxious to sell a number of its fighter-bomber jets to South Korea. However, the South Koreans were willing to buy U.S. jets only on the condition that the aircraft be assembled in Korea. This would require the transfer of some important aeronautical technology to Korea. In this case, the United States was anxious to make the sale and so it agreed to the transmittal of important military technology. In less spectacular fashion, many industries are anxious to establish manufacturing plants in nations where wages are low. When they do so, however, they must transfer some of their manufacturing and technological capacity to these nations. These companies proceed with such transfers in order to remain competitive by gaining lower manufacturing costs. One result, however, is that the host nations gain access to the new technology. This sort of transfer is an important facet of the process of economic development. Hence, the pressures of global endeavor encourage the dissemination of intellectual property.

Computers present yet another challenge to maintaining close control of information and technology, even as their increasing importance in business, government, military applications, and ordinary life gives people even greater incentive to control dissemination of computer technology. Computers themselves pose a threat to the control of technology and information because they become vastly more useful when they are linked to other computers, and the more dense their links to other machines, the more useful they become. Computers' value lies in their ability to store and transfer vast quantities of information. People who deal with computers are aware that once information is entered into a computer network, it is dismayingly easy to strew far and wide, nearly instantaneously. Hence, computers, by their nature, work against efforts to keep strict control over intellectual property.

One basic difficulty is that violation of copyright and patent laws sometimes brings benefits to people in several nations while harming people in others. For example, many people in developing nations benefit from entire industries devoted to violating international copyright laws. Mass production of American movies and television shows is a case in point, because ordinary people in many developing nations, such as Egypt or China, benefit from having access to very cheap movie and television cassettes, and those running the industries enjoy great profits. However, the American movie and television industries, and their employees, are harmed by this activity, because counterfeiting causes them to lose the benefits of royalties or product sales.

Some in developing nations have argued that the information and technology protected by patents and copyrights should be like education, that is, resources freely available to all. They assert that those who wish to strictly enforce copyright and patent protection worldwide have no moral justification for their views, noting that much of the intellectual and cultural heritage of humanity is considered the common property of all mankind. Since legally protected intellectual property is immensely important for economic and cultural development (not to mention influence) in the world today, there is even greater reason to make these materials readily available to all, particularly as they might be useful to those seeking to extract themselves from poverty and social disorder. This is particularly so in cases where this expertise is needed to help bridge the economic and political gap between developed and developing nations. Hence, many who offer these arguments believe that justice is best served by making technology and information easily available to all, since these are important tools that will allow the poorer nations of the world to gain some of the power and wealth of the more privileged ones.

Those opposed to loosening or eliminating copyright and patent protections offer several arguments. They claim that persons, nations, and corporations would lack motivation to develop new technology or amass new information or create literature or films if they could not be assured control over, and profits from, their dissemination. People and institutions are not often motivated to work for free and do not care to lose control of the products they have created. Furthermore, development of intellectual property requires enormous investments of time, talent, and money. Without the prospect of some financial return from their efforts, people are unlikely to make such investments. The costs of such undertakings need to be paid somehow, and an important way to do so is to recycle profits generated by previous efforts.

Even corporations and governments that are disposed to transfer technology and information to others are willing to do so only on the condition that they gain some benefit in return, and this would be impossible if they did not enjoy legally sanctioned control over their intellectual property. Furthermore, these corporations and governments note that the very power and utility of much intellectual property would make it very dangerous if it fell into the hands of terrorists, lunatics, or rogue governments. Of course, there is no way to completely safeguard such material, but they assert this is no reason to dismantle the barriers to its dissemination. As much control as can be achieved, after all, is better—and safer for humanity—than none at all.

Those opposed to loosening copyright and patent laws also argue, in response to the claim that technology and information are needed to reduce the gap between the wealthy and powerful and the underprivileged nations of the world, that these intellectual resources are of no value unless they can be put to use. A major criterion of whether these resources are likely to be put to use in fruitful fashion is whether corporations are willing to invest their resources in a nation to exploit these intellectual resources. Without the prospect of this useful employment of information, it will do little good for the nations seeking to gain possession of intellectual resources.

Moreover, those opposed to loosening copyright and patent laws assert that many of the nations anxious to proclaim intellectual property the common heritage of mankind are rich in natural resources that they wish to exploit and use for their own profit. Those nations would be highly unlikely to agree to the proposal that their natural resources should be deemed the common heritage of all mankind, even though they may, in contrast to developers of intellectual property, have done nothing to bring their resources into being, and may have to rely on the technology of others in order to exploit those resources.

Information and technology are likely to gain even greater importance for human life in years to come, particularly as computers become more powerful and more widely used in daily life. As a practical matter, however, it is also most likely that even more rigorous protection of patents and copyrights will be established. The reason is partly that these patents and copyrights are in the hands of the most powerful nations of the world, which are anxious to protect their status. But it is also partly that the profit incentive will be needed to prompt persons, corporations, and governments to continue to energetically seek technological advances and accumulate more information. Neither governments nor corporations are likely to be motivated to offer generous financial support to research if they cannot be confident of gaining control of successful discoveries. Such regulation is seen as necessary for the smooth and efficient functioning of the global economy, since corporations will be hesitant to place their expertise in nations where it will not be safeguarded.

**For further reading:** Benko, Robert B. 1984. *Protecting Intellectual Property Rights: Issues and Controversies.* Washington, DC: American Enterprise Institute for Public Policy Research.
Gadbaw, R. Michael, and Timothy J. Richards. 1988. *Intellectual Property Rights: Global Consensus, Global Conflict?* Boulder, CO: Westview Press.
Homet, Roland S. 1983–1985. *The International Dimension: New Technologies and Intellectual Property Rights.* Washington, DC: Congressional Office of Technology Assessment.
Jussawalla, Meheroo. 1992. *The Economics of Intellectual Property in a World without Frontiers: A Study of Computer Software.* New York: Greenwood Press.
Lury, Celia. 1993. *Cultural Rights: Technology, Legality, and Personality.* London and New York: Routledge.
Organization for Economic Cooperation and Development. 1989. *Competition Policy and Intellectual Property Rights.* Paris: Organization for Economic Cooperation and Development.
Sherwood, Robert. 1990. *Intellectual Property and Economic Development.* Boulder, CO: Westview Press.
Smith, Gordon. 1993. *Intellectual Property: Licensing and Joint Venture Profit Strategies.* New York: J. Wiley.
Stewart, George R., et al. 1994. *International Trade and Intellectual Property: The Search for a Balanced System.* Boulder, CO: Westview Press.
Sullivan, Neil F. 1995. *Technology Transfer: Making the Most of Your Intellectual Property.* Cambridge, England: Cambridge University Press.
Wallerstein, Michael, et al. 1993. *The Global Dimension of Intellectual Property Rights in Science and Technology.* Washington, DC: National Academy Press.

# International Government

The governments of nations have caused much of the suffering and turmoil that human beings have endured in the course of history. The Nazi Holocaust, Stalin's brutal dictatorship in the U.S.S.R., and the program of genocide carried out by the Pol Pot regime in Cambodia are among the most notorious examples of cruel and lawless government. When the additional toll of war, repression, and economic disaster caused by national governments is added to the balance, the ills they have caused loom large indeed. In view of this dismal record, many argue that the human race would be better off without governments of any sort. However, others respond that human beings have devised governments because these institutions perform necessary functions, and they argue that human beings would be worse off without governments.

Proponents of the utility of governments point to the turmoil in Lebanon in the 1970s and 1980s as well as the present chaos and suffering in Somalia, Rwanda, and Bosnia as instances of the sort of life human beings can expect when they lack a governing body with the power to preserve order, prosperity, and stability. Therefore, the solution to the ills caused by national governments, they assert, is not to eliminate government, which is in any case likely to be impossible, but to establish the right sort of government.

Although national governments have been the cause of many of the world's ills, the cases of Bosnia and Somalia are vivid illustrations of the consequences of a lack of effective national government. Hence, some argue that the solution to the problems caused by national governments is the creation of an international government that would possess sufficient power to prevent the abuses caused by the governments of individual nation-states while allowing those governments to preserve order within their territories. To perform its functions effectively, this international government would have to possess sovereignty over the governments of the world's nations; have its own sources of revenue (rather than depending on dues paid by nation-states, as the United Nations now does); and command the powers to enact, adjudicate, and enforce laws, and to maintain and deploy its own military forces.

In addition, as many of the discussions in this book illustrate, the world is plagued by problems that require a coordinated and vigorous response by humanity as a whole. Pollution control, arms reduction, management of multinational corporations, and international crime all require a deliberate response and direction from the world community. A genuine international government, its proponents assert, could address these concerns far more efficiently and effectively than the present patchwork array of treaties, international governing agencies, and international conferences.

The civil war in Bosnia demonstrates the difficulties that attend the lack of an effective international government. Bosnia has been the scene of mass slaughter, brutal siege of cities, atrocious abuses of inmates in prison camps, forced relocation of many citizens from their homes, and countless other outrages. Through the medium of television, the people of the world and the world's political leaders were able to witness concrete evidence of the brutality of this war. It seemed obvious to all that people could not in good conscience allow the slaughter to continue, but the most powerful nations of the world dithered ineffectually for several years while many people died, several cities remained under siege, and many more people were forcibly evicted from their homes. Only after this lengthy period did the powerful nations begin to work seriously to bring peace to the region, but the peace that resulted is unstable and unsatisfactory, with several notorious war criminals still at large and an aggressor group retaining control of much of the territory it gained by force. Lack of an international governing authority with power to make and enforce decisions toward ending the violence in Bosnia no doubt contributed to the delay in bringing even this tenuous peace to the region. Furthermore, a powerful international governing body might well have achieved a more satisfactory and stable peace. Such a body could have intervened in forceful fashion far earlier in the civil war than did the voluntary assembly of nations.

In view of the above considerations, it is unsurprising that several writers and organizations strongly urge the creation of a genuine international government, a government that would have far more sovereign authority and unity than the United Nations now possesses. A government of this sort could prevent nations from initiating wars. It would also have the means to prevent individual governments from abusing their citizens as the government of Pol Pot did in Cambodia in the 1970s. It would be able to respond forcefully and decisively to problems that are global in nature, such as pollution, arms transfer, crime, disease, and population growth. Given the harm and suffering that unregulated national governments have caused their people and the ills that might befall the human race if it fails to respond effectively to global problems, it is not merely prudent but it is the moral obligation of humanity to create a genuine international government.

Proponents of international government acknowledge that national governments will be loath to yield their sovereign authority to an international governing body. However, they claim in response that this is the only effective means of addressing many of the problems humanity is facing. In addition, they argue that national governments are mistaken when they claim that they represent the collective wills of their citizens, as so many governments have so clearly abused their citizens in the course of human history and embarked on courses of action that their citizens did not desire. In addition, governments rarely consult their citizens when undertaking courses of action or devising new policies. When they do consult their citizens by means of polls or elections, they often make elaborate efforts to sway their populations to their own viewpoints. Hence, the claim that national governments inevitably represent the collective will of their citizens is false. It is also erroneous to say that national governments are concerned for the welfare of their citizens, once again because so many governments have caused their citizens harm. Furthermore, they claim that there is no reason to believe that an international government will be either more or less responsive to the wishes of ordinary persons than national governments. In fact, the collective will of all the people of the world would be a far more effective means of exerting pressure on an international government than are the separate and often competing wills of the various nations.

Many other people, however, argue that creation of an international government is both unwise and unjustified. In their view, the effort to create an international government is unlikely to succeed because the governments of the world's nations are highly unlikely to yield their sovereign prerogatives to an international government. Hence, the whole project is futile. However, even if an international government were created, it would most likely be ineffectual because the national governments of the world would remain in existence, would retain much of their power, and would not hesitate to use that power to prevent an international government from interfering with their domains of interest.

Opponents also argue that an international government is unnecessary because the present arrangement of allowing the national governments of the world to come together to address global problems can be equally effective—as, for example, when many nations united against Saddam Hussein's invasion of Kuwait. When the nations have good intentions and are firmly united, their collective action will be successful. Hence, what is required to deal adequately with global crises is not international government but additional measures to induce national governments to cooperate effectively and additional refinement of the measures already present for these purposes.

Opponents of international government also argue that national governments would be unjustified in yielding their sovereignty to an international government. This is because the human beings of the world are now organized into peoples, groups of individuals sharing a common language, common values, and common cultural practices. The peoples of the world are too diverse and lead lives that are far too distinctive to allow a single international government to represent the interests and desires of all equally effectively. National governments, however, have the obligation to represent the interests and seek the welfare of the people of their nation. To give this sovereignty away is to give away the main opportunity for effective representation of national interests.

For these reasons, it is highly unlikely that the world's national governments will ever be willing to yield their sovereignty to an international government. However, because there are many problems that must soon be addressed by the world as a community, these national governments will likely come to recognize that some form of international governing structure is needed to cope with them. Hence, it is most likely that a variety of international governing structures, with a variety of purposes and authorities, will emerge as the years pass. Though there probably will not be a movement to a single world government, the community of nations is likely to develop a whole array of governing entities that have sufficient authority to carry out their responsibilities without demanding a total abdication of sovereignty on the part of national governments.

**For further reading:** Bull, Hedley. 1995. *The Anarchical Society: A Study of Order in World Politics.* New York: Columbia University Press.

Claude, Innis L. 1988. *States and the Global System: Politics, Law, and Organization.* New York: St. Martin's Press.

Falk, Richard. 1992. *Explorations at the Edge of Time: The Prospects of World Order.* Philadelphia: Temple University Press.

Walker, Barbara, Norman Cousins, and the World Federalist Association. 1991. The *World Federalist Bicentennial Reader and Study Guide.* Washington, DC: World Federalist Association.

Weatherford, Roy. 1993. *World Peace and the Human Family*. London and New York: Routledge.

Yunker, James. 1993. *World Union on the Horizon: The Case for Supernational Federation*. Lanham, MD: University Press of America.

# International Systems of Law

In June 1997, authorities of Cambodia's government announced that Pol Pot had been detained by his followers. Pol Pot is among the most notorious figures of the twentieth century. Though his government held power in Cambodia for only a few years in the 1970s, well over a million Cambodians died as a result of his rule. Some members of the Cambodian government believed that he should be put on trial for his crimes. However, they felt that the trial should not be held in Cambodia, both because Cambodian legal institutions were in disarray and because it might have been impossible to ensure his physical security, since most Cambodians had lost one or more family members during his rule and might seek vengeance. Hence, the Cambodian leaders asserted that Pol Pot should be tried by an international court. The difficulty is that no international tribunal exists that could serve this purpose.

Although the above example is extreme, it illustrates a compelling case of the need for an international legal structure. As it happens, many different systems of international law have grown up during this century; however, the case of Pol Pot demonstrates that important gaps remain in these varied systems of law. The difficulty is that several systems of international law have evolved in separate domains, each independent of the other and none functioning under a sovereign global authority. Hence, the full range of the international legal system encompasses laws governing commercial relations, the conduct of war, the violation of human rights, and relations between the governments of nations. Furthermore, there is not simply one system of international law covering each of these domains. Rather, there are often several systems, each with its own range of jurisdiction and its own source of judicial authority.

These systems of law are evolving for the same reasons that systems of law have been created in all human societies, that is, to provide mechanisms for settling disputes, to enforce standards of conduct on the members of a community, and to provide mechanisms enabling the members of a community to accomplish certain tasks, such as establishing corporations or clarifying the meaning of laws. Hence, systems of international law emerged in the previous half century because of the increasing web of relations that binds the various peoples of the globe together.

International legal systems differ from domestic systems of law in several important respects. One is that international legal systems do not emerge from an international sovereign authority. There is no international government with sovereign authority similar to that existing on the level of the national state. Rather, there are a variety of international governing bodies (such as the United Nations), most of which exist as the instruments of the nations that created them, and which do not have any coercive power over national governments. Rather, these bodies generally depend for their effectiveness on the cooperation of the governments that participate within the organizations, or more often on the ability of one or several governments to sway others to their will. A second difference, related to the first, is that the various international legal systems lack the range of coercive powers of enforcement available to those created by sovereign governments. The bulk of enforcement is generally provided by peer pressure or the desire to preserve opportunities for cooperation. Even where more elaborate methods of enforcement are available, they generally depend on the support of national governments for their effectiveness. Third, these systems of law have generally grown up independently of one another. They do not result from a systematic effort to create a unified system of law to meet the needs of a defined society. As a result, there are overlapping jurisdictions. Some branches of law are more highly developed and more effectively enforced than others. Also, there is no single set of principles on which the entire body of international law rests.

It is clear that a system of international law modeled after the systems of law of individual nations would require an international government with the sort of sovereign authority possessed by the governments of nations. A system of law of this sort would enjoy several advantages over the present patchwork of legal systems. It could be based on a single, cohesive set of legal principles; it could have authoritative powers of enforcement; it could be independent of the goodwill of national governments; and it could have a cohesive structure of courts, jurisdictions, and institutions for altering and enacting laws. However, the major weakness of this sort of legal system is that nations are not likely to yield full sovereignty to any entity resembling a world government at any time in the near future. Hence, the world is most likely faced with the option of retaining the system of law it possesses at present, perhaps refined and extended as circumstances require.

Whatever system of international law emerges in the future will confront a serious issue, that of whether national governments are obliged to respect the judgments of such courts and provide them with means to enforce their decisions. The problem is illustrated by two cases from recent history.

In 1984, the International Court of Justice in The Hague, The Netherlands, agreed to hear charges that the Sandinista government of Nicaragua presented against the United States. The International Court of Justice was created by the United Nations to adjudicate accusations that national governments have violated international law. Though the United States was not at war with Nicaragua, it fervently desired the overthrow of the latter's government and was actively supporting a revolutionary group dedicated to this cause. As part of its effort to undermine the Nicaraguan government, the United States placed mines in one of Nicaragua's harbors to prevent shipping from entering or leaving. Nicaragua charged that this was clearly an act of war, even though the two governments were not at war and had not made any declarations of war. The United States rejected the charges and fought the issue in the Court. In 1986, the Court found in favor of Nicaragua's charges, determined that the United States was guilty of violating international law, and imposed punishment on the U.S. government. In response, the U.S. government simply ignored the verdict and refused to pay the penalty. Such behavior is ironic, given that the Court was created partly at the behest of United States, and various functionaries of the United States had often spoken in favor of a clear rule of law in the international realm. It is clear that U.S. actions in this case undermined the rule of law in the international domain and reduced the authority of the Court. Had the United States accepted the verdict, that country's power and influence in the world are such that the stature and authority of the Court would have been significantly enhanced. Other nations brought before the Court would have been far more likely to cooperate and far less likely to ignore its verdict.

The second example is provided by the World Tribunal on Human Rights, also housed in The Hague and under the authority of the United Nations. This court is charged with trying crimes against human rights around the world, and it recently was called into session to hear charges against various participants in the civil war in the Balkans. The parties on all sides of the war appear to have engaged in outrageous violations of human rights, from rape to deliberate starvation, to forced removal of people from their homes, to mass murder. Several people have been brought to trial, but the crucial issue was whether the governments of Bosnia, Croatia, and Serbia would cooperate with the process, since they would be required to assist in delivering persons charged with crimes, presenting witnesses, and gathering evidence at the scenes of purported crimes. Though citizens of all three nations are believed to have been involved in violations of human rights, all have given some degree of cooperation, though without any great enthusiasm. They have cooperated only because of intense pressure from powerful nations. Hence, to the extent that this series of war crimes trials succeeds, the achievement will be due to the committed support of the great powers of the world. If the trials are at least modestly successful in bringing war criminals to trial and punishing them, they will constitute a considerable step forward toward the creation of an international rule of law. Modest success also might augur well for another round of trials, this one on war crimes committed in Rwanda, where some of those thought to have taken part in the massacre of Tutsi several years ago are awaiting trial, though others remain at liberty.

Given the importance of a system of law in an increasingly interdependent world, many argue that nations are obligated to yield a portion of their sovereignty so that these international judicial systems may function effectively. They argue that nation-states should also work enthusiastically to establish a more organized system of law that will have greater independence of the governments of nation-states and will be able to hear grievances of citizens against their own governments. Such measures, they argue, will to a significant degree support the rights and liberties of ordinary people, help establish a rule of law among nations, and create a more stable climate for international business. In their view, the potential benefits to ordinary people, governments, and business corporations would justify the loss of sovereignty by national governments. They argue that governments have the obligation to serve the best interests of their people and of the institutions associated with them. Governments also have the obligation to help create a more stable world order. Hence, they are obligated to yield whatever portion of their sovereignty is necessary to serve these ends.

Many, in contrast, believe that governments are never justified in yielding any portion of their sovereignty. This is partly because governments are charged with looking after their citizens. If they lack full sovereignty, they will not be able to carry out this obligation as effectively as they otherwise might. Just as no one is justified in selling him- or herself into slavery, no matter what the benefit, no government is justified in bartering away any of its sovereign prerogatives, since this is the collective will of its people.

Governments are particularly unjustified in yielding sovereignty to help create an international system of law, because application of laws is one of the most important responsibilities governments possess. Further, yielding sovereignty in this matter is likely to lead to greater pressure to give away additional sovereign prerogatives as the international system of law develops further. The system of nations has served the world reasonably well for nearly 500 years, so there is little reason to begin to subvert that system by taking steps toward the creation of something quite different and completely untested.

Since it is quite unlikely that national governments will allow the creation of a sovereign world government, it appears that the present array of narrowly focused systems of law will continue to evolve in piecemeal fashion. It is also likely that new systems of law will emerge to direct world affairs in particular areas. For example, the world's nations are creating a dense network of treaties and agreements designed to protect the environment. No doubt there will be disagreements concerning the obligations created by these treaties and disputes over harm to one or several nations by pollutants coming from another nation. These disputes will have to be resolved in some judicial setting if they are to be addressed by means other than war. Similar measures probably will be taken to enforce arms control agreements and control of nuclear materials. In the commercial realm, agreements covering intellectual property are likely to result in disagreement and claims regarding harm done. Hence, various judicial systems likely will emerge to address these needs. It is quite possible that in the distant future, this patchwork of legal bodies will merge into a single, organized unit. For the next several years, however, it is probable that an international legal system will continue to emerge gradually and in piecemeal fashion, and will gain increasing authority only as the nations, people, and corporations of the world become accustomed to dealing with it and relying on its judgments.

**For further reading:** Falk, Richard, et al. 1985. *International Law: A Contemporary Perspective.* Boulder, CO: Westview Press.

Fitzpatrick, Joan. 1994. *Human Rights in Crisis: The International Systems for Protecting Human Rights during Time of Emergency.* Philadelphia: University of Pennsylvania Press.

Gill, Terry. 1989. *Litigation Strategy at the International Court: A Case Study of the Nicaragua v. United States Dispute.* Dordrecht and Boston: M. Nijhoff.

Grotius, Hugo. 1962 (first published in 1625). *The Law of War and Peace.* Tr. Francis Willey Kelsey. Indianapolis: Bobbs-Merrill.

Levi, Werner. 1991. *Contemporary International Law: A Concise Introduction.* Boulder, CO: Westview Press.

McWhinney, Edward. 1987. *The International Court of Justice and the Western Traditions of International Law.* Dordrecht and Boston: M. Nijhoff.

Nardin, Terry, and David Mapel. 1992. *Traditions of International Ethics.* Cambridge, England: Cambridge University Press.

United States Congress. Commission on Security and Cooperation. 1996. *The War Crimes Trials for the Former Yugoslavia: Prospects and Problems.* Washington, DC: Commission on Security and Cooperation.

# Intervention

Intervention in a nation's affairs by other nations is among the most contentious and difficult issues in international ethics. Consider the long civil war in Bosnia: While many people were being slaughtered and many others were being tortured and abused in concentration camps, other nations dithered for years before finally deciding to send military forces to attempt to restore order and end the violence. At present, fighting is at a standstill, and a semblance of peace has returned. The world community has spent billions of dollars to restore peace and begin rebuilding this devastated land. However, foreign troops cannot remain in Bosnia forever, and many fear that armed conflict will erupt again after they leave.

The debate over intervention in Bosnia was waged with arguments that were stark and compelling. Nearly every day, during the war, newspapers and television news programs were filled with accounts of horrible death, enormous suffering, and vicious cruelty. Television in particular made the human suffering in Bosnia immediate and compelling. Bosnia's misery could not be avoided. Many people in other nations began to wonder whether they were acting as barbarously as Bosnia's vicious combatants by failing to intervene. The message seemed simple and clear: The endless round of atrocities would not halt without outside intervention.

On the other hand, few wanted their sons and daughters to face death in a remote part of the world, which after all, was largely responsible for its problems. No one could say how many foreign troops might be killed or injured in an effort to end the Bosnian conflict. No one could say with any certainty how long outside forces might be needed to establish an enduring peace, or whether war might erupt again after the foreign peacekeeping troops left.

Also, the world's governments were, as they always seem to be, short of cash and faced with other compelling demands on their finances. The effort to end the fighting in Bosnia and help restore it to normalcy would certainly be costly, but none could say precisely how costly it might become. So the conflict continued until NATO forces were dispatched to establish a semblance of peace. Even now, no one can say with certainty that the NATO effort will succeed and that violence will not erupt again in Bosnia.

Meanwhile, although Bosnia is now comparatively quiet, other troubled portions of the world have attracted attention. A few years ago, there was a terrible slaughter of Tutsi by Hutu tribesmen in Rwanda. In 1997, there apparently was a slaughter of Hutu by Tutsi in the Congo (formerly Zaire). Afghanistan remains embroiled in vicious civil war, as it has been for several decades. Hence, the nations are faced with the dilemma of wishing to respond to human suffering but fearing the cost, danger, uncertainty, and possible futility of efforts to help. Controversies over intervention are still with us and are likely to remain with us for the foreseeable future.

In the broadest terms, intervention is simply the *interference* by others in the affairs of a person or a nation. This interference can take many forms. One form is coercion, forcing a nation or individual to conform to others' wishes. The coercion can be physical, as when nations employ, or threaten to employ, military force to alter the behavior of other nations, societies, or individuals, but it may also take other forms. Economic embargoes and blockades (such as that currently imposed by the United States against Cuba) are types of coercion commonly used against nations. For individuals, economic pressure can include the threat of being fired or fined. Interference may also be more subtle. Social pressure is frequently used to shape the behavior of individuals, and nations use a form of social pressure when they attempt to manipulate other nations' activity. For example, nations can ostracize other nations by excluding them from international conferences or international organizations; pressure them by making speeches and passing resolutions condemning their activities; and recruit other nations or international organizations, such as the United Nations, to engage in these activities. All of these methods of social pressure were employed in order to convince South Africa to dismantle its policies of apartheid.

The discussion of intervention began at the level of the relations between persons, or between individual persons and society, receiving a vigorous boost when the English philosopher John Stuart Mill wrote his famous essay *On Liberty* in the mid–nineteenth century. Mill argued that individuals and society as a whole are morally unjustified in intervening in an individual's life for any other purpose than to prevent harm to others. Mill based this argument on his belief that adult human beings in full possession of their faculties are rational and able to use their rational decisions to guide their actions. They are, in other words, free, rational beings. These capacities enable them to govern their own lives but also make them morally responsible for their actions. If others intervene, they override these capacities, and this overriding denies the essential human nature of the person whose life has been infringed upon. The concept of intervention has been at the center of many discussions of freedom of speech and religion in this century. There has been much discussion of what counts as intervention in individuals' lives and the circumstances under which it may be justified.

In debates on international ethics, the concept of intervention is applied to questions of whether other nations or the world community may justly intrude in the affairs of a sovereign state. Discussion of intervention is closely linked with nationalism and sovereignty, because nation-states often claim their possession of sovereignty entitles them to control their own affairs, free from meddling by other nations. The argument is thus akin to the individual person's right to live the life he or she desires. In fact, state sovereignty is sometimes claimed to be *based on* the right of self-governance enjoyed by individual persons, since states (democratic states, at any rate) are supposed to serve as the representatives of their people (and even totalitarian states claim to rule on behalf of the best interests of their people). Hence, those who oppose intervention often claim that to intrude in the affairs of a sovereign state is to override the wishes and interests of its citizens and is wrong for the same reasons that make intrusions into individual lives wrong.

The past several decades have seen vigorous discussion of intervention in the affairs of sovereign states. The discussion has been particularly heated on those occasions when the world community has debated how it should respond to a government that is causing great suffering to its people. For example, after the Khmer Rouge swept into power in Cambodia in 1975, it began a systematic massacre of the population. Of the total population of 4 million to 5 million Cambodians, between 1 million and 2 million were either killed directly or died as a result of the Khmer Rouge's brutal policies. Many argued that the world community had a moral obligation to use military force if necessary to halt these enormous crimes. As it happened, no international military intervention took place. However, some years after the Khmer Rouge were removed from power by the Vietnamese army, the United Nations was allowed entry. Since then, it has played a central role in attempting to restore democratic government and a semblance of normal life to Cambodia. Though practical concerns prevented the international community from intervening with armed force in Cambodia, few argued that an armed intervention would have been morally unjustified. Most believed that military intervention would be justified by saving many lives and that the Khmer Rouge, by virtue of its bloody policies, had lost any claim to representing the Cambodian people.

The U.N. Charter neatly encapsulates the difficulties surrounding the topic of intervention. On the one hand, Paragraph 7 of Article 2 in Chapter 1 unambiguously states: "Nothing contained in the present Charter shall authorize the United Nations to intervene in matters that are essentially within the domestic jurisdiction of any state. . . ." On the other hand, the Charter's Preamble affirms the United Nations' commitment "to reaffirm faith in fundamental human rights, in the dignity and worth of the human person, in the equal rights of men and women of nations large and small. . . ." Hence, the Charter both forswears intervention in the internal affairs of nation-states *and* affirms the United Nations' commitment to uphold the rights of individual persons. The problem is that national governments sometimes violate the rights of their citizens, and in cases of civil war, when groups of citizens battle one another, the rights and dignity of some citizens may be violated by other citizens. This occurred in Bosnia, for example, where the Serb and Muslim ethnic groups were at war and commonly violated one another's rights (though the Serbs' record is apparently considerably worse than that of the Muslims).

Given nations' abysmal record of intruding in one another's affairs primarily from motives of greed or vengeance, the United Nations' commitment to refrain from intrusion seems perfectly reasonable. Furthermore, some argue that governments must be presumed to represent their citizens in dealings with other nations. Hence, to intrude in their affairs is equivalent to overriding the wishes and desires of their people. Furthermore, many practical difficulties lie in the way of intervening when national governments abuse their citizens. The international community did not intervene in Cambodia during the Khmer Rouge's bloody rule in part because of enormous problems involved with assembling an international military force, transporting it to Cambodia's isolated and rugged terrain, and subduing a force hardened to life in the jungle and accustomed to the fluid, hit-and-run fighting of guerrilla warfare. Intervention is complicated in a different way when the rights of individual persons are being violated as a result of a civil war in which two or more ethnic groups or clans are battling one another. In light of these considerable practical and theoretical difficulties, some have argued that intervention in any nation's affairs is unjustified on both moral and practical grounds.

However, the vast suffering of the Cambodians or of the innocent people caught between the contending armies in Bosnia has prompted others to argue that intervention is sometimes morally required and even sanctioned by international law. Intervention, it is often argued, is required in order to honor the United Nations' commitment to protect the rights and dignity of all human beings. Proponents of this belief often argue that the many cases in which nations have wrongly intruded into the affairs of other nations do not give support to the belief that intervention is never justified. They insist that intervention by the community of nations on behalf of human well-being should be distinguished from selfish and unjust intervention. They argue, in addition, that nations that brutally violate the rights of their citizens or of certain citizen groups can hardly be pursuing the desires and interests of their citizens. The practical difficulties of assembling a large international military force are considerable, but some point out that international military forces have functioned successfully in many cases, including during World War II and in the Korean War. Moreover, the proponents of intervention point out that alternatives to military intervention exist and have been used successfully, such as the economic boycott and diplomatic pressures the world community employed against South Africa during the period of apartheid.

South Africa's policy of apartheid was particularly vicious. Apartheid means simply "apartness" of the black and white races, but this was not its true intent or practice. The policy not only ensured that the two races lived in different areas but also that blacks would remain economically dependent on whites, who then used their labor and skills to create comfortable lives for themselves. Blacks, under this policy, had essentially no civil rights and were manipulated at will, and often with great cruelty, by the white government. Even though the white government was clearly in power in South Africa, the world community determined that its violation of the basic human rights of its black population was too unjust to be overlooked. Hence, the world community enforced an embargo on trade with South Africa, and in particular, sought to prevent military weapons from reaching it. In addition, multinational corporations with operations in South Africa were pressured to withdraw. After a good bit of hesitation, the great majority (including several American corporations) did agree to cooperate. In addition, South Africa was barred from a number of the communal activities of the world's nations, such as the Olympics. After some years of these pressures, the white South African government voluntarily gave up its policy of apartheid, and following free elections in which all citizens could vote, allowed a black majority government to take power. There are many reasons why South Africa finally abandoned its policy of apartheid, but the incessant pressure from the international community surely played a significant role. The important point, though, is that the community of nations and peoples believed it was morally obligated to intervene in South Africa's affairs in order to halt its unjust policies.

The end of the cold war has eliminated many factors—particularly the tendency of the Great Powers to frame all issues in terms of the rivalry between them and the efforts of nonaligned nations to seek solidarity among themselves in order to free themselves from the influence of the Great Powers—that prevented the members of the United Nations from intervening in nations to protect the welfare of individual human beings. One result is that the United Nations has recently become far more active in promoting peacemaking and in working to relieve human suffering. In addition, other international groups, such as NATO and the Association of American States in the Western Hemisphere, have intervened on behalf of beleaguered people on several occasions. Moreover, the expanding global economy and enormously improved travel and communications have strengthened the ties people have to one another and made it more difficult to ignore human suffering wherever it occurs. Hence, although international intervention, as occurred in Somalia or Bosnia, has been plagued by difficulty, it appears that the community of nations is apt to continue to intervene on behalf of suffering people in troubled portions of the world. In addition, there have been a number of important successes, as in Haiti, Cambodia, and South Africa, which may serve to strengthen the resolve of the community of nations to intervene on behalf of human rights.

**For further reading:** Benn, S. I., and R. S. Peters. 1965. First published in 1959. *The Principles of Political Thought.* New York: Free Press.

Boutros-Ghali, Boutros. 1993. "U.N. Peacekeeping in a New Era." *The World Today* 49 (April): 66–69.

Brown, Peter G., and Douglas MacLean, eds. 1979. *Human Rights and U.S. Foreign Policy: Principles and Applications.* Lexington, MA: Lexington Books.

Greenwood, Christopher. 1993. "Is There a Right of Humanitarian Intervention?" *The World Today* 49 (February): 34–40.

Lefever, Ernest W. 1970. "The Perils of Reform Intervention." *Worldview* (February): 7–10.

Mill, John Stuart. 1947. (First published in 1859.) *On Liberty.* Ed. Alburey Castell. New York: Appleton-Century-Crofts.

Rieff, David. 1995. *Slaughterhouse: Bosnia and the Failure of the West.* New York: Simon & Schuster.

Shawcross, William. 1984. *The Quality of Mercy: Cambodia, Holocaust and Modern Conscience.* New York: Simon & Schuster.

Vincent, R. J. 1974. *Nonintervention and International Order.* Princeton, NJ: Princeton University Press.

# Multinational Corporations

Multinational corporations are among the most powerful forces driving the process of global unification. Multinational corporations are difficult to define precisely because there are so many differing forms of multinational economic activity and because few business enterprises today can afford to remain entirely aloof from world markets. However, a serviceable though necessarily imprecise definition would encompass all business enterprises that have significant portions of their organizations located in more than one nation. Merely trading goods across national boundaries would not make a business a multinational corporation, but having manufacturing or distribution centers would. Although difficult to define, multinational corporations are energetically and ceaselessly knitting the ties of trade, manufacturing, labor, and expertise that are binding nations more closely together.

The unifying forces exerted by multinational corporations are sufficiently strong that it is difficult for even the most isolated and recalcitrant governments to offer more than fleeting resistance to their activities. This is because national governments are aware that their nations' prosperity and stature depend on active participation in the global economy. Nations such as North Korea or Myanmar (formerly Burma), which have sought to remain aloof from the global economy, are among the poorest and most backward in the world. Even the recalcitrant leaders of these nations are becoming aware that they have no choice but to enter the global economy, however reluctantly, if their countrymen are to escape dismal poverty and gain an opportunity to become influential members of the world community. Today, most nations are so deeply enmeshed in the global economy that they would seriously harm their own economies were they to attempt to withdraw. For example, the United States must import more than half of the petroleum it uses. If it were to attempt to close its borders and rely only on the petroleum available domestically, its economy would be crushed, because much economic activity in the United States depends on cheap and plentiful fuel.

Though multinational corporations are enormously important to nations' relative prosperity and stature, they also have created a number of difficult moral issues. Some believe that multinational corporations bring considerably more grief than benefit to nations, as these powerful corporations frequently succeed in evading effective control by national governments. In addition, certain multinational corporations have used their enormous wealth and power to manipulate governments and people into serving their corporate interests. Huge corporations like General Motors or United Brands have considerably more wealth than do many nations; they have vast armies of lawyers at their disposal; and they can shift accounts, inventory, and records rapidly from nation to nation to escape taxes or governmental oversight. The problems of taxation and legal oversight are exacerbated by the difficulty of determining whether a particular corporation is U.S., British, Japanese, or German. For example, Coca-Cola is a prominent symbol of American life. However, it generally receives 80 percent of its profits from its overseas operations, and the great majority of its employees, bottling plants, and distribution systems are located outside the United States. As a result, from Coca-Cola's perspective, the United States is simply one market among many. The late corporate president was a naturalized U.S. citizen of Cuban descent, but many other chief executives are not U.S. citizens. Hence, Coca-Cola is more a global corporation than a U.S. corporation. In light of these circumstances, the central moral issues are whether multinational corporations can and should be held morally accountable for their activities, and whether people would be better off without them.

The difficulties posed by multinational corporate activities are nicely illustrated by the case of Nike, a manufacturer of athletic shoes. Though its corporate headquarters are in the United States, most of its manufacturing plants are abroad. Recently, controversy arose because it was reported that a Nike plant in Indonesia provided wages and working conditions that were scandalously low by U.S. standards. As a result, there was an outcry against its exploitation of Indonesian workers (who were mostly young women). However, further investigation revealed that the wages Nike paid, and the working conditions it offered to Indonesians, were better than Indonesian laborers could hope to receive at other workplaces. Hence, jobs at the Nike plant were eagerly sought and highly prized by Indonesians. Furthermore, attracting plants and jobs of the sort that Nike offered was viewed by many Indonesians, particularly those in government, as a necessary step toward economic development and joining the ranks of the world's advanced nations. From this perspective, Nike was not exploiting Indonesia or its people but was offering them a valuable opportunity.

Another case, less well known and more bizarre, is perhaps even more revealing. Following World War II, International Telephone & Telegraph (IT&T) filed a claim with the U.S. government, seeking restitution for damage to its manufacturing plants by Allied bombers during the war. It seems that the Focke-Wulff fighter-bomber plant in Germany was among the corporation's subsidiaries. IT&T continued throughout the war to own and to receive profits from the plant, which was churning out materiel to be used against the Allied forces. Consequently, some argued that IT&T's conduct was a scandalous violation of corporate responsibility and that IT&T had violated its obligation to contribute to the Allied war effort. However, according to several commentators, no corporate enterprise can or should be expected to pursue any end other than maximizing corporate profits, because any loss in the efficiency of the free market would bring greater harm to humanity than greater patriotism on IT&T's part would bring benefits.

There are three major views on the moral status of multinational corporations. One is that multinational corporations neither can nor should be held morally accountable for their actions, and that unfettered corporate profit seeking greatly benefits humanity. The argument that corporations cannot be held morally accountable for their actions rests on two claims. One is that only individual human beings have the freedom of conduct and rationality of thought that allow them to be morally responsible for their activities. Only individual human beings are able to grasp principles of moral conduct and make decisions that will bring their acts into accord with their moral standards. Because corporations are abstract, artificial creations, they have neither the freedom nor the ability to grasp abstract moral principle that individual human beings enjoy. Furthermore, corporations are created solely to make profits for their owners. People invest money in corporations or buy them in the hope that they will profit from their actions, and they expect corporate managers and employees to pursue the same goal. Hence, if corporations refrain from seeking maximal profit because they wish to uphold moral ideals, they will have violated the trust that investors have placed in them. Lastly, some argue that corporations will benefit humanity only if they seek profits aggressively and single-mindedly, for the efficiency and prosperity generated by unbridled competition result in more jobs, more opportunities, and a greater array of goods available to consumers. The unconstrained choice of participants in the free market is key to this array of benefits. Any attempt to restrict or redirect the array of choices available to consumers distorts the operation of the market, and therefore makes it less efficient and less responsive to the desires of consumers.

A second major view is that multinational corporations both can and should be held morally responsible for their activities, and that they will benefit humanity only if they are held accountable to standards of moral conduct. Those holding this view point out that corporations are held responsible for violations of law. Therefore, they have the resources of freedom and rationality necessary to be morally accountable for their endeavors. They also point out that many corporations do uphold standards of moral conduct and make this adherence known to investors. People who buy stock in corporations that they know adhere to moral codes cannot claim to be unjustly treated. Many also claim that corporations known to be morally upright are more likely to prosper than those known to be willing to violate moral constraint in pursuit of financial advantage. No one, no matter how profit hungry, is anxious to do business with entities known to violate moral scruples in pursuit of economic advantage. Trust, mutual respect, and integrity are linchpins of commercial endeavor. Far from being impediments to competitive success, these qualities are necessary preconditions of free market activity. Lastly, while partisans of this view agree that economic competition in a free market brings many benefits to humanity, they argue that it is false that any and all restrictions on economic endeavor will harm humanity or undermine the efficiency of the market. They point out, for example, that pollution regulations have created many opportunities for corporate endeavor, and there is now a thriving market for pollution-control services and products. Hence, pollution control results in two kinds of benefits, creating a better environment for human life as well as increasing economic opportunities.

A third view develops the position that multinational corporations cannot be expected to serve any interests other than their own and that efforts on behalf of corporate profits will always be harmful to the interests of the nations in which corporations conduct their operations. Partisans of this view claim that multinational corporations are not bound to any particular nation or people and will seek economic benefit where and when they can. They will shuffle jobs and expertise from one nation to another, without regard for the interests of any of the nations or people who will be affected by their conduct. When they exhaust resources in one nation, they will simply move elsewhere. If their actions create social unrest in a nation, they will simply move to more congenial surroundings. They are glad to offer any expertise they possess to whomever is able to pay them for it, without regard to the ultimate use of the expertise or the interests of the nations whose institutions may have generated it. Furthermore, corporations will not hesitate to use their power and influence to pressure nations and individuals to serve their ends, whether or not these ends benefit the people concerned. Hence, partisans of this position conclude, multinational corporations are, in the long term, a menace to people and nations and must either be rigorously controlled by nations or put out of existence altogether so that business corporations will grow and function strictly within national boundaries, serving the interests of their home nations.

Whether multinational corporations significantly benefit humanity or not, they are unlikely to disappear. In fact, they are likely to grow more numerous and powerful in coming years. This is because business activity thrives on opportunities, and benefits from the power and efficiency offered by large size. Whatever doubts national leaders have about the benefits of multinational corporate activity, in the past several decades, they have generally concluded that they must actively participate in the world economy if their nations are to thrive. In fact, the most prosperous and dynamic nations at present—those deemed models of economic development—gained their prowess by moving aggressively into international commerce. Also, the tempo of multinational commerce seems to quicken as more nations and more corporations enter the global fray. The ties these endeavors create appear to nurture the creation of yet more ties, which speed the process of globalization along that much more quickly. Moreover, nations and individuals are learning to channel the activities of multinational corporations in ways that benefit them. Nations are developing systems of law better suited to coping with multinational business activity; a system of international commercial law is developing to serve the same purpose; and nations are learning to pool their resources toward coping with multinational corporations. The United Nations is also serving as an important center for pooling expertise and resources needed for dealing with multinational corporations. In addition, the ever increasing number of multinational corporations seeking new arenas of opportunity has given nations the ability to force corporations to compete with one another for access to their markets, labor, or expertise. Individuals also have learned to group together to influence huge corporations, as when the concerted efforts of consumer groups forced Nestlé to withdraw its infant formula from markets where it was unsuitable. Thus, the long-term prospect is that there will be more multinational corporations, that they will become active in more areas of the world, and that their endeavors will continue to stitch the world more closely together economically and socially. However, it also appears that nations and people are learning to cope with multinational corporations and to use them to their own advantage.

**For further reading:** Collins, Glenn. 1997. "Profits at Coca-Cola Rose by 18% during 4th Quarter." *New York Times* (1 February): A35:3

DeGeorge, Richard T. 1993. *Competing with Integrity in International Business.* New York: Oxford University Press.

Donaldson, Thomas. 1989. *The Ethics of International Business.* New York: Oxford University Press.

Elfstrom, Gerard. 1990. *Moral Issues and Multinational Corporations.* London and New York: Macmillan and St. Martin's Press.

Houck, John, and Oliver Williams, eds. 1996. *Is the Good Corporation Dead? Social Responsibility in a Global Economy.* Lanham, MD: Rowman & Littlefield.

Mydans, Seth. 1996. "For Indonesians at Nike Plant: Just Do It." *New York Times* (9 August): A4.

National Conference on Business Ethics. 1986. *Ethics and the Multinational Corporation: Proceedings of the Sixth National Conference on Business Ethics, October 10 and 11, 1985.* Lanham, MD: University Press of America.

Sampson, Anthony. 1973 *The Sovereign State of I. T. T.* London: Hodder & Stoughton.

Shue, Henry. 1996. *Basic Rights: Subsistence, Affluence, and U.S. Foreign Policy.* 2d ed. Princeton, NJ: Princeton University Press.

Vernon, Raymond. 1977. *Storm over the Multinationals: The Real Issues.* Cambridge, MA: Harvard University Press.

# National Sovereignty

National governments guard few things as jealously as their national sovereignty. Sovereignty has two aspects: the external (in relation to other nation-states) and the internal (in relation to citizens). In its external aspect, sovereignty includes the ideas that no other nations or institutions have legal authority over national governments or are morally justified in coercing them or intruding into their domestic affairs. Internally, from the perspective of ordinary citizens and their governments, sovereignty includes the ideas that national governments are the highest legal authority in a nation and that citizens owe them obedience.

Sovereignty is a relatively recent arrival on the world's political scene. It was first discussed barely 500 years ago, when it was given theoretical formulation by Jean Bodin, a French political theorist and theologian. Its significance has increased in parallel with the rise of the modern nation. During Europe's Middle Ages, the concept of sovereignty would have been nonsensical because all human beings, including human monarchs, were believed to owe their authority to God and to be subservient to God's will. The idea that monarchs or governments could have sovereignty apart from divine authority would have been unthinkable for medieval Europeans.

In this century, sovereignty has prompted much discussion and has been the center of considerable controversy, partly as a result of notorious violations of national sovereignty in several wars and partly as a result of the efforts of colonies of Europe to escape imperialist control and gain a status equal to the other nations of the world. Following World War II, sovereignty was thought sufficiently important in international affairs and international law that respect for sovereignty was enshrined in the charter of the United Nations.

Though most politicians, academics, and lawyers agree that sovereignty is of considerable importance, it is currently the focus of several moral controversies. One is whether any and all governments are entitled to sovereign status. For example, many deny that a tyrannical government that has gained power through brute force and without the approval of its people is entitled to sovereign status either with regard to other nations or to its own citizens. A second moral problem is whether national governments are ever entitled to give up portions of their sovereign authority. For example, at present, nations commonly make agreements on matters of trade, ecology, arms control, and finance that require that they cede a portion of their sovereignty. However, if national governments are morally entitled to their sovereignty, or if sovereignty is the moral entitlement of a nation's citizens, then an agreement that yields a portion of national sovereignty may be morally illegitimate. A third issue is whether other nations are ever justified in intruding in the sovereign affairs of nations. (For an examination of this question, *see* Intervention.)

Most people agree that citizens and nations should recognize sovereign status only of national governments that have the moral entitlement to rule over their citizens. However, the tendency in international diplomacy in this century has been to award sovereign recognition to any government that is clearly in physical control of a particular nation, and most individuals likewise would acknowledge that any government with physical control over them has sovereign authority. There are exceptions to this general practice, but they are rare and gain attention in part because they are exceptions to the usual rule. For example, Saddam Hussein gained control of Iraq by military coup and has ruled his nation with ruthless dictatorial force ever since he fought his way to power. His citizens have essentially no civil rights or protections, and Hussein has not hesitated to kill them whenever it suits his purposes. In addition, the Iraqis have suffered greatly as a result of the U.N. embargo on trade with Iraq that followed the Persian Gulf War. Nonetheless, there are few signs of overt opposition to Hussein's regime inside Iraq, and most nations, including the United States, had recognized his rule prior to the Gulf War. Hussein remains in power, despite the fact that his regime has displayed none of the qualities that would morally entitle him to rule.

The same point is also well illustrated by U.S. relations with Communist China. The United States refused to grant recognition of China following its successful revolution in 1948 on the grounds that it had gained power by force (and because the United States was allied with the overthrown government of Chiang Kai-shek). The United States continued to withhold recognition following the Communist revolution on grounds that the Marxist government was not democratic and did not respect its citizens' civil rights (and also because the United States was opposed to Communist nations in general). However, after several decades had passed, the United States finally established relations with Communist China (thereby acknowledging its sovereignty) on the grounds that it was simply too important a nation to be ignored, given U.S. interests.

Some argue that it is proper for nations and governments to routinely recognize the sovereign status of any government that is clearly in power in a nation. They argue that governments in firm control of a nation should have their sovereign status recognized both by the world community and by their own citizens. This is because they believe that moral standards beyond a commitment to the recognition of actualities have no place in the affairs of nations. They support their view with several arguments. One begins with the assertion that the only means that nations have of exercising influence on a rogue nation is war or economic embargo, both of which are extremely dangerous, difficult to control with precision, and likely to cause great suffering to the very people they are designed to help. In addition, the interests of a nation's citizens might necessitate good relationships with even a renegade nation. For example, given Iraq's great oil reserves, many nations were anxious to be on good terms with Hussein in order to gain access to the resource that he controlled. In addition, they frequently argue, should those in other nations really wish to assist the beleaguered citizens of a rogue nation, the best way of doing so is by establishing firm ties with its government, then employing these ties to attempt to improve the welfare of the nation's people. The rogue nation's citizens have the choice of either accepting the authority of a dictatorship or rising up in armed rebellion. Rebellion is sure to be costly in lives and economic damage, may fail, and even if successful, may produce another dictatorship as bad as the previous one. These citizens have no good options, but the least difficult and dangerous course may be to remain quiescent.

Many are not persuaded by these arguments. They argue that there must always be a difference between governments that in fact have power over a nation and governments that are morally entitled to power. They argue that it is always reasonable to ask whether a particular government is entitled to power, even in circumstances where people and nations have little option other than to attempt to get along in a tyrannical system. The murderous regime of the Khmer Rouge in Cambodia is estimated to have killed more than a million of its own citizens during its years in power in the 1970s. It had no moral claim to rule and was granted official recognition by only a few nations. On the other hand, the United States had diplomatic relations with the Baltic states of Latvia, Lithuania, and Estonia during the entire cold war, a period when these nations were firmly controlled by the Soviet Union and their governments existed only as shadow governments in exile. The U.S. government had several reasons for its policy, among them the belief that these governments in exile were morally entitled to reign over these nations, even though their prospects for gaining control of their nations appeared hopeless for most of the cold war.

Furthermore, many argue that it is reasonable to ask whether the people of a nation are morally entitled to rise in rebellion even when prudence would dictate that they refrain from doing so. It also makes sense to ask whether a national government has a moral entitlement to recognition of its sovereignty even under circumstances where prudence requires that ties be created and maintained.

There is considerable divergence of opinion over what moral standards governments must satisfy in order to possess a valid entitlement to rule. Some argue that governments are entitled to rule only when they have been elected by democratic means. Others believe that governments that gain power by the will of the people, even when this will is expressed through armed revolution, are entitled to sovereign authority. Yet others believe that governments are entitled to claim sovereign authority only when they preserve and protect the basic civil rights of their people, such as the rights listed in the U.N. Universal Declaration of Human Rights. In this view, even a government with considerable popular support would be illegitimate if it failed to honor human rights. (This might occur in a nation where a majority of citizens enthusiastically endorsed the suppression of a minority.) Yet others believe that governments that succeed in preserving and promoting the well-being and prosperity of their people deserve sovereign status. Hence, they may argue that governments such as that of Singapore, which is tyrannical and corrupt, are entitled to their sovereignty so long as they maintain a high level of prosperity for their people. Nonetheless, all proponents of this position believe that national governments must uphold a set of moral standards, whatever it might be, in order to claim title to sovereignty.

In recent years, as the nations of Europe have moved toward greater political and economic unity, they have become embroiled in debates about whether governments are ever justified in yielding portions of their sovereignty. For example, they are taking measures to create a single currency for the nations that choose to become part of the European Union. However, control over currency is among the most important facets of a nation's sovereignty. This is because the value of a nation's currency determines both how much money a government has to spend and also how much money is circulating through its economy and hence available to be employed for business and personal finance. Thus, control of its currency's value (by regulating interest rates that banks may charge and by simply printing or not printing more money) is a central feature of governments' power. When the European Union proposes to create a common currency, to bind its nations' economies together more tightly and ease economic transactions among them, it is threatening a significant portion of its member nations' sovereignty.

Some, particularly in Great Britain and in France, argue strongly that a common currency represents an unjustified loss of sovereignty. Sovereignty, they claim, represents the will of a nation's people. To yield sovereignty, therefore, is to forsake a portion of the people's power to control their own affairs. They argue that such action—even if undertaken freely and with consent—is as unjustified as an individual's selling him- or herself into slavery. That is, it is morally equivalent to an individual's giving away the entitlement to control his or her own affairs, and is equally unjustified. Respect for human dignity, whether at the level of the individual or of the entire nation, demands that such activity be avoided and brands it immoral. Further, they argue, it would be immoral for political leaders to agree to this loss of sovereignty, because the sovereign authority that is yielded to the central European government could be used in ways that harm the interests of the people in individual European nations. As the primary responsibility of political leaders is to preserve the security and welfare of their citizens, this would obviously be unjustified.

Others—some in Great Britain and France, but mainly in Germany and Italy—argue that this loss of sovereignty is necessary to preserve the security and welfare of the people of Europe. They argue that greater economic unity is needed to allow European corporations to compete more effectively on the world market and to attract more foreign investment to Europe. At present, the global market rewards size, both because greater size provides greater efficiency and economies of scale and because large corporations are able to compete more effectively against other large corporations. In addition, the current variations in national currencies and regulations, particularly in nations with markets of modest size, might make European countries comparatively unattractive to corporations seeking investment opportunities, because a manufacturing plant established in one nation might have difficulty selling products to other nations nearby. However, corporations would have greater incentive to invest in Europe if they knew that products manufactured in one nation could be sold easily in other nations. Hence, the governments' obligation to look after the security and well-being of their citizens, in this case, requires yielding sovereignty rather than jealously protecting it. Failure to take these measures toward economic unification will, they argue, erode Europe's ability to compete in the global economy along with its wealth and erode its power and influence in the world. It may be worth noting that many European political leaders are persuaded by these arguments, for they, rather than ordinary citizens, are at the forefront of the movement for greater economic integration.

In addition, proponents of the European Union argue that the loss of sovereignty will be felt only by the national governments. A government's loss of sovereign authority does not amount to a loss in the self-control of individuals unless this sovereignty is transferred to a dictatorial government, or the governing entity that receives sovereignty is unresponsive to the wishes of citizens. Were this not so, then individuals would be morally remiss to grant authority to any government, whether local, national, or international.

Disagreements over issues of sovereignty are likely to increase in coming years, as nations find themselves bound more tightly together and find it necessary to cooperate more closely with one another through binding treaties that address mutual concerns, such as trade or pollution. Further, to the extent that international governing bodies, such as the United Nations, and international standards of conduct become more firmly entrenched in world affairs, questions of which standards nations must satisfy in order to claim title to sovereignty will be more frequent and heated. Nonetheless, it appears at present that the view that any government in power is entitled to its sovereignty, no matter how brutal it is or how it came into power, is waning in influence. However, there is another strand of thought that merits consideration. This is the view that the emerging global economy is making the nation obsolete, and that the era to come is the era of far more international cooperation. If this prediction is correct, then questions of sovereignty will become less important because nations will become less important and less consequential for global affairs.

**For further reading:** Barker, Rodney. 1990. *Political Legitimacy and the State*. Oxford: Clarendon Press.

Beitz, Charles. 1979. *Political Theory and International Relations*. Princeton, NJ: Princeton University Press.

Dobriansky, Paula. 1989. "The Baltic States in an Era of Soviet Reform." *Department of State Bulletin* 89 (June): 35–39.

Falk, Richard. 1981. *Human Rights and State Sovereignty*. New York: Holmes & Meier Publishers.

Green, Leslie. 1988. *The Authority of the State*. Oxford: Oxford University Press.

Hinsley, F. H. 1986. *Sovereignty*. 2d ed. Cambridge, England: Cambridge University Press.

Hoffmann, Stanley. 1993. "Good-Bye to a United Europe." *New York Review of Books* 40 (27 May): 27–31.

James, Alan. 1986. *Sovereign Statehood*. London: Allen & Unwin.

Newman, Ronald. 1994. "Overview of U.S. Policy Toward Iraq." *U.S. Department of State Dispatch* 5 (7 February): 66–68.

Wriston, Walter. 1992. *The Twilight of Sovereignty*. New York: Charles Scribner's Sons.

# Nationalism

Nationalism is the view that the welfare and interests of members of one's own national group should be given greater weight in one's moral deliberations than those of people outside one's nation. This view is among the major barriers to the full-fledged development of international ethics.

Extreme examples of this position hold that people outside one's nation should count for very little when making decisions that affect them. A more moderate belief is that the members of one's own nation should always be given preference over foreigners. This issue arises each year in the United States when Congress is deliberating over spending money for foreign aid. Some often argue that any money available to the United States should be put to use for the welfare of U.S. citizens rather than to aid those in other lands, unless doing so will serve the interests of U.S. citizens in some way.

To the extent that people find nationalism compelling, they will concern themselves less with the interests of people in other parts of the world, and the ethics of international relations will have very little attraction for them.

However, there are some difficulties with the concept of nationalism. For one thing, it is a relatively new idea on the world scene. It is some 250 years old, considerably younger than the idea of the nation-state. Nationalism began to receive attention when the leaders of some nations attempted to create a sense of unity among their citizens. Sometimes the concept served the purpose of territorial expansion. At other times, it was evoked in service of increasing military strength, as national leaders needed a means of enticing large numbers of people to enlist in the ranks of their armed forces. The appeal to nationalism served these purposes well, and as a result, it became part of the standard political rhetoric. In other words, nationalism has not always been a part of human psychology and culture, and it might well cease to be so at some point in the future.

Even now, many people identify more closely with their region or their ethnic group than with the nation where they live. Some, such as the Kurds or Albanians, may feel greater kinship with members of their own ethnic group who are scattered among several nations than with the citizens of the nation where they reside. It was partly for this reason that the nation of Yugoslavia fell apart a few years ago, resulting in the brutal civil war in the Balkans. Lacking a strong dictatorial government to hold them together, the people of Yugoslavia found that they identified themselves more as Croats, Serbs, or Muslims than as Yugoslavians. Even the United States has not always had a strong sense of national identity. In the view of scholar Garry Wills, the United States did not achieve a sense of national identity until the

Civil War. Wills credits Abraham Lincoln with having created this sense, calling it one of Lincoln's most important accomplishments.

A more basic problem with the concept of nationalism is that it is unclear what qualities a group of people must possess in order to consider itself a nation. For example, a nation must differ from an ethnic group, since many nations, such as the United States and Russia, contain many different ethnic groups. Neither does possession of a common language suffice to create ties of nationhood. The United States and Great Britain, for example, share a common language but obviously consider themselves two separate nations. Even within one nation it is often possible to find several different linguistic groups. Switzerland, for example, has groups of German speakers, others who speak Italian, and still others who speak French, yet the Swiss enjoy a strong sense of national identity. The United States contains groups of Spanish speakers, Chinese speakers, and so on, yet few members of these groups would think of themselves as anything other than Americans. Most often, nations are patched together by means of military conquest or merger. National boundaries are generally artificial creations that could easily have been drawn differently. Hence, it is not easy to see why great moral weight should be placed on the fact of common membership in a nation or why people should believe they have moral obligations to their fellow citizens that they do not have to other people.

It is easy to imagine a case in which one nation attacks another, with the avowed intention of annexing the target nation and absorbing its institutions. A person within the target nation might then be called upon to fight to save his or her home nation. But this person might have no reason to believe the government of the attacking nation will be worse than that of his or her home nation. In fact, there might be reason to believe that this citizen's prospects in the new nation would be somewhat improved if the attack were successful. Such an individual could plausibly claim that he or she had no obligation to fight on behalf of his or her home nation simply to preserve it and its identity.

Nonetheless, many people do believe that nationalism is sufficiently important that members of one nation should give greater moral weight to the interests of fellow citizens than to people in other nations. They may point out, for example, that members of a particular nation pay taxes to that nation for the purpose of improving the lot of the nation as a whole. Hence, citizens of a nation can claim aid from other citizens on the grounds that all are engaged in a common enterprise and generally have accepted the obligation to look after one another's interests. Furthermore, in times of war or economic hardship, the members of a single nation are likely to share a common fate and will have to work together to repair the damage. Moreover, even though most nations are artificial creations, the fact that most nations have been in existence for some time has had the effect that most members of a nation feel a sense of emotional bonding with other members of their nation. Hence, Americans will often be more troubled by news that an airline crash claimed the lives of U.S. citizens than if it had killed people from, say, Brazil or Australia.

Without some emotional bonding of this sort, talk of ethics is likely to be ineffectual. People are moved by their emotions and feel a sense of obligation based on their emotional ties. Furthermore, the fact that people have lived together in a given nation for a period of time means that they are genuinely likely to have developed some ties, since people's bonds of education, economic interdependence, governmental service, and so on are likely to be confined within the boundaries of their home nation.

In addition, governments and political leaders generally explicitly accept the responsibility to look after the welfare and interests of the people of a single nation. The citizens of that nation rely on governments and governmental leaders to carry out these responsibilities, and they would feel betrayed if political leaders gave equal weight to the interests of other nations. They would feel particularly outraged if governmental leaders of their home nation sacrificed their interests for the sake of the welfare of people in other nations.

Nonetheless, some people respond that giving great weight to national bonds is mistaken. Even if there is some justification for placing somewhat greater emphasis on the interests of members of one's home nation, there is no justification for failing to give considerable weight to the welfare of people in other nations, particularly when their needs are very great, as in times of famine or epidemic.

Most religions and moral philosophies of the world hold that qualities such as rationality, freedom of action, consciousness, possession of a soul, or ability to suffer are the most relevant criteria when considering whether a being is legitimately of moral concern or not. None of these intellectual movements gives support for the position that national identification is relevant to moral decision making. In ancient times or among primitive cultures, many believed that people living in other cultures were not fully human and therefore did not deserve the same concern that was owed to a member of one's own group. However, most people now recognize that these views are false, that human beings everywhere in the world are equally human, and that none are semihuman.

Although those opposed to nationalism might concede that living in a particular nation creates bonds among members of that nation, they assert that this fact does not conclusively prove that the interests of the members of one's own nation should always be given greater weight than any interests or concerns of people in other nations. Furthermore, they argue that a common principle of moral obligation is that people should be of assistance to the extent that they are able. Hence, not all people in all nations will be able to aid all people in all nations with any or all problems they may have. National ties often make a difference, because governments are among the primary instruments for assisting people; for this reason, it is generally more difficult to assist people in alien nations than people in one's home nation. However, the wealthy people of the world, acting collectively, could do a great deal to assist the starving, and at very little expense to themselves individually.

Furthermore, opponents of nationalism are apt to point out that many problems of international ethics are common to all people. They believe that if these problems are to be addressed effectively, all the people and all the governments will have to cooperate and acknowledge their common interests and common concerns. People are unlikely to be eager to cooperate with people in other nations if they believe that these aliens do not regard them as full moral equals and if they do not give great moral weight to their concerns. As a purely practical matter, therefore, the people of the various nations of the world will have to give equitable weight to the interests of all human beings if they are to succeed in solving the problems that they jointly face.

Although nationalism has been an extremely powerful force in the world for the past century or so and remains very powerful in many places today, several other forces at work in the world today are likely to undermine it. The most important corrosive factor is the rise of the global economy, which is creating thick webs of ties binding people, companies, and even nations in all parts of the world. Individuals may soon come to live and work in several nations in the course of their careers. Even if they remain in their home nation, they may find themselves working for a corporation owned by a foreign company. In the course of their work, they may well find they have more in common with others in their profession or corporation than with many of their countrymen. They may also find that their personal interests, determined by the corporation where they work, differ from the interests of their nation as a whole. They may be employed by a firm that imports automobiles into their nation, for example, and will prosper as more of these automobiles are sold. However, the government of their home nation may be struggling to reduce its balance of payments deficits, and therefore make an effort to reduce the number of foreign automobiles sold within its boundaries. Furthermore, travel, communication, and problems of global concern all are likely to conspire to make national boundaries less important to people and make them more willing to recognize the concerns and interests of those living elsewhere. Hence, it is likely that nationalism will recede in importance in years to come and that people will be more willing to recognize the interests and concerns of people living elsewhere.

For further reading: Greenfeld, Liah. 1992. *Nationalism: Five Roads to Modernity.* Cambridge, MA: Harvard University Press.

Hobsbawm, Eric. 1990. *Nations and Nationalism since 1780.* Cambridge, England: Cambridge University Press.

Hoffmann, Stanley. 1984. *Duties beyond Borders: On the Limits and Possibilities of Ethical International Politics.* Syracuse, NY: Syracuse University Press.

Horseman, Matthew. 1994. *After the Nation-State: Citizens, Tribalism, and the New World.* London: HarperCollins.

Judt, Tony. 1994. "The New Old Nationalism." *The New York Review of Books* 41 (26 May): 44–51.

Katzenstein, Peter, ed. 1996. *The Cultures of National Security: Norms and Identity in World Politics.* New York: Columbia University Press.

Tamir, Yael. 1993. *Liberal Nationalism.* Princeton, NJ: Princeton University Press.

Walzer, Michael. 1983. *Spheres of Justice.* New York: Basic Books.

Wills, Garry. 1992. *Lincoln at Gettysburg.* New York: Simon & Schuster.

# Natural Resources

Two fundamental trends probably will dominate the world in the next century. One is the expanding global economy and the attendant economic development of many less developed nations of the world. The other is the continued increase in human population, particularly in the less developed nations. These two trends will have profound effects on human life. In particular, however, they will place vastly greater demands on the world's natural resources.

Advanced, industrialized societies use far more resources per person than do impoverished ones. As the less developed societies join the ranks of the industrialized, they, too, will make greater demands on the world's natural resources. Even without the effects of economic development, the expanding human population will require more resources than in past centuries.

Wars have been fought over control of land, petroleum, and water. If supplies of these resources become depleted, human beings and their governments are likely to become desperate, and war or social turmoil are even more likely to result from disputes over control of or access to natural resources.

More than 25 years ago, a report by the Club of Rome caused a great stir by concluding that the world would essentially exhaust its store of vital resources by the end of the twentieth century. As is now apparent, the Club of Rome's report, *The Limits to Growth*, first published in 1972, was overly pessimistic. However, with sufficient time, its warnings will prove correct if human beings do not take steps to preserve the resources they need to live.

The resources in greatest demand include water, petroleum, and land. But materials vital for human life also include mineral and vegetable resources, such as trees. Even now, many of these resources are readily available only to the comparatively wealthy people of the world. Eventually, all these resources will be in short supply, and the world's population will have to make decisions about how scarce resources will be distributed and how to ward off further depletion. Hence, many assert that at the present time humans have the obligation to begin to consider a response to conditions of shortage as well as to consider questions of how to cope with conditions of moderate scarcity, such as exist at present.

There are several issues to be considered here. The first is that of who should have control of the world's resources. Traditionally, the nations where resources are located are deemed to have title to control them. Within nations, private persons who have deeds of ownership to resources are generally believed to have the right to control them. The second set of moral issues concerns the question of how these resources should be distributed. The contemporary arrangement is to allocate resources to those with sufficient money to pay for them. However, those without large amounts of money may have greater needs; therefore, some argue that the world's poor have a stronger claim to vital resources than do the wealthy. The third set of issues encompasses the question of what measures should be taken to respond to the depletion of natural resources. Some argue that conservation measures are morally obligatory to prevent the hardship that will accompany depletion of the world's resources. Others argue that conservation is insufficient, that it will only postpone inevitable shortages. Hence, they assert, human beings must change their ways and learn to live from sustainable resources. These issues are international in scope because shortages of resources affect people all over the world. Consequently, if they are to have any prospect of being effective, measures taken to address the problems caused by a shortage of resources must be international in scope.

The moral issues posed by the tightening supplies of natural resources are nicely illustrated by conditions in the Middle East. The Middle East has been a hotbed of war and turmoil for many years. Wars have been fought there over religion, politics, and control of land. However, several astute commentators have argued that the next war in the Middle East will be fought over water. Water has always been in short supply in this arid portion of the world; today, water supplies are under far greater strain than in the past because of economic development, use of water to irrigate agricultural crops, and increasing population. The issue comes into sharp focus on the Jordan River, upon which Syria, Lebanon, Israel, and Jordan all rely for water. The river is thoroughly exploited, and it simply stops in the Dead Sea, which in turn is shrinking because less of the Jordan River's water flows into it with each passing year. All of the nations bordering the river have an increasing need for its water, and each has long-standing claims to it, but clearly, the Jordan does not have sufficient water to meet all these demands. The situation is complicated by the fact that these nations generally distrust one another and have fought wars with one another in the recent past. However, they will have no choice but to cooperate if they are to avoid catastrophe resulting from lack of water. It seems clear that any effective response to the problem will have to be multinational and binding on all the nations dependent on the Jordan's water.

Traditionally, nations have controlled the natural resources found within their boundaries. This tradition dates from the time when monarchs controlled states and were deemed also to control all that lay within their domains. At present, however, world circumstances do not permit such a clear-cut arrangement. For example, rivers commonly flow through or along the borders of several different nations, each of which depends on the water for its needs. In eras when water was plentiful and people were scarce, each nation bordering a lake or river could draw as much water as it desired without affecting its neighbors. However, this is no longer the case in many parts of the world.

Petroleum, too, is often a problem in this regard. Although oil fields often lie clearly within national boundaries, many important supplies of petroleum lie under seabeds, where national boundaries are disputed. In addition, wherever the deposits are located, petroleum is of no use to humanity so long as it is pooled deep underground. Substantial investments of equipment, money, and human expertise are required to discover oil reserves, bring them to the surface, and then refine and transport them to places where they can be put to use. The efforts, skills, and cooperation of many groups of people and organizations are needed to complete these various steps, and almost all of those people and organizations can claim to own the oil at some point or another in the process of making it available to consumers. So when the entire picture is viewed, the question of who controls oil is not so clear.

Furthermore, the seabeds are now thought to be rich in many other natural resources of great importance to humanity. Generally, these resources lie far beyond the boundaries claimed by any single nation, and only in recent years have the technology and expertise been developed to exploit these resources. Vast amounts of money will be required to recover the seabeds' wealth. Many nations argue, with the traditional concept of the control of natural resources in mind, that nations should control the exploitation of these resources and gain the lion's share of the benefits from them. However, corporations argue that they cannot be expected to take the risks and make the expenditures required to exploit seabed resources unless they have control over the use of these resources and gain a substantial share of the profits from them. However, others argue that neither nations nor corporations should control the world's resources. Rather, the people of the world as a whole should be the beneficiaries of its natural wealth.

The present system of distributing the world's natural resources is controlled by wealth. That is, those with sufficient wealth can gain access to the world's resources, whereas those lacking money are left out. However, some argue that the world's poorest people should be given preference in gaining access to its natural wealth, since they have the greatest and most desperate needs. Those who are wealthy will suffer little if a part of their resources is taken from them. For example, with fewer resources, the world's wealthy might have to travel by bus rather than by private car or live in apartment buildings rather than single-family houses. However, for many people, control of resources is a matter of life or death. Hence, when human life and well-being are at stake, these should take precedence over matters of convenience or lifestyle.

Some argue that the present generation has an obligation to itself and to future generations to prevent the depletion of the world's resources. Those making this assertion claim it is unfair and irresponsible to use up all the resources of the world now, when the need for them is likely to be much greater in the future. Many of the world's resources, like petroleum, cannot be regenerated, and once used, they are gone for good. Therefore, humans are morally required to conserve the world's resources in order to stave off, for as long as possible, the time when those resources are exhausted. However, others argue that these measures are insufficient and that conservation merely delays resource depletion and ensuing disaster. They argue that humans are therefore obligated to change their ways of life to make minimal use of resources and to focus on developing resources that can be renewed in sufficient amounts that the world will never exhaust the supply.

Both views are opposed by two camps. One argues that conservation or reliance on sustainable resources unfairly harms the less developed nations because they will be asked to slow their pace of economic progress for the sake of preserving resources. Proponents of this view argue that because the wealthy nations are largely responsible for the impending depletion, they should bear most of the cost of preventing that depletion. The other camp argues that the only rational approach to the question of managing the earth's resources is to rely entirely on market forces. Markets are composed of a series of transactions between individuals who make exchanges they believe to be mutually beneficial. This system ensures that resources will go where they are most needed and at the most reasonable costs. Therefore, relying on the market will be the most efficient way of making use of the world's resources. Any other means will be hopelessly inefficient, likely corrupt, and probably futile.

It seems obvious that increasing population and economic advancement will place ever greater burdens on the earth's resources in coming years. Many of these problems will require international cooperation, if human beings are to avoid resorting to warfare or lapsing into turmoil. One significant factor is that large multinational corporations will likely gain even more control than they now possess of much of the world's petroleum and minerals. Although nations once had firm control of these resources, the global economy is reducing the importance of national governments and increasing the importance of multinational corporations, which are adept at functioning in the circumstances of the global economy. Although the world community has taken only tentative steps toward gaining effective control over the world's resources, increasing pressure on natural resources in coming years likely will force it to adopt stricter measures.

In the long run, it is likely that human beings will have to change ways of life that rely on vast amounts of energy and replace them with ways of life that make minimal use of energy and water, and in ways that allow these crucial resources to be renewed. This course appears to be the only sure means of staving off eventual disaster.

**For further reading:** Bauer, P. T. 1981. *Equality, the Third World, and Economic Delusion.* Cambridge, MA: Harvard University Press.

Commoner, Barry. 1971. *The Closing Circle.* New York: Bantam Books.

Hardin, Garrett. 1980. *Promethean Ethics: Living with Death, Competition, and Triage.* Seattle: University of Washington Press.

Kennedy, Paul. 1993. *Preparing for the Twenty-first Century.* New York: Random House.

Meadows, Donnella, et al. 1974. *The Limits to Growth: A Report for the Club of Rome on the Predicament of Mankind.* 2d ed. New York: Universe Books.

Partridge, Ernest. 1981. *Responsibilities to Future Generations.* Buffalo, NY: Prometheus.

Sebenius, James. 1984. *Negotiating the Law of the Sea.* Cambridge, MA: Harvard University Press.

Wolf, Aaron. 1995. *Hydropolitics along the Jordan River: Scarce Water and Its Impact on the Arab-Israeli Conflict.* Tokyo and New York: United Nations University Press.

# Pollution Control

Few issues are more intensely debated than that of global pollution. There is considerable evidence that pollution and environmental degradation often do not remain confined within the boundaries of the nation in which they originate, but cause harm far beyond. For example, many believe that acid rain, generated by industrial activity in the northeastern United States, is degrading portions of Canada's forests. The cloud of radioactive gases accidentally released during an explosion at a nuclear power plant in Chernobyl, Ukraine (formerly part of the Soviet Union), brought death and radiation sickness to the surrounding area, and then drifted northwestward, across northern Europe. Radioactive fallout from the cloud contaminated milk and water supplies in several nations and may have long-term effects on the health of the people living there. On the basis of examples like these, many environmental activists argue that pollution is a global problem. They believe that an effective solution to the problem of pollution might well require a collective response from the world's nations.

The difficulties of redressing global pollution are numerous and complex. The first is the problem of gaining accurate factual information on the array and concentration of pollutants in the environment and whether they are likely to cause problems for humanity. For example, there is considerable debate on whether the world has entered a period of global warming, and if it has, whether the destruction of the atmosphere's ozone layer is a significant factor. Though many scientists agree that the world probably has entered a period of global warming and that depletion of the ozone layer in the atmosphere has played a causal role in this trend, other respected scientists disagree. Nearly all acknowledge that further information is needed before these questions can be answered conclusively. Hence, it is necessary to accumulate additional factual data on the amount and spread of pollutants in the environment and the degree to which they genuinely threaten human well-being.

Second, many are concerned over the issue of whether the environment has value in and of itself, and therefore should be protected for its own sake, or whether it is important only insofar as it affects human life.

Third, because pollutants originating in one nation often cause harm in other nations, there is the issue of who should be responsible for cleaning up the damage. An additional complication is that many believe that the most important contributing causes of global pollution are increased industrial production and the effects of economic advancement. Hence, human beings may face the choice of controlling pollutants only at the cost of reducing their standard of living or closing off avenues of economic opportunity. In consequence, the representatives of many developing nations argue that the poor nations are being asked to carry an unfair share of the burden of addressing pollution. Their argument is that the wealthiest nations have contributed most to the load of pollution in the environment, but the poorest nations are being asked to slow their pace of economic development for the sake of reducing the world's pollution. National sovereignty is another factor that has complicated efforts to address global pollution. Many environmental activists argue that global pollution, if it is to be successfully controlled, must be addressed by agreements that will be binding on all nations. However, many nations (the United States included) are loath to yield portions of their national sovereignty to serve these goals.

These various difficulties are aptly illustrated by the practice of clearcutting in the Brazilian rain forest. Brazilians are destroying their vast rain forest at the rate of millions of acres every year. However, forests play a vital role in maintaining the earth's environmental balance. Green plants take carbon dioxide from the environment and return oxygen to it. Animals, including human beings, need the oxygen in the atmosphere to live. On the other hand, increases in the amount of carbon dioxide in the atmosphere are thought to boost the amount of heat retained by the earth and thus to contribute to global warming. It has recently been discovered that the vast Brazilian rain forests, with their spectacular arrays of vegetation, play a key role in maintaining the global balance of carbon dioxide and oxygen. Because of this, many of the world's nations are urging Brazil to halt its destruction of the rain forests. However, some Brazilians respond that exploitation of the land covered by the rain forests is necessary to provide a means of living for many Brazilians, most of whom are crowded into the narrow strips of land along the Atlantic coast. Furthermore, they argue, exploitation of the rain forests is required to carry out Brazil's program of economic advancement. As a final blow, they also assert that by far the largest destruction of forest lands has occurred in the developed areas of the world, such as the United States and Europe. Without this destruction, Brazil's forests would lack the importance they possess for the environment at present. Therefore, many Brazilians argue, it is unjust to demand that their nation alone carry the burden of preserving the environmental balance. Instead, Brazil should receive compensation from the developed nations in return for delaying or abandoning its rain forest exploitation.

Some argue that such ambitious and far-reaching measures to preserve the environment would be premature. They argue, for example, that it is still unproven that the world is undergoing global warming, and it is not clear what effect, if any, the depletion of the ozone layer has on this process. Opponents of strict environmental protection point out that under these circumstances, stringent measures to protect the environment will certainly bring harm to humanity—the economic cost of the regulations taken to protect the environment and the political cost of the loss of national sovereignty resulting from global, mandatory standards of environmental protection. They assert that the potential benefits, in contrast, are far less certain, both because there is insufficient information on the nature of the problem and because it is possible that even strict regulations will be ineffective in stopping or reversing the damage.

Yet others assert that economic advancement must always take precedence over protection of the environment. In an age when most of the world's population lives in dismal poverty, they argue that the first priority should be to take measures that allow them to advance economically. People who are dying of starvation or diseases resulting from poor sanitation or lack of proper nutrition, or enduring lives without the prospect of productive labor, should not be asked to make sacrifices on behalf of the minority of the human race that lives in comfort and can afford to worry about the quality of human life 50 or 100 years in the future.

Some commentators argue as well that it is a mistake to urge national governments to yield portions of their sovereignty to global efforts to curb environmental problems. It is the duty of national governments to look after the welfare of their citizens, and national governments are better situated than outsiders to know their citizens' needs. Hence, even if pollution requires a governmental response of some sort, this responsibility should be carried by individual national governments, not by multinational institutions or international treaties.

However, environmental activists contend that determined global action to address pollution must be taken now. Although many concede that several environmental issues require further study and more precise data, they generally assert that conclusive information is available about the harm of other types of pollution and that the harmful effects of other types are reasonably certain. Furthermore, the likely outcome of failing to take prompt action is global catastrophe, including the prospect of human extinction. Hence, these environmentalists conclude that the responsible course is to take action now, even with incomplete information and unanswered questions. They argue that diligent environmental protection measures will benefit all humanity, not simply the wealthy. Environmental degradation makes it more difficult for extremely poor people to feed themselves, since pollution degrades the fertility of the soil and harms the growth of plants and animals. Furthermore, the extremely poor are more vulnerable to the health problems caused by pollution because they are more likely to live amid polluted areas and to be weakened by poor nutrition and lack of access to adequate medical care.

Finally, environmental activists contend that global environmental problems require a global response, even if nations must yield some portions of their sovereignty to do so. Nations can, at most, control the pollution that originates within their borders. In some cases, where pollution originates from a single source beyond their borders, they may be able to negotiate bilateral agreements to control it. However, if they are poor and weak and the polluting nation is wealthy and powerful and stands to suffer economic loss by controlling pollution, it might be impossible to obtain an effective agreement. Most importantly, however, most types of pollution originate from several sources and affect many parts of the world. Hence, environmental activists conclude, the great problems of global pollution can be adequately addressed only by multinational arrangements that are binding on the nations involved. Multinational agreements that are binding on all eliminate the argument that control of pollution yields an unfair economic advantage to those nations less scrupulous in matters of environmental care. Although erosion of national sovereignty will result, the benefits of increased human welfare are well worth the cost. In addition, many national governments are not notably concerned about the welfare of their citizens, and many cater primarily to the concerns of a small, wealthy minority. Hence, many environmental activists argue that preserving national sovereignty in matters of environmental protection will not necessarily serve the best interests of the ordinary people of the world.

It seems highly likely that the world's pollution problems will significantly increase in coming years unless determined action is taken. Two major trends give credence to this view. First, the world's population is likely to enlarge significantly in the foreseeable future. More human beings generate more pollution and place a greater strain on the world's resources. Second, more nations of the world will industrialize and become increasingly prosperous. China's 1.2 billion citizens are a case in point. Their economy is growing at breakneck speed, and it is reasonable to presume that many Chinese will soon be able to afford automobiles and will require greater amounts of energy to power the appliances and machinery that their prosperity will allow them to acquire. More energy usage and more automobiles imply significantly more pollution.

Many national governments have shown that they are aware of the need for more aggressive global measures to address the problems caused by pollution. Hence, they recently agreed to negotiate a treaty to slow the depletion of the ozone layer and eventually reverse the trend. They have become aware that they must make global, binding initiatives to address these problems. Otherwise their efforts will have scant chance of success. However, it is not yet certain that national governments are prepared to take vigorous action to address all the problems of global pollution. Hence, it is not yet clear that they will take sufficiently aggressive measures to address the greater burdens the human race is likely to place on the environment in the future. It is possible that only impending environmental catastrophe will finally compel them to take action sufficient to address global pollution problems.

**For further reading:** Elsom, Derek M. 1992. *Atmospheric Pollution: A Global Problem.* Oxford: Blackwell Publishing.

Foster, Bruce A. 1993. *The Acid Rain Debate: Science and Special Interests in Policy Formation.* Ames: Iowa State University Press.

National Geographic Society. 1995. *The Emerald Realm: The Earth's Precious Rainforests.* Washington, DC: National Geographic Society.

Ray, Dixie Lee. 1993. *Environmental Overkill: Whatever Happened to Common Sense?* Washington, DC: Regnery Gateway.

Silver, Cheryl Simon, et al. 1990. *One Earth, One Future: Our Changing Global Environment.* Washington, DC: National Academy Press.

Soroos, Marvin. 1986. *Beyond Sovereignty: The Challenge of Global Policy.* Columbia: University of South Carolina Press.

———. 1997. *The Endangered Atmosphere: Preserving a Global Commons.* Columbia: University of South Carolina Press.

Turco, Richard P. 1996. *Earth under Siege: Air Pollution and Global Change.* New York: Oxford University Press.

# Population Control

For the past two centuries, the world's population has been expanding at a rate unprecedented in human history. Moreover, for much of the twentieth century, the world's population has exploded at an even greater rate than it did during the nineteenth. According to the United Nations Population Division, world population reached 1 billion people in 1804; it doubled to 2 billion by 1927 but reached 3 billion in 1960 and 4 billion by 1974. By 1987, the world population reached 5 billion and is now estimated to be 5.8 billion and may double in size by the end of the next century.

Even though some parts of the world are not burdened with rapidly expanding populations, the overall population increase is of global concern for several reasons. More people use more resources, generate more pollution, and place greater burdens on governmental and social services. Increased demands on the world's resources will eventually result in fewer resources available for all. Pollution is notoriously mobile, and it spreads readily across national boundaries. In addition, rapid increases in global mobility are allowing people in impoverished or turbulent nations to move to calmer, more prosperous parts of the world in search of employment and better lives. Hence, those who are secure in well-off nations with stable populations cannot afford to ignore the difficulties of people in overcrowded nations, for those desperate people may soon migrate to the lands of the prosperous.

However, the unprecedented number of human beings living at the present time is not the primary cause of ills related to population. The real difficulties result from the rate of human population increase and the lack of social resources adequate to deal with such rapidly increasing human needs. For example, the most densely populated places in the world include Japan, Singapore, Hong Kong, and The Netherlands. These places are obviously neither impoverished nor disorderly. On the contrary, they are models of prosperous, carefully managed societies and are the envy of many less populous nations. In contrast, many areas of the world where people are starving or where there is great social turmoil and eroded social order—sub-Saharan Africa, for example—are relatively unpopulated. Even a nation as densely populated as India suffers ills related to population only because its government and its society are having difficulty coping with the rate of increase, not because of the overall size of its population. India is certainly not densely populated in relation to Japan or Singapore, for example, and it has far greater natural resources than either. Although Japan is densely populated, its population is not growing quickly, and its social structures are well equipped to address the difficulties that its large population brings.

A high rate of population increase strains a society's resources in several ways. For example, a rapidly expanding population will contain a disproportionately larger number of young people than will societies with stable or decreasing populations. But young people need jobs and social services, and they are prone to social unrest. Societies must create jobs for them, provide them with places to live, and offer the services needed by growing families. Few societies with rapidly expanding populations have the social or economic resources to accommodate the needs of vast numbers of young people. Social turmoil and decay frequently result.

Many argue that if rapid population increase is overwhelming the nations globally, then global population control measures must be taken. Population control programs already have been initiated by some nations, such as China (where the program is mandatory) and South Korea (where it is not). However, population control is freighted with complexities. There are issues of which measures should be used to control population and what sort of measures are most likely to be safe and effective in the less developed portions of the world. There are questions of whether these measures should be made mandatory or whether systems should be devised to allow individuals to make their own choices on matters of reproduction. Choices regarding reproduction are among the most important decisions individuals make. Most families are loath to yield control of decisions about reproduction to a government or community. Furthermore, mandatory control of reproduction is a significant intrusion into the autonomy of individuals. However, if birth control programs are designed to depend on voluntary decisions, they might be ineffective in areas of the world where national culture is such that people value large families.

Cultural and religious factors further complicate these matters. For example, in many of the nations where population is increasing at an astounding rate, large families are eagerly sought, and ordinary people strongly resist efforts to restrict the number of children they may have. For most of human history, the problem has been lack of people rather than an oversupply. Hence, most persons in the world and most cultures view large populations as a sign of a prosperous and orderly society. Throughout most of human history, population has been stable or has grown only slowly. The population explosion is a relatively recent trend in human history, having begun barely 200 years ago. Most human cultures and social attitudes took shape in eras when the most pressing human problems resulted from too few people rather than too many. Hence, rigorous population control measures must address long-standing cultural biases that favor large families. Moreover, several methods of population control, such as abortion, are viewed with disfavor by many societies and many people, while other methods are unsuitable for use in the less developed, impoverished nations that are apt to need them most.

An additional area of complexity is the role and status of women in many societies. As a practical matter, women will have to play a central role in carrying out programs of population control, for they have the burdens of bearing and raising children. However, in many traditional societies, women's status is such that they are unable to exercise effective control over reproduction. Numerous studies have shown that as women gain greater education and play a more important role in economic activity, they become able to exercise greater control over reproduction. Hence, societies in which the lives and social status of women are improving generally discover that birth rates decrease. Therefore, programs aimed at controlling population must give consideration to the status of women.

Efforts at population control often produce unexpected difficulties. Mainland China, for example, is keenly aware of the hazards posed by excessive population growth, and it has undertaken a vigorous program of population control. It has placed a strict limit of one child per couple on the Chinese people, which it enforces with great rigor, and this policy has caused considerable resentment. It also has brought other difficulties, for Chinese culture values male children far more than female. Hence, many have resorted to abortion or infanticide to avoid having female children. One poignant consequence is that there is now an imbalance between males and females in the generation approaching marriageable age, with far more males than females. It is difficult to imagine what social stresses might result from this state of affairs, but this imbalance of the sexes is sure to cause more than minor difficulty. An additional complication is that many in the United States are opposed to China's policy of condoning abortion as a method of birth control as well as to the mandatory and inflexible character of its program. Hence, the U.S. Congress has passed several measures designed to press the Chinese to alter their policies.

Many are vigorously opposed to any international program of population control. They offer several arguments to support their point of view. First, they argue that the earth still holds plenty of empty space and enormous quantities of natural resources. To the extent that there are shortages in these domains, they argue that a better solution than birth control is conservation and careful management of the use of resources. The problem, therefore, is not the number of people present or even the rate of population increase but the lack of social organization competent to provide for the people who are alive. Hence, the appropriate response is social and institutional reform rather than birth control. They argue further that a successful program of birth control would almost certainly have to be mandatory, and therefore would be a significant intrusion into the autonomy and private lives of individuals. Because decisions about reproduction are deemed highly important by most people and are often emotionally charged, mandatory controls or even significant coercion in matters of reproduction would be morally unjustified.

A related objection is grounded on the claim that effective population control measures would have to impinge on national sovereignty, because they would require that nations meet certain standards of population growth. Such measures would also encounter the problem mentioned above, conflicting with the moral standards and cultural practices of many of the world's peoples. Hence, opponents of birth control measures are apt to conclude that efforts at mandatory population control would amount to a type of cultural imperialism, and they are certain to vigorously resist such measures.

The burdens of global population control will fall unequally on the nations of the world. The wealthy and industrially advanced nations generally have stable populations or populations that are growing at only a modest rate. Several nations, such as Italy, actually have declining populations, and little would be required of them by a global population control effort. However, the poorer and less developed nations, which are also the most likely to have rapidly expanding populations, would bear most of the burden of restrictions on population growth.

Opponents of international population control measures argue that efforts at population control thus far generally have produced mediocre results. They are often effective for only a short period before people revert to their usual habits (the exceptions being nations, like China, that are willing to resort to draconian measures of control); and not infrequently, these programs backfire, with population explosions occurring after initial, modest successes. At best the programs are ineffectual in controlling population and often carry the burden of being coercive.

Those who favor international population control programs counter these assertions with vigorous responses of their own. They argue that population control programs need not be mandatory or inflexible to be effective. They claim that people (particularly women) are frequently eager to escape the burdens of more children, particularly when they are unable to provide adequately for them. Frequently all that is necessary to gain the enthusiastic cooperation of such women is education and the provision of suitable birth control methods.

These proponents argue that an international program of population control is necessary both because some coordination of measures and goals is necessary and because many impoverished and disorganized nations lack the resources needed to effectively carry out such programs. Hence, an international program is needed to provide resources and support to the neediest nations. Furthermore, these impoverished nations are not bearing an undue burden from these programs. Quite the opposite, the poorer nations are carrying the burden of populations expanding more rapidly than they can handle, and these nations in particular will clearly benefit from programs that might help them get their populations under a measure of control.

Partisans of these methods may concede that many programs of population control have been ineffectual or counterproductive, but this should not imply that all such efforts must be. In fact, they point to examples of quite successful programs of population control. However, they also agree that in the long term, the most effective methods of controlling population are economic development of impoverished nations and education for women, for these are the factors most strongly associated with successful population control.

If demographers' projections of future population growth are to be believed, the world's population is likely to continue growing at an explosive rate for the foreseeable future. Furthermore, it is unlikely that the poorest nations, those most likely to have high birthrates, will be able to provide for the anticipated vast legions of people. Hence, it seems likely that most people in the world will come to view efforts at population control as necessary to stave off disaster. Clearly, this problem will not solve itself, and the world community eventually will be forced to take active measures to address it.

**For further reading:** Banister, Judith. 1987. *China's Changing Population.* Stanford, CA: Stanford University Press.

Ginsburg, Faye, and Rayna Rapp, eds. 1995. *Conceiving the New World Order: The Global Politics of Reproduction.* Berkeley: University of California Press.

Hardin, Garrett. 1993. *Living within Limits: Ecology, Economics, and Population Taboos.* New York: Oxford University Press.

Harkavy, Oscar. 1995. *Curbing Population Growth: An Insider's Perspective on the Population Movement.* New York: Plenum Press.

Harris, Marvin. 1987. *Death, Sex, and Fertility: Population Regulation in Preindustrial and Developing Societies.* New York: Columbia University Press.

Hartmann, Betsy. 1995. *Reproductive Rights and Wrongs: The Global Politics of Population Control.* Boston: South End Press.

Moffett, George. 1994. *Critical Masses: The Global Population Challenge.* New York: Viking Press.

Sen, Amartya Kumar. 1994. "Population: Delusion and Reality." *New York Review of Books* 41 (22 September): 62–71.

Wongaman, J. Philip, ed. 1973. *The Population Crisis and Moral Responsibility.* Washington, DC: Public Affairs Press.

# Refugees

In some ways, refugees are not controversial at all. Refugees are people who have been forced from their homes and means of livelihood by war, political upheaval, ethnic animosity, or natural disaster. They include the very young and very old, the sick and the disabled, and in most cases they are innocent victims of forces that have uprooted their lives. Because they have been displaced, they frequently suffer greatly from lack of food, medical care, and shelter and are unable to tend to their own needs. They rarely wish to remain where they have sought refuge and desire only to return to their homes in safety so that they may begin rebuilding their lives. Hence, most people and most nations unambiguously agree that refugees should be helped. Both international law and the United Nations have conventions and treaties that affirm the world community's obligation to assist refugees.

Beyond this point of common agreement, however, refugees spark intense controversy and recrimination. The disagreement results in part from the huge number of refugees in the world today and in part from the difficulty of returning many groups of refugees to their homes. The world community is reasonably well equipped to accommodate modest numbers of refugees for relatively brief periods. The U.N. High Commission on Refugees, various nongovernmental organizations, such as the International Red Cross or Doctors without Borders, and national governments customarily attempt to aid those who are displaced. So long as refugees' numbers are relatively small and they are uprooted for a short period of time, these groups are generally able to give refugees reasonably adequate food, shelter, medical care, and assistance in returning to their homes.

However, tens of millions of refugees are scattered across the world at present. Moreover, considerable numbers have been stranded in refugee camps for many decades, and these camps are often located in nations ill equipped (or ill disposed) either to assimilate them into their own populations or to provide them with the means to earn livelihoods. Furthermore, refugee populations often become pawns for nations' political intrigues or warring groups' maneuvering. For example, millions of Palestinians languish in refugee camps that were established in Lebanon in 1948. Many of them were born in these camps and know no other life. However, they cannot return to their ancestral homes, which are now in Israel. They cannot establish new lives for themselves in other nations because several nations wish to use the camps to maintain political pressure on Israel.

Afghanistan is another difficult case. A considerable portion of Afghanistan's population was forced abroad after the Soviet Union intruded into a civil war there. However, although the Soviets departed several years ago, many Afghans remain encamped in Pakistan or Iran. They linger abroad because bitter civil war continues in their homeland and millions of land mines, booby traps, and unexploded munitions pose grave hazards to any who venture back to their native villages. Meanwhile, Pakistan and Iran are bearing much of the burden of housing the Afghans. These two nations are poor and fractured by ethnic, political, and religious hostility. Neither is prepared to make an effort to assimilate yet another fractious group into its population. Yet powerful groups within both nations wish to influence politics within Afghanistan and are doing so by supporting one armed faction or another and providing military and economic assistance to groups that support their aims. Thus, both Afghan refugees and Afghanistan itself have become hostage to other states' political aims.

Hence, although there is little controversy over the fundamental question of whether refugees should be helped, there is much disagreement on who should bear the burdens of assisting them; how long the world community should continue to support refugees who cannot return to their homes; whether the impoverished nations, who often shoulder much of the burden of coping with refugees, should receive compensation from the community of nations; whether places should be sought for refugees in other nations when they cannot return home; and whether the world community is obligated to work to remove obstacles in the way of refugees' attempts to return to their homes.

A common response to these questions is to declare that the entire world community is indeed obligated to help refugees for as long as they need assistance, and to take whatever measures are necessary to remove obstacles in the way of their return to their homelands. The basis for this argument is the fact that the refugees often suffer greatly, have very serious needs, are unable to support themselves, and therefore deserve the help of all who are able to give aid.

Opponents of this view offer practical as well as theoretical objections. The practical objections focus on the absence of any global authority with financial resources and physical means sufficient to provide haven and shelter for all who might need it. The financial resources that nations and individuals contribute to refugee aid are insufficient to meet the needs of all the world's refugees, and national governments are unlikely soon to give authority to any international agency to use taxation or gain control of other means necessary to assist refugees. Furthermore, addressing the needs of refugees often requires the further use of political or military force, because the refugees were driven from their homes by military or political upheaval and they cannot return until these conflicts are resolved, or they are marooned in camps because they have become pawns in the political intrigues of others.

International efforts to address refugees' problems cannot be successful unless or until the international community commands sufficient resources to provide long-term and large-scale assistance to refugees and secures the power to use diplomatic and military force to bring military and political conflicts to a halt so that refugees may return to their homelands. Given that the international community lacks these resources and is unlikely to acquire them in the near future, any effort to achieve such goals is likely to be futile and might even result in greater harm to those languishing in refugee camps.

However, even if these practical difficulties could be addressed, some argue that more basic and more intractable theoretical difficulties remain. The theoretical difficulties involve other concepts of international ethics, those of nationalism and sovereignty. Arrangements that would enable the world community to properly care for and resettle huge numbers of refugees require something approximating international governing structures that would have legal authority over national governments. The peoples of the world would have to make an explicit commitment to preserve the well-being of all humans and to assist them when they are unable to help themselves. Since the first requirement amounts to a vestige of world government, it conflicts with the principle of national sovereignty, the view that nations are the ultimate masters of their fates and cannot be subject to any higher authority. The commitment to national sovereignty is a mainstay of diplomacy and international relations in this century, so much so that respect for national sovereignty was mandated by the charter of the United Nations. In addition, a commitment by all of the world's peoples to concern themselves with the welfare of all others would conflict with the principle of nationalism—the view that national boundaries mark an important border of significant human concern and moral obligation. As with national sovereignty, a commitment to nationalism is deeply entrenched in the political consciousness of this century, and many are strongly resistant to any commitments that might undermine it.

It is difficult to say whether there are likely to be more or fewer refugees in coming years than at present. Refugees with the greatest need and in the greatest peril—in other words, the overwhelming majority—are those displaced by political upheaval or military conflict. Political refugees are most commonly found in the politically unsettled and unstable regions. To the extent that the nations in those parts of the world achieve stability and avoid warfare, refugees will cease to be a problem. The major areas where political refugees are found include Africa, the Middle East, and Southeast Asia. These regions remain volatile and could erupt without warning. Although encouraging signs of emerging stability have appeared in each region recently, they remain vulnerable to turmoil.

In contrast, many of the distressing nationalist conflicts that erupted in central Europe following the collapse of the Soviet Union now appear on the way to resolution. In past years, many political refugees were generated by the dictatorships of South America, but many of these nations now appear committed to democratic institutions and are developing a growing, though still tenuous, concern for human rights. Thus, to the extent that there is hope for greater political stability in these parts of the world, there is also hope that fewer refugees will be generated in future years.

With the collapse of the Soviet Union and the fading of the cold war, the nations of the world have been more willing to cooperate for humanitarian concerns and support a larger role for the United Nations in addressing these concerns. However, the United Nations has suffered failures along with successes, and it remains to be seen whether the community of nations will be willing to give it resources and power sufficient to address the needs of the world's refugees.

In addition to refugees displaced by warfare or political turmoil, new categories of refugees—economic and ecological refugees—have become prominent in recent years. Economic refugees are those who leave their home nations to escape abysmal poverty or to seek greater opportunity elsewhere. Europe and North America have been awash in economic refugees in recent years. Economic refugees have been generated by the collapse of the Soviet Union and advances in transportation that greatly ease movement across national borders. The developed nations of the world have generally been less sympathetic to economic refugees than to political refugees and less disposed to assist them. However, these refugees are often able to find jobs in their host nations that native citizens shun, and therefore they are welcomed by employers, although often exploited by them. To the extent that economic disparities between nations remain, transit across national boundaries is allowed, and employers face labor shortages, the number of economic refugees is likely to increase despite grumbling in their host nations.

Ecological refugees are people who have been driven from their homes and livelihoods by environmental degradation. To the extent that human degradation of the environment continues, the number of environmental refugees is likely to increase. Although their plight is less dramatic than that of refugees from war, their suffering and the obstacles to their living normal lives are very serious. Because this is a relatively new and as yet rarely reported problem, the world has given little attention to the plight of ecological refugees. However, if the world does not take effective measures to address environmental pollution, the numbers of ecological refugees and their hold on our attention are likely to increase. Indeed, some have argued that in coming years, environmental problems will so disrupt social and economic life that they could well ignite widespread and violent turmoil.

Hence, both the future of refugees and that of the world's response to their difficulties remain uncertain.

**For further reading:** Abramowitz, Morton I. 1994. "Exodus: The World Refugee Crisis." *Foreign Policy* 95 (Summer): 175–183.

Deng, Francis Mading. 1993. *Protecting the Dispossessed: A Challenge for the International Community.* Washington, DC: Brookings Institution.

Farer, Tom J. 1995. "How the International System Copes with Involuntary Migration: Norms, Institutions, and State Practice." *Human Rights Quarterly* 17 (February): 72–100.

Gorman, Robert F., et al. 1993. *Refugee Aid and Development: Theory and Practice.* Westport, CT: Greenwood Press.

Loescher, Gil. 1993. *Beyond Charity: International Cooperation and the Global Refugee Crisis.* New York: Oxford University Press.

Rogers, Rosemarie. 1992. "The Future of Refugee Flows and Policies." *International Migration Review* 26 (Winter): 1112–1143.

Suhrke, Astri. 1994. "Environmental Degradation and Population Flows." *Journal of International Affairs* 47 (Winter): 473–496.

Zolberg, Aristide. 1994. "Commentary on Current Refugee Issues." *Journal of International Affairs* 47 (Winter): 341–349.

# Terrorism

Few issues have captured people's attention in the past several decades as keenly as international terrorism. People around the world have been moved by pictures of innocent victims, including small children, killed or maimed during terrorist acts. Most people around the world are repulsed by acts of terrorism and express contempt for those who practice it. However, international terrorism raises two significant moral concerns. One is whether it can ever be morally justified. The other is what measures the nations of the world are justified in taking to combat it.

Before an examination of terrorism can get under way, we must understand what terrorism is. Terrorism is distinct from acts of war, common criminal acts, or the twisted violence of the mentally deranged. Not all acts of terrorism are violent. For example, a terrorist group might disrupt computer communications in technologically advanced societies. Probably no lives would be lost and no physical damage would follow, but sabotage of this sort could cause great economic and social disruption.

Not every act intended to cause harm or fear is terrorist. Criminal extortion, for example, is not. Most terrorists claim that their activity serves some political purpose, calling attention to a particular viewpoint or movement, disrupting a repressive government, or pressuring a government to change its policies. Hence, terrorism, in most cases, is activity intended to cause harm of some sort in order to achieve a political end. Sometimes, of course, it is difficult to see what political goals acts of terror are designed to achieve and even more difficult to believe that these acts will be effective in achieving them. Sometimes terrorism lapses into common banditry, and at other times terrorist groups will continue their violent acts even when those acts serve no clear purpose. The motives for this futile violence might include simple inertia, the desire to keep a movement intact, or a primal addiction to violence.

Acts of terrorism need not be directed at governments, however. They may be intended to coerce businesses or private individuals. For example, a case in which a minority family moves into a racially segregated neighborhood and is met with violent acts intended to instill fear and drive them away is also an instance of terrorism. Governments and leaders, too, have resorted to terrorism to keep their populations docile and subservient, as did Josef Stalin in the Soviet Union. However, politically motivated terrorism is the variety most apt to cross national boundaries, and hence, it will be our focus here.

The first issue is whether terrorist acts can ever be justified. We must note, of course, that even if some terrorist acts can be justified in moral terms, many more cannot; so the theoretical issue of whether any particular act of terror can ever be justified may not address the question of whether most acts of terror have moral justification.

Many people will quickly respond that acts of terror are never morally justified. They will point to pictures of innocent people killed in airline bombings as the archetypes of actions that are gravely, morally wrong. Furthermore, they may assert that if terrorism is harm intended to achieve a political end, then terrorists must always ask whether other modes of pursuing their political ends are likely to be as effective. In most cases, it is likely that they will be. If this is so, then the nonviolent course should be chosen, and the violent act is morally unjustified. Moreover, even if these nonterrorist alternatives are likely to be less effective in achieving political ends, they should generally be chosen if they avoid the probability of harming innocent people.

In addition, opponents of terrorism point out that political goals, even very worthy ones, do not suffice to justify any and all actions designed to further them. For example, it might be very good to replace a repressive government with one that is democratic. However, this worthy goal would not justify killing or endangering the lives of large numbers of innocent people. For example, the present government of Peru, led by President Alberto Fujimori, is disconcertingly undemocratic in many ways, and the Shining Path guerrilla movement is clearly dedicated to his overthrow. However, this certainly does not imply that the Shining Path's many acts of violence are justified. Furthermore, it is often difficult to explain precisely how any given act of terrorism is likely to help bring about any particular political goal. For example, Islamic militants have occasionally bombed buses in Israel in pursuit of their goal of gaining a Palestinian state. However, it is generally difficult to see how attacking a bus loaded with innocent people will help bring about the goal of greater autonomy for an ethnic group.

In addition, critics of terrorism point out that the bloodiest and most spectacular acts of terror are commonly believed to be instances of so-called state terrorism—that is, acts of terror financed or supported in other ways by national governments. Certainly national governments cannot claim that acts of terror are the only means available to them to further their goals.

However, those who are tempted to resort to terrorism often retort that acts of terror are sometimes the only means available to small and relatively powerless groups. In some circumstances, violent acts will be the only means dissident groups have of drawing attention to their cause. In other cases, these acts are the only means opponents possess for striking a blow at an oppressor government. Furthermore, they point out that conventional warfare between nations commonly results in the death or injury of many innocent people. The destructiveness of bombs and missiles is so vast and so difficult to control precisely that their use in war is almost certain to result in the death of many innocent people. Moreover, acts of terror do not result in anything approaching the social upheaval and misery resulting from this century's wars. Therefore, partisans of terrorist violence may assert, the terrorist act that results in the death of innocent people is not wildly different from nation's acts of war and, in fact, that such activity brings far less harm to humanity than does conventional warfare. They may then conclude that acts of terror are vastly easier to justify because they cause less harm overall than acts of war.

Also, some proponents of terrorist activity claim that under the conditions of contemporary warfare, no one is innocent; all contribute in one or another way to the cause of war, because contemporary wars involve all sectors of society. For example, even farmers who grow food needed to support fighting troops are giving vital support to the war effort. Without food, the fighting would soon cease. Hence, terrorists may argue that they are merely mirroring the conditions of contemporary warfare when they engage in activities that result in harm even to people who are not actively fighting.

Some argue that terrorism is so great and vile a menace to contemporary societies that nearly any measures to eradicate it would be justified, including torture and the wholesale revocation of the civil rights of an entire society. Extreme measures are justified, these opponents may say, both because terrorism is a serious threat to the societies at which it is directed and because only very aggressive measures will combat it effectively. They may assert that no society can function in a climate of fear, in which anyone may be killed or maimed at any time. Moreover, if terrorists find they can succeed in acts of terror of one type in one area, they may move on to other types of terrorism and other targets, with the consequence that eventually no segment of society will be secure from terrorist acts. In addition, success will likely breed conditions for more terrorist acts, since terrorists will be captivated by their success. Also, terrorist acts will likely draw the allegiance of psychotic people who are attracted by the idea of death and destruction and wish to be part of it.

Extreme measures, strict opponents of terrorism may say, are also justified because only determined responses, even including the wholesale revocation of the civil rights of a population, will suffice to effectively combat terrorism.

Terrorists operate in small groups and easily blend back into society when they are finished with their acts. Hence, only measures that intrude on the privacy of all people are likely to be effective in ferreting them out.

Those opposed to extreme measures in stopping terrorist activity may begin by questioning the significance of terrorist acts or the amount of harm they cause to societies. They point out that far more people are killed in automobile accidents, accidents with fireworks, or airplane crashes than are killed by terrorist acts. Yet no one is advocating mobilizing an entire nation to fight the menace caused by cars, fireworks, or air travel. Though spectacular acts of terror capture the public imagination, they do relatively little damage to society as a whole and do not greatly disrupt any domain of social activity. In advanced, democratic nations, no terrorist groups face the likely prospect that they or their political programs will enjoy success.

Thus, moderates may claim, since the threat posed by terrorists is small, there is little justification for extreme measures intended to combat them. In fact, wholesale revocation of civil rights, as through the declaration of martial law, would likely be a far greater menace to social life than the terrorist activity it is intended to combat. Not only would these measures cause great harm by removing civil rights from people, they would introduce the possibility of greater harm by opening the way for a tyrannical government to take advantage of the lapse in civil rights and install itself in power. Once civil rights are removed, there is little to prevent military cabals or dictators from taking control of the society.

Terrorism is likely to be with us for some time. The state terrorism supported by rogue nations is not likely to disappear until these states collapse or change their ways. Even lesser methods of terror, such as bombing and sabotage, are easily employed. It is a safe bet that when the means are available, someone will find a convenient excuse to put them into practice. Furthermore, there is not likely to be any shortage of disaffected groups in human societies at any time in the future. Disaffection is part of human life and is not likely to be erased in even the most benevolent and prosperous society. It is sobering that West Germany, as supportive of its population and solicitous of civil rights as any nation on earth, was the home of radical terrorist groups in the 1970s and 1980s. Even a single event, such as a successful coup by the Shining Path terrorist group in Peru, might spawn imitators in other parts of the world.

However, two factors appear destined to have a long-term effect on acts of terror. One is that the emerging global economy is dividing the world's population into two groups: those who function successfully as part of the global economy and those who do not. Participants in the global economy are likely to enjoy the lion's share of wealth and power in the years to come, but nonparticipants will find their lives becoming more desperate with each passing year. Thus, the chasm between these two groups may well provide a hospitable domain for terrorist groups. The world's population explosion adds to this social volatility. The greatest rates of increase of population are occurring in the least prosperous portions of the world. Hence, these unfortunate domains will have increasing numbers of young, active people who live in miserable circumstances but have little hope for improving their lives. Once again, these desperate youngsters are likely to be attracted to terrorist groups.

The second factor likely to have a significant impact on terrorism is the likely availability of new instruments of terror. These range from nuclear material lifted from the remnants of the Soviet Union to chemical and biological agents of death and destruction that are simple to manufacture and deploy but capable of causing devastating, large-scale injury and loss of life.

It is likely that nation-states will cooperate ever more closely to combat terrorism. They will be forced to do so in order to address the global threat that terrorism poses. However, no matter what measures national governments adopt, determined terrorists are likely to find ways to inflict damage. Hence, this greater cooperation must be combined with determined efforts to remove the social conditions that breed terrorists.

**For further reading:** Fotion, Nicholas. 1981. "The Burdens of Terrorism." *Values in Conflict: Life, Liberty, and the Rule of Law*, ed. Burton M. Leiser, 463–470. New York: Macmillan.

Leeman, Richard. 1991. *The Rhetoric of Terrorism and Counter-Terrorism*. Westport, CT: Greenwood Press.

Netanyahu, Benjamin. 1995. *Fighting Terrorism: How Democracies Can Defeat Domestic and International Terrorists*. New York: Farrar, Straus & Giroux.

Nielsen, Kai. 1981. "Violence and Terrorism: Its Uses and Abuses." *Values in Conflict: Life, Liberty, and the Rule of Law*, ed. Burton M. Leiser, 435–449. New York: Macmillan.

Purver, Ronald. 1997. *Chemical and Biological Terrorism: New Threat to Public Safety?* London: Research Institute for the Study of Conflict and Terrorism.

United States. Department of State. Bureau of Public Affairs. 1990. *International Terrorism*. Washington, DC: Department of State, Bureau of Public Affairs.

Wardlaw, Grant. 1989. *Political Terrorism: Theory, Tactics, and Counter-Measures*. Cambridge, England: Cambridge University Press.

Wilkinson, Paul. 1986. *Terrorism and the Liberal State*. 2d ed. London: Macmillan.

# War

War is sustained violent conflict between organized bodies in which each party seeks to cause the other to submit. Armies attempt to gain their ends through destruction or intimidation. Military forces are created to destroy human beings and property. The destruction of the opposing forces allows armies to gain control of a territory, government, and people, or prevents an alien army from gaining control of a nation. Warfare's methods are brutal and imprecise, and they generally result in far more destruction and suffering than are necessary to achieve military or political aims.

War is among the great scourges of human life. It has caused millions of deaths and horrible injuries in this century alone. In addition, it wreaks vast devastation on the societies that it envelops. However, despite all that may be said against it, war is distressingly common. The United States has been at war for approximately one year of every four in this century. There are scores of wars in the various corners of the world at the present time—as many as 40, by some counts.

It is rare to find a political leader or ordinary human being willing to speak unreservedly in favor of war. Almost all declare themselves wholeheartedly opposed to it. Yet these same leaders are all too willing to go to war, and these same ordinary people are frequently eager to fight in war. War is thus simultaneously repulsive and attractive to people. As in the matter of arms control, although most people agree the human race would be better off without war, they often find what they believe are good reasons to engage in it.

Nations have various reasons for going to war. Sometimes they do so to gain territory, punish enemies, assist allies, fight off aggressors, or suppress domestic revolutions. At other times they resort to war to overthrow oppressive governments, as in the case of the American Revolutionary War. Nations that wage successful wars occasionally gain wealth and influence, and these are part of the lure of war.

It is not always easy to distinguish war from other types of armed confrontation; however, perhaps the following example will help to clarify the difference. In fall 1996, the United States showered cruise missiles on Iraqi air defense installations on several occasions in response to Iraqi attacks against the Kurds in the northern portion of Iraq. The Kurdish enclave had been designated a protected area for the Kurds by the United Nations following the Persian Gulf War. When Saddam Hussein's forces attacked the area, the United States determined that he must be punished. It did so by sending Tomahawk cruise missiles into Iraq to attempt to destroy Iraqi air-defense installations. Due to the circumstances that preceded the shelling, neither Iraq nor the United States viewed this as an act of war, and the incident was forgotten after a few weeks. However, had Iraq responded to the assault and the exchange continued, it would have been difficult to distinguish this activity from warfare.

Although nations and people have often found it reasonable to make war, all agree that its eradication is a desirable goal. The difficulty is that given the attraction of war for nations and for people, the control of war or its prevention will have to be international in scope. Control of war will require treaties, to be sure, but genuinely effective control will require the support of the great and influential nations of the world and may also require the creation of an international armed force capable of responding violently to the threat of violent conflict between nations.

Since war's eradication would relieve much human suffering and prevent much evil, it is plausible to argue that political leaders and ordinary people have the obligation to work to prevent it. The instruments of warfare are in the hands of the political leaders of nations. As a result, they have far more control over whether war occurs or is prevented than do ordinary people. Hence, they have a more pressing obligation to work for the elimination of warfare than do ordinary people. However, history shows that political leaders are easily tempted by the prospect of warfare. Furthermore, even leaders who avoid the temptation to initiate war may find themselves thrust into violent conflict when other nations launch aggressive attacks against them. In addition, it sometimes happens that nations seeking to remain at peace are drawn into other nations' wars, as the United States was drawn into the war in Europe during World War II. Hence, national leaders cannot simply disavow the resort to armed combat if they are to avoid war. They must work to create conditions that will prevent any and all nations from resorting to war.

There are sharp differences of opinion over whether it is possible for any nation to forswear the resort to war and over the question of what measures nations should adopt if they do make the attempt to disavow war.

One group, called realists, argues that nations cannot be bound by moral constraint. They point to the sorry history of the violent relations among nations and note that even the best-intentioned nations are often driven to war. In particular, they point out that there is no mechanism for forcing pacifism on nations. Without some external restraint, nations are unlikely to escape the temptation to indulge in warfare, but at the same time, nations are unlikely to allow any other bodies to gain power over them. Hence, war will remain a distressingly common feature of the world scene, and there is little that can be done to remedy this condition. In fact, realists assert that any attempts to reduce the incidence of war are likely to result in more human suffering, since the responsible and humane nations will agree to restrain themselves, while the greedy and brutal nations will continue in their violent ways.

A second group believes that nations can effectively eliminate most of the causes of war if they act in concert and employ the mechanisms already in place for preventing war. They believe that the present system of treaties, alliances, and machinery for applying international peer pressure to recalcitrant nations need only be improved and refined. In any case, they argue, only measures that elicit the cooperation of the world's nations can bring about peace, because nations control the instruments of war and there is no authority with sufficient power at present to control nations. In particular, they argue that the United Nations can be enormously helpful in helping to preserve or restore peace by providing machinery to assist nations who are seeking peaceful resolutions to their conflicts. However, the United Nations can never be more successful or powerful than the nations of the world allow. Without the cooperation and money of national governments, the United Nations can achieve little. However, those nations teetering on the brink of war but genuinely seeking a way to avoid violent conflict can turn to the United Nations for its assistance in restoring peace, and in such a case, the United Nations might be effective.

A third group agrees with realists, holding that individual nation-states and groups of nations cannot be expected to exercise sufficient restraint to avoid warfare. However, this group differs from realists in its belief in the feasibility of creating international armed forces for the prevention of war between nations. Some prominent members of the United Nations have already urged the creation of a standing U.N. force that would be available at a moment's notice to intervene in trouble spots. The force envisaged would be sufficient only for small-scale intrusion into low-intensity conflict and would be effective only when both warring parties desire its involvement. However, it is not difficult to imagine that this force could be expanded to the point where it would have sufficient power to deter even very powerful nations from going to war. All that is required is that the powerful and influential nations of the world exercise their influence to support the creation of such a force.

Yet another group believes that political leaders cannot be counted on to exercise the initiative to genuinely eradicate war. Political leaders tend to be highly attached to their nation's military forces, and they have a great deal of power to lose if they yield control of their national armed might. However, members of this fourth group believe that the united will of the ordinary people of the world would suffice to pressure political leaders into taking the initiative. Most advanced and wealthy nations are democracies, and therefore, at least in principle, receptive to the will of their people. If a sufficient number of people in enough nations genuinely and vigorously worked for peace, their political leaders would have little choice but to yield to their wishes.

Although war continues to be distressingly common, there are reasons to believe it may not be as prevalent in the future as in the past. Right now, the prospect of a major war among the great and influential nations of the world is extremely remote. This is not because these nations have become more enlightened or saintly. Rather, it is partly because the global economy continues to knit the nations of the world together in so many ways that war between them has become quite difficult to imagine. Also, the major source of state power at the end of the twentieth century is economic might. Japan and Germany have only vestigial military forces, yet they are among the most influential and admired nations of the world due to their economic success. Thus, in the present era, great wealth and power do not result from control of territory but rather from command of technology, with computers being an obvious example of the latter. Traditional warfare is best suited to making gains in geographic territory. It is not at all suited to gaining control of technology or generating technological expertise. Hence, to the extent that future power and wealth result from technology and human expertise, armed conflict will be irrelevant.

It is for these reasons that some bold authors have predicted that war has become obsolete in the present era, at least for the major nations of the world. These authors may be overly optimistic, but they offer intriguing reasons to believe that in the future the great nations of the world will find warfare less useful as an instrument of national policy than in the past. In addition, most of the less developed nations are now striving mightily to embark on programs of economic development and they are aware that warfare will only get in the way of these ambitions. Furthermore, the more actively and deeply these nations become involved in the global economy, the more difficult it will be for them to find reasons to go to war, and the more war will be seen as a detriment rather than an asset to national prosperity.

Hence, it is possible that major warfare among the world's great powers will lose its attractiveness and that no special measures will be needed to eradicate it. However, the dark side of the cloud is that the minor wars, such as those in Bosnia or Somalia, will continue; and it remains to be seen whether the world's influential nations will develop the political will to create effective machinery to halt or prevent these minor wars. On one hand, the world's nations have little incentive to do so, since the minor wars affect relatively few people and tend to remain confined within small areas. On the other, the spirit of international cooperation—one of the legacies of the end of the cold war—and the desire to eliminate the primary causes of human suffering might suffice to motivate them to create the machinery for eliminating these small conflicts.

**For further reading:** Boutros-Ghali, Boutros. 1993. "U.N. Peacekeeping in a New Era." *The World Today* 49 (April): 66–69.

Hamilton, Lee, et al. 1993. "A U.N. Volunteer Military Force: Four Views." *New York Review of Books* 40 (24 June): 58–60.

Holmes, Robert. 1989. *On War and Morality.* Princeton, NJ: Princeton University Press.

Johnson, James T. 1982. *Just War Tradition and the Restraint of War.* Princeton, NJ: Princeton University Press.

Kagan, Donald. 1995. *On the Origins of War.* New York: Doubleday.

Kaysen, Carl. 1990. "Is War Obsolete?" *International Security* 14 (Spring): 42–64.

Mueller, John E. 1989. *Retreat from Doomsday: The Obsolescence of Major War.* New York: Basic Books.

Urquhart, Brian. 1989. *Decolonization and World Peace.* Austin: University of Texas Press.

———. 1993. "For a U.N. Volunteer Military Force." *New York Review of Books* 40 (10 June): 3–4.

Walzer, Michael. 1977. *Just and Unjust Wars.* New York: Basic Books.

# Weapons Control

The cold war between the world's superpowers has left many troubling legacies. The huge mass of deadly weapons circulating in the various troubled parts of the world must be counted among its more dangerous remnants. The United States and the Soviet Union manufactured enormous quantities of weapons and shipped them in generous amounts to their client states. Many of the unused weapons continue to circulate the globe today, available to the highest bidder.

Another particularly troubling legacy of the cold war are the stockpiles of nuclear weaponry and radioactive materials. These have caused difficulty in two ways. First, some of the world's lesser powers acquired nuclear weapons in emulation of the great powers, and several others attempted to do so. A handful of nations are now generally believed to have nuclear weapons, although they have not publicly admitted to this. In particular, several rogue nations, such as Libya and Iraq, are believed to be attempting to create such weapons. Second, the Soviet Union's control over nuclear weapons and material crumbled as the state fell into disarray. Many in Soviet military forces and government are believed to be seeking quick profits by selling stolen nuclear materials to criminal or terrorist groups, according to experts testifying before several U.S. Senate committees. Several shipments of nuclear materials have been intercepted in Germany and Eastern Europe, but experts believe that much additional material has escaped the former Soviet Union undetected. Hence, considerable amounts of nuclear materials might well be at large in the world today, at risk of falling into the hands of outlaw governments or terrorist groups. Part of the difficulty is that nuclear weapons are not particularly difficult to make, given the proper materials.

Another particularly troubling legacy of the cold war are the vast armament industries many nations of the world have constructed. Although the demise of the cold war has erased their primary purpose for existing, these industries retain hundreds of thousands of employees and make significant contributions to their national economies. They are politically well connected and influential, and many nations deem them important to long-range national security. Although the nations in which these industries reside are not currently at war, many fear that they will find themselves at war in the future and will need a functioning munitions industry if they are to prevail. Hence, nations are loath to dismantle their arms industries.

In times of peace, however, nations buy relatively few arms, and their munitions makers must seek other ways of remaining profitable. The most common way of doing so is to continue to sell weapons in whatever markets are available. For example, although the government of the United States has taken many measures to advance the cause of arms control, it simultaneously works to encourage other nations to buy weapons from American corporations. As a result, the United States remains a major source of arms on the global market. The activities of the munitions industries of the former Soviet Union also are particularly troubling in this regard. The economies of the nations formed from the remains of the U.S.S.R. are in such desperate condition that industries are willing to resort to extreme measures to remain viable. Hence, they are offering extremely sophisticated and deadly weaponry in the world market to anyone with the money to buy it.

Chemical and biological weaponry constitute another serious threat. Several nations of the world, such as Iraq and Libya, are believed to be seeking the ability to manufacture chemical weapons, such as poison gases, as well as biological weapons, which kill or injure by causing disease or cause turmoil by making vast tracts of territory uninhabitable.

All of the above classes of weapons are capable of causing enormous amounts of death and injury. Furthermore, these weapons may cause tragedy if they are detonated by accident or as a result of improper maintenance. Because of the dangers posed by these weapons of mass destruction, few responsible persons or governments can fail to be wholeheartedly in favor of strict measures to control their manufacture and distribution. Given the fact that these weapons circulate throughout the world and are capable of wreaking global devastation, many assert that the problem is clearly international and must be addressed by means of international treaties and oversight groups.

At present, various groups are devoted to attempting to control the manufacture and disposal of these weapons. These groups are composed largely of national governments and seek to gain their objectives by treaties that will be binding on all, although it is clear that enforcing the provisions of these treaties on sovereign governments will be very difficult. In fact, the success of these treaties depends on the continued goodwill and cooperation of all the governments involved, as well as on their achieving reliable methods for inspecting suspected manufacturing sites and safe means for destroying weapons caches. Without continued inspection and pressure to enforce these agreements, it is all too likely that one or another nation will find good reason to begin manufacture of these weapons. Even if arms control measures enjoy reasonable success, there remains the possibility that terrorist or nihilist groups will gain control of these materials and use them for their own purposes. Hence, to ensure that people remain free of the threat posed by these weapons, the agreements among nations to rein in the manufacture of such weapons will have to be combined with measures to prevent raw materials from falling into the hands of outlaw groups.

The difficulty with arms control agreements is twofold. First, although all can agree that the entire world and all its peoples would be better off if all these weapons could be eliminated, or at the very least, kept under tight control by the community of nations, any particular nation or revolutionary group will gain a significant advantage if it possesses such weapons at a time when the other nations of the world lack them. Hence, any nation can gain a strong advantage over the others by cheating or seeking some special exemption for itself. In particular, some nations have reason to feel particularly vulnerable, especially if they are surrounded by powerful and hostile neighbors or if they have a long history of difficult relations with neighboring nations. These nations may decide that, given their vulnerability, they have no recourse but to develop the most powerful and fearsome weapons possible, in hopes that this may be sufficient to ward off an attack by hostile neighbors. Second, since each nation will be aware that it can gain an advantage for itself by cheating, it will recognize that other nations have the same incentive. Hence, each nation will have to acknowledge that all other nations will have considerable motivation to cheat, and if they are genuinely concerned about the security of their people, a nation's leaders might believe that the most prudent course of national policy is to proceed on the assumption that all other nations are cheating.

The above difficulties are illustrated by two examples. The nation of Israel is extremely small, much smaller than the average American state. It is surrounded by hostile and heavily armed neighbors with vastly larger populations and far more land than it possesses. Based on the experience of a series of deadly wars in the past 50 years, it has every reason to believe that these surrounding nations would welcome the opportunity to eradicate it. As a way of attempting to ward off this outcome, Israel is widely believed to have developed a small cache of nuclear arms. This is noted by, among others, the analysts affiliated with the Stockholm International Peace Research Institute. Although Israel has never admitted to possessing these arms, many Israelis believe it has them and would be willing to use them in the event of a catastrophic attack by its neighbors. Hence, although the people of Israel have as much reason as others to welcome a world free of nuclear weapons, they have equal reason to wish to keep a supply of such weapons on hand.

The United States is also in a quandary. It is among the leaders in pressing for strict control on the sale and manufacture of arms. As one of the most powerful nations in the world, it has considerable influence on others and can provide a strong impetus to the success of weapons control programs by setting a good example. However, the United States also has one of the largest arms industries in the world. These companies have many employees and have an enormous impact on the economies of the areas where they have manufacturing plants. In addition, they are wealthy, influential, and well connected politically. Hence, they have vast means available to them to look after their own best interests and gain government support. In addition, the United States is aware that it might be involved in a major war at some point in the future, and thus, that it needs efficient and sophisticated weapons industries in place if it hopes to prevail. Hence, to help sustain its munitions industries, the United States has become the world's largest exporter of arms and munitions. Although the U.S. government has formulated guidelines to prevent the sale of arms to certain nations and regions, it has proven willing to sell arms to nations, such as Argentina and Singapore, that have no clear need of them, and there are no guarantees that U.S. weapons will not be resold. Once U.S. arms enter the world market, they become available to the highest bidder—even when the highest bidder may be a bitter enemy of the United States. Furthermore, the flood of U.S. arms on the world market contributes to instability, flowing to insurgent or disgruntled groups and providing the means for violent upheavals or civil wars. Thus, the desire of the United States to protect and preserve its own industries conflicts with its desire to protect its citizens and to contribute to peace in the world.

As the above examples make clear, the world's national governments face a profound conflict. On the one hand, rigorous and effective arms control is in the best interests of all nations and peoples. On the other hand, all have powerful and plausible motives for desiring to make exceptions of themselves. India, for example, has a long history of strongly supporting a world treaty to rigorously control nuclear arms. However, in 1996, when most of the nations of the world were willing to sign such a treaty, India refused, claiming that the treaty was unfair to nations like itself. Many observers believe that the real reason for India's refusal was that it did not want to forgo the possibility of developing nuclear weapons in view of potential threats from Pakistan and mainland China.

The end of the cold war has removed some of the pressure from issues of arms manufacture and control. The great powers of the world no longer see themselves as locked in a bitter fight to the death. Hence, they no longer need to amass ever larger quantities of arms for themselves and their allies. No longer locked into an arms race, they have less need to produce new generations of more sophisticated and deadlier types of arms. Now they are free to cooperate wholeheartedly in removing the threats posed to human life by powerful weaponry. However, the end of the cold war also has created instability, with several nation-states fragmenting into warring factions and other states locked in mutual, escalating hostilities. Although the cold war was a fearsome period, many now look back on it with nostalgia because it was more orderly and predictable; that is, instead of many small, unstable, warring groups and new ones popping up each year, the world had only two armed camps, which had studied each other carefully and which were sufficiently responsible that they refrained from unleashing their nuclear weapons on each other.

With the wholehearted support of the major powers, there is now a far greater possibility of creating the conditions for effective control of the world's masses of arms. Hence, although considerable dangers remain, there is now greater hope that the world's nations will eventually succeed in setting aside their single interests and taking determined action on behalf of the welfare of the world as a whole.

**For further reading:** Art, Robert, and Kenneth Waltz. 1993. *The Use of Force: Military Power and International Politics*. 4th ed. Lanham, MD: University Press of America.

Bailey, Kathleen. 1991. *Doomsday Weapons in the Hands of the Many: The Arms Control Challenge of the '90s*. Urbana: University of Illinois Press.

Gray, Colin. 1992. *House of Cards: Why Arms Control Must Fail*. Ithaca, NY: Cornell University Press.

Jervis, Robert. 1993. "Arms Control, Stability, and Causes of War." *Political Science Quarterly* 108 (Summer): 239–253.

Kosta, Tsipia. 1989. *New Technologies: Defense Policy and Arms Control*. New York: Harper & Row.

Sopko, John. 1996–1997. "The Changing Proliferation Threat." *Foreign Policy* 105 (Winter): 3–20.

Ulrich, Albrecht. 1987. "Conversion of Military Industries to Alternative Production." *World Futures* 24: 263–284.

United States Congress. Senate Committee on Armed Services. 1995. *Intelligence Briefing on Smuggling of Nuclear Material and the Role of International Crime Organizations, and on the Proliferation of Cruise and Ballistic Missiles*. Washington, DC: U.S. Government Printing Office.

United States Congress. Senate Committee on Governmental Affairs. 1992. *Weapons Proliferation in the New World Order*. Washington, DC: U.S. Government Printing Office.

United States House Committee on Foreign Affairs. Subcommittee on Arms Control. Library of Congress. Congressional Research Service. 1992. *The Future of Arms Control: A Report*. Washington, DC: U.S. Government Printing Office.

# Women's Status

Different cultures and different nations have very different conceptions of the proper status and role of women. Some, such as the United States and much of Europe, have moved to widespread acceptance of the idea that women should have a status in society equal to that of men. Although discrimination against women continues to occur in these parts of the world, there does appear to be a general consensus that women should have the same opportunities and responsibilities as men, that they should be free from sexual harassment, and that there are no essential differences between men and women in terms of basic abilities and talents. Other cultures (as in India and many Islamic nations) hold deep-seated beliefs that women are inferior to men or that women should be strictly isolated from public life and should be kept from most of the activities that are available to men outside the home. In many nations, women are expected to carry the greatest share of the burden of child rearing, while they have very limited access to education, little claim to rights of their own that they may enforce against their husbands or other males in their families, and no culturally sanctioned role in public life.

There are considerable factual data supporting the view that the conditions of women are distinctly worse than those of men in many societies of the world. For example, in advanced societies, the life expectancy of women is generally greater than men. However, in most parts of the world, women's life expectancy is distinctly less than men's. Part of the explanation is found in the greater hazards of childbirth women face in many societies, but another part lies in the higher incidence of malnutrition among women in many parts of the world and in the larger numbers of women laboring in hazardous or undesirable occupations. In addition, in many parts of the world, the educational levels of women are far lower than those of men. Because educational levels are closely allied to levels of general well-being and education provides the key to opportunity and power in most human societies, the lack of education indicates a distinctly lower standard of living. In addition, in many nations of the world, women are apt to be physically abused and exploited by men. In some cultures, women are valued considerably less than men, so much so that it is believed that there is a high rate of female infanticide in many nations (see, for example, the work of Amartya Sen). Its purpose is apparently to get rid of unwanted females and free family resources for the more desirable male children.

The inferior cultural status of women in many societies results in considerable suffering and loss of opportunity for decent and productive lives. Hence, many argue that humanity cannot enjoy the luxury of claiming, in relation to the status of women, that human beings must respect the cultural differences of varying societies, even when these differences result in practices that are morally repugnant to many in other societies. The physical suffering and the ruined lives resulting from these practices are evils too great to be overlooked or tolerated, even if an effective response requires active intervention to attempt to change traditional cultures.

However, there are further complications to this issue. In several cases, the question has arisen, whether Western women should set aside their own cultural expectations when they live amid traditional non-Western cultures.

For example, many women have positions of responsibility in multinational corporations, and as part of their duties, they are sent to live and work in traditional societies where women are allowed no public role, even including being forbidden to drive automobiles. Many ask whether these women should be required to conform to the traditional role for women when they live and work in these societies, or whether women with these responsibilities should even be sent to positions in such societies. A related question also arises: How should Western societies deal with immigrant groups from traditional societies that wish to maintain their traditional practices while living and working in Western nations?

A particularly poignant example of these problems arose in the United States in 1996, when a young woman from an African nation applied for asylum in the United States on the grounds that she would be subjected to genital mutilation if she returned to her home country. In her native country, clitoridectomy and related rituals are routinely performed on young women at the age of puberty. These processes are intended to prevent them from gaining pleasure from sexual activity and to make them faithful, dutiful wives who will participate in sexual activity only within marital relations and only for the purpose of bearing children. The additional, unintended results are terrible pain, often serious injury and infection, and, occasionally, death.

The facts in this particular case are beyond dispute: First, there is no question that this practice is firmly entrenched in the traditional culture of the woman's home nation and is endorsed by most people there, including many women. Only a small fraction of the members of the society condemn the practice or wish to avoid it. Second, it is quite clear that the young woman in question ardently wished to avoid the procedure. She went to the trouble of escaping her home nation, took refuge in Europe for a time, and finally made her way to the United States, at which point she applied for asylum. The members of her family in her home nation desired that she return so that the procedure could be performed. However, several groups in the United States provided her with financial, moral, and legal support in her battle to avoid returning to have the operation performed. The U.S. courts eventually ruled in favor of her desire and allowed her to remain in the United States. The court decision is a clear repudiation of the traditional values and practices of her culture, at least insofar as it applies to people living in the United States. It is also likely that her traditional culture would not allow the sort of individualism that she displayed in seeking to avoid her fate. It is far more likely that her home culture would presume that she, like all other members of the society, should submit without question to the dominant social practices.

Understandably, however, opinions sharply differ on such matters. Some argue that the practices of traditional societies regarding women should be left alone, even when these practices result in harm to them. They offer several arguments to support their views. One argument rests on the claim that it is impossible to demonstrate conclusively that one set of cultural practices is right and others are wrong. Because this is so, there can be no justification for one cultural group to make moral judgments on the practices of other cultural groups or to interfere with these practices. A second train of argument holds that it would be morally unjustified to intrude into the affairs of an alien culture even if it could be demonstrated that some cultural practices are mistaken. Those who develop this argument point out that respect for the autonomy of particular human beings requires that other people and the rest of society refrain from intruding into the life of an individual even when the outsiders are quite convinced that a person's activities are morally wrong and harmful. The same principle, they argue, should apply to cultures. It is morally unjustified, they claim, for one culture to intrude into the affairs of another even if the latter's practices are clearly wrong. It is unjustified because respect for the autonomy of these cultures requires that they be left alone. Lastly, appealing to the same principle of respect for autonomy, they argue that traditional cultural practices should be respected even when they result in clear harm to some members.

Part of the problem is that there is difficulty in determining just what counts as harm to a particular individual. Those who accept Western ideas about medical practice, for instance, believe that the cutting, pain, and trauma caused to the body by surgery is not harmful to the patient but is helpful because it is believed that these measures will restore the patient to health. However, for societies that do not accept the validity of Western medicine, Western surgical practices would be considered harmful. Another part of the problem is that there is a clear difference in values separating societies. In the traditional society discussed above, very great value is placed on the freedom from sexual desire that the genital mutilation offers to women. The practice is seen as harmful only by people who do not share a belief in this supreme value.

Those who are opposed to traditional treatments of women argue that the harm that women suffer as a result of some practices is too great to overlook. They point out that the eradication of Jewish people might be claimed to be an entrenched cultural practice of Nazi Germany, but this would not suffice to convince other nations that the Nazi practices should be ignored. Similarly, the killing and maiming that women suffer as a result of some traditional practices are too weighty to be overlooked. In this vein, opponents of traditional treatment point out that there are limits to what autonomous persons can expect the larger society and other human beings to condone. Killing other persons, making their lives miserable, or abusing them would certainly place these persons beyond immunity from social pressure. In the same vein, there must be limits to what customs even independent and ancient societies can be allowed to practice without intrusion from outside. Furthermore, they argue that if respect for autonomy is important, then respect for the autonomy of individuals should outweigh concern for that of traditional practices, since human beings are of ultimate importance in the world and cultural practices can claim value and respect only insofar as they are in conformity with the wishes and values of individual human beings.

Therefore, individuals should have their wishes respected in cases where they do not desire to conform to the traditional social values of their homelands. However, in some cases this nonconformity may make it impossible for an individual to function as a respected member of a particular society, as in the case of the African woman. In such instances, some assert that those who choose not to conform should be allowed the option of leaving the society and finding another life elsewhere. This would be the case particularly in societies where the individual is expected to remain subservient to the society as a whole.

In the past several decades, women around the world have begun to unite across national and cultural divides to press for the common cause of the improvement of the lot of women. As part of this effort, the United Nations has devoted several conferences to examining the global status of women. As the world's peoples and nations continue to be drawn closer together by communications and transportation and by the advancing global economy, clashes of values across cultural boundaries probably will increase both in frequency and in intensity. At present, however, it appears likely that many values and practices of traditional cultures will give way in the face of the pressures of globalization. The modernization of societies that accompanies economic development is also likely to improve the status of women. Societies that are more advanced in economic development are more apt to offer educational opportunities to women, encourage smaller families, find places for women in national economies, and expose women to ideas different from those of their native cultures. The increasingly united and powerful women's movement is likely to help speed this process along.

**For further reading:** Dorkenoo, Efua. 1994. *Cutting the Rose: Female Genital Mutilation: The Practice and Its Prevention.* London: Minority Rights Group.

Dugger, Celia. 1996. "U.S. Grants Asylum to Woman Fleeing Genital Mutilation Rite." *New York Times* (14 June): A1.

———. 1996. "A Refugee's Body Is Intact but Her Family Is Torn." *New York Times* (11 September): A1.

Heyzer, Noeleen, et al., eds. 1995. *A Commitment to the World's Women: Perspectives on Development for Beijing and Beyond.* New York: UNIFEM.

Mies, Maria. 1986. *Patriarchy and Accumulation on a World Scale: Women in the International Division of Labor.* London: Zed Books.

Sen, Amartya Kumar. 1990. "More than 100 Million Women Are Missing." *New York Review of Books* 37 (20 December): 61–66.

———. 1993. "The Economics of Life and Death." *Scientific American* 268 (May): 40–47.

Turshen, Meredith, and Briavel Holcomb. 1993. *Women's Lives and Public Policy: The International Experience.* Westport, CT: Greenwood Press.

# CONTEMPORARY ETHICAL ISSUES

## Chapter 5:
## Significant
## Documents

The Helsinki Accords and the U.N. Universal Declaration of Human Rights are the two crucial documents in international ethics.

The U.S. Bill of Rights, or the first ten amendments to the U.S. Constitution, were ratified on 15 December 1791 after being accepted by nine states. Though they are among the most important and interesting parts of the U.S. Constitution, they were not part of the original Constitution, which was ratified on 21 June 1788. The French Declaration of the Rights of Man and of the Citizen was approved by its National Assembly on 26 August 1789. These documents have been enormously influential on political thinking around the world in the past 200 years. Together, they gave strong support for the ideas that all human beings are equal and that all have moral rights simply in virtue of being human.

The Geneva Conventions contain the international humanitarian laws governing warfare. The series of Geneva Conventions began in the last century and are of vital importance not only because they establish legal principles and rules to govern the conduct of war but also because they establish international legal recognition of moral constraints on the treatment of all human beings. As such, they are an important milestone in the development of international ethics.

The Helsinki Accords, ratified by representatives of 35 nations gathered in Helsinki, Finland, for a Conference on Security and Cooperation, also have played a crucial role but within somewhat narrower limits. The Final Act of the Conference, which has come to be known as the Helsinki Accords, lists a number of fundamental rights. Though the rights listed in the Accords mirror many of the principles found in the U.N. declaration, they were signed by the major powers locked in the cold war, including the United States and the Soviet Union. Because of this, the Accords served two functions. First, they were an explicit affirmation of a commitment to human rights by the superpowers. Second, because they had been accepted by the governments of the Soviet bloc, they served as a rallying point for dissidents in Eastern Europe who opposed their nations' totalitarian regimes. Hence, the Accords played a role in the demise of the cold war. Today, they remain an important point of reference for political movements and governments in nations once under Soviet dominion that have been laboring to create democratic institutions.

The U.N. Universal Declaration of Human Rights has become the keystone of international ethics. It serves as the primary point of reference for most humanitarian aid organizations, including dissident political groups battling for human rights and democracy, the international women's movement, ecology, and movements opposed to war and violence.

The Vienna Declaration and Programme of Action was adopted by the World Conference on Human Rights on 25 June 1993 at the conclusion of its meeting in Vienna, Austria. This conference was held under the aegis of the United Nations and charged with the responsibility of assessing the world's observance of human rights and making recommendations for improving the attainment of human rights. Hence, the Vienna Declaration and Programme of Action does not have the force of law; it contains only recommendations addressed, variously, to the secretary-general of the United Nations, the General Assembly of the United Nations, the nations of the world, and nongovernmental organizations active in the area of human rights. This document is notable for several reasons. For one, it both reaffirms commitment to the rights contained in the U.N. Universal Declaration of Human Rights and gives recognition to issues not emphasized (and, in some cases, not mentioned) in the Universal Declaration of Human Rights, such as the rights of women, children, indigenous people, and migrant workers. In addition, it contains a number of specific recommendations for measures designed to attain the rights it endorses. Also, it has specific recommendations to gain information on the degree to which rights are realized and it makes provision for follow-up reports to be made to the United Nations that will examine the degree to which progress has been made.

# U.S. Constitution

## Bill of Rights

### Amendment I

Congress shall make no law respecting an establishment of religion, or prohibiting the free exercise thereof; or abridging the freedom of speech, or of the press; or the right of the people peaceably to assemble, and to petition the government for a redress of grievances.

### Amendment II

A well regulated militia, being necessary to the security of a free state, the right of the people to keep and bear arms, shall not be infringed.

### Amendment III

No soldier shall, in time of peace be quartered in any house, without the consent of the owner, nor in time of war, but in a manner to be prescribed by law.

### Amendment IV

The right of the people to be secure in their persons, houses, papers, and effects, against unreasonable searches and seizures, shall not be violated, and no warrants shall issue, but upon probable cause, supported by oath or affirmation, and particularly describing the place to be searched, and the persons or things to be seized.

### Amendment V

No person shall be held to answer for a capital, or otherwise infamous crime, unless on a presentment or indictment of a grand jury, except in cases arising in the land or naval forces, or in the militia, when in actual service in time of war or public danger; nor shall any person be subject for the same offense to be twice put in jeopardy of life or limb; nor shall be compelled in any criminal case to be a witness against himself, nor be deprived of life, liberty, or property, without due process of law; nor shall private property be taken for public use, without just compensation.

### Amendment VI

In all criminal prosecutions, the accused shall enjoy the right to a speedy and public trial, by an impartial jury of the state and district wherein the crime shall have been committed, which district shall have been previously ascertained by law, and to be informed of the nature and cause of the accusation; to be confronted with the witnesses against him; to have compulsory process for obtaining witnesses in his favor, and to have the assistance of counsel for his defense.

## Amendment VII

In suits at common law, where the value in controversy shall exceed twenty dollars, the right of trial by jury shall be preserved, and no fact tried by a jury, shall be otherwise reexamined in any court of the United States, than according to the rules of the common law.

## Amendment VIII

Excessive bail shall not be required, nor excessive fines imposed, nor cruel and unusual punishments inflicted.

## Amendment IX

The enumeration in the Constitution, of certain rights, shall not be construed to deny or disparage others retained by the people.

## Amendment X

The powers not delegated to the United States by the Constitution, nor prohibited by it to the states, are reserved to the states respectively, or to the people.

# Declaration of the Rights of Man and of the Citizen

*Approved by the National Assembly of France, 26 August 1789*

The representatives of the French people, organized as a National Assembly, believing that the ignorance, neglect, or contempt of the rights of man are the sole cause of public calamities and of the corruption of governments, have determined to set forth in a solemn declaration the natural, unalienable, and sacred rights of man, in order that this declaration, being constantly before all the members of the Social body, shall remind them continually of their rights and duties; in order that the acts of the legislative power, as well as those of the executive power, may be compared at any moment with the objects and purposes of all political institutions and may thus be more respected, and, lastly, in order that the grievances of the citizens, based hereafter upon simple and incontestable principles, shall tend to the maintenance of the constitution and redound to the happiness of all. Therefore the National Assembly recognizes and proclaims, in the presence and under the auspices of the Supreme Being, the following rights of man and of the citizen:

### Articles

1. Men are born and remain free and equal in rights. Social distinctions may be founded only upon the general good.
2. The aim of all political association is the preservation of the natural and imprescriptible rights of man. These rights are liberty, property, security, and resistance to oppression.

3. The principle of all sovereignty resides essentially in the nation. No body nor individual may exercise any authority which does not proceed directly from the nation.

4. Liberty consists in the freedom to do everything which injures no one else; hence the exercise of the natural rights of each man has no limits except those which assure to the other members of the society the enjoyment of the same rights. These limits can only be determined by law.

5. Law can only prohibit such actions as are hurtful to society. Nothing may be prevented which is not forbidden by law, and no one may be forced to do anything not provided for by law.

6. Law is the expression of the general will. Every citizen has a right to participate personally, or through his representative, in its foundation. It must be the same for all, whether it protects or punishes. All citizens, being equal in the eyes of the law, are equally eligible to all dignities and to all public positions and occupations, according to their abilities, and without distinction except that of their virtues and talents.

7. No person shall be accused, arrested, or imprisoned except in the cases and according to the forms prescribed by law. Anyone soliciting, transmitting, executing, or causing to be executed, any arbitrary order, shall be punished. But any citizen summoned or arrested in virtue of the law shall submit without delay, as resistance constitutes an offense.

8. The law shall provide for such punishments only as are strictly and obviously necessary, and no one shall suffer punishment except it be legally inflicted in virtue of a law passed and promulgated before the commission of the offense.

9. As all persons are held innocent until they shall have been declared guilty, if arrest shall be deemed indispensable, all harshness not essential to the securing of the prisoner's person shall be severely repressed by law.

10. No one shall be disquieted on account of his opinions, including his religious views, provided their manifestation does not disturb the public order established by law.

11. The free communication of ideas and opinions is one of the most precious of the rights of man. Every citizen may, accordingly, speak, write, and print with freedom, but shall be responsible for such abuses of this freedom as shall be defined by law.

12. The security of the rights of man and of the citizen requires public military forces. These forces are, therefore, established for the good of all and not for the personal advantage of those to whom they shall be intrusted.

13. A common contribution is essential for the maintenance of the public forces and for the cost of administration. This should be

equitably distributed among all the citizens in proportion to their means.

14. All the citizens have a right to decide, either personally or by their representatives, as to the necessity of the public contribution; to grant this freely; to know to what uses it is put; and to fix the proportion, the mode of assessment and of collection and the duration of the taxes.

15. Society has the right to require of every public agent an account of his administration.

16. A society in which the observance of the law is not assured, nor the separation of powers defined, has no constitution at all.

17. Since property is an inviolable and sacred right, no one shall be deprived thereof except where public necessity, legally determined, shall clearly demand it, and then only on condition that the owner shall have been previously and equitably indemnified.

# Geneva Convention for the Amelioration of the Condition of the Wounded and Sick in Armed Forces in the Field, of 12 August 1949 (First Geneva Convention)

*The following excerpts are taken from the First Chapter of the First Geneva Convention of 1949. These selections include the main principles of the Geneva Conventions.*

Entry into force: 21 October 1950.

## Chapter I. General Provisions

**Art. 1.** The High Contracting Parties undertake to respect and to ensure respect for the present Convention in all circumstances.

**Art. 2.** In addition to the provisions which shall be implemented in peacetime, the present Convention shall apply to all cases of declared war or of any other armed conflict which may arise between two or more of the High Contracting Parties, even if the state of war is not recognized by one of them. The Convention shall also apply to all cases of partial or total occupation of the territory of a High Contracting Party, even if the said occupation meets with no armed resistance. Although one of the Powers in conflict may not be a party to the present Convention, the Powers who are parties thereto shall remain bound by it in their mutual relations. They shall furthermore be bound by the Convention in relation to the said Power, if the latter accepts and applies the provisions thereof.

**Art. 3.** In the case of armed conflict not of an international character occurring in the territory of one of the High Contracting Parties, each Party to the conflict shall be bound to apply, as a minimum, the following provisions:

(1) Persons taking no active part in the hostilities, including members of armed forces who have laid down their arms and those placed hors de combat by sickness, wounds, detention, or any other cause, shall in all circumstances be treated humanely, without any adverse distinction founded on race, colour, religion or faith, sex, birth or wealth, or any other similar criteria. To this end, the following acts are and shall remain prohibited at any time and in any place whatsoever with respect to the above-mentioned persons:

    (a) violence to life and person, in particular murder of all kinds, mutilation, cruel treatment and torture;

    (b) taking of hostages;

    (c) outrages upon personal dignity, in particular humiliating and degrading treatment;

    (d) the passing of sentences and the carrying out of executions without previous judgement pronounced by a regularly constituted court, affording all the judicial guarantees which are recognized as indispensable by civilized peoples.

(2) The wounded and sick shall be collected and cared for.

An impartial humanitarian body, such as the International Committee of the Red Cross, may offer its services to the Parties to the conflict. The Parties to the conflict should further endeavour to bring into force, by means of special agreements, all or part of the other provisions of the present Convention.

The application of the preceding provisions shall not affect the legal status of the Parties to the conflict.

**Art. 4.** Neutral Powers shall apply by analogy the provisions of the present Convention to the wounded and sick, and to members of the medical personnel and to chaplains of the armed forces of the Parties to the conflict, received or interned in their territory, as well as to dead persons found.

**Art. 7.** Wounded and sick, as well as members of the medical personnel and chaplains, may in no circumstances renounce in part or in entirety the rights secured to them by the present Convention, and by the special agreements referred to in the foregoing Article, if such there be.

**Art. 8.** The present Convention shall be applied with the cooperation and under the scrutiny of the Protecting Powers whose duty it is to safeguard the interests of the Parties to the conflict. For this purpose, the Protecting Powers may appoint, apart from their diplomatic or consular staff, delegates from amongst their own nationals or the nationals of other Neutral Powers. The said delegates shall be subject to the approval of the Power with which they are to carry out their duties.

## Chapter II. Wounded and Sick

**Art. 12.** Members of the armed forces and other persons mentioned in the following Article, who are wounded or sick, shall be respected and protected in all circumstances.

They shall be treated humanely and cared for by the Party to the conflict in whose power they may be, without any adverse distinction founded on sex, race, nationality, religion, political opinions, or any other similar criteria. Any attempts upon their lives, or violence to their persons, shall be strictly prohibited; in particular, they shall not be murdered or exterminated, subjected to torture or biological experiments; they shall not willfully be left without medical assistance and care, nor shall conditions exposing them to contagion or infection be created.

Women shall be treated with all consideration due to their sex. The Party to the conflict which is compelled to abandon wounded or sick to the enemy shall, as far as military considerations permit, leave with them a part of its medical personnel and material to assist in their care.

**Art. 13.** The present Convention shall apply to the wounded and sick belonging to the following categories:

(1) Members of the armed forces of a Party to the conflict, as well as members of militias or volunteer corps forming part of such armed forces.

(2) Members of other militias and members of other volunteer corps, including those of organized resistance movements, belonging to a Party to the conflict and operating in or outside their own territory, even if this territory is occupied, provided that such militias or volunteer corps, including such organized resistance movements, fulfil the following conditions:

    (a) that of being commanded by a person responsible for his subordinates;

    (b) that of having a fixed distinctive sign recognizable at a distance;

    (c) that of carrying arms openly;

    (d) that of conducting their operations in accordance with the laws and customs of war.

(3) Members of regular armed forces who profess allegiance to a Government or an authority not recognized by the Detaining Power.

(4) Persons who accompany the armed forces without actually being members thereof, such as civil members of military aircraft crews, war correspondents, supply contractors, members of labour units or of services responsible for the welfare of the armed forces, provided that they have received authorization from the armed forces which they accompany.

(5) Members of crews, including masters, pilots and apprentices, of the merchant marine and the crews of civil aircraft of the Parties

to the conflict, who do not benefit by more favourable treatment under any other provisions in international law.

(6) Inhabitants of a non-occupied territory, who on the approach of the enemy, spontaneously take up arms to resist the invading forces, without having had time to form themselves into regular armed units, provided they carry arms openly and respect the laws and customs of war.

**Art. 14.** Subject to the provisions of Article 12, the wounded and sick of a belligerent who fall into enemy hands shall be prisoners of war; and the provisions of international law concerning prisoners of war shall apply to them.

**Art. 15.** At all times, and particularly after an engagement, Parties to the conflict shall, without delay, take all possible measures to search for and collect the wounded and sick, to protect them against pillage and ill-treatment, to ensure their adequate care, and to search for the dead and prevent their being despoiled.

Whenever circumstances permit, an armistice or a suspension of fire shall be arranged, or local arrangements made, to permit the removal, exchange and transport of the wounded left on the battlefield. Likewise, local arrangements may be concluded between Parties to the conflict for the removal or exchange of wounded and sick from a besieged or encircled area, and for the passage of medical and religious personnel and equipment on their way to that area.

**Art. 16.** Parties to the conflict shall record as soon as possible, in respect of each wounded, sick or dead person of the adverse Party falling into their hands, any particulars which may assist in his identification.

## Chapter III. Medical Units and Establishments

**Art. 19.** Fixed establishments and mobile medical units of the Medical Service may in no circumstances be attacked, but shall at all times be respected and protected by the Parties to the conflict. Should they fall into the hands of the adverse Party, their personnel shall be free to pursue their duties, as long as the capturing Power has not itself ensured the necessary care of the wounded and sick found in such establishments and units.

## Chapter VIII. Execution of the Convention

**Art. 45.** Each Party to the conflict, acting through its Commanders-in-Chief, shall ensure the detailed execution of the preceding Articles, and provide for unforeseen cases, in conformity with the general principles of the present Convention.

**Art. 46.** Reprisals against the wounded, sick, personnel, buildings or equipment protected by the Convention are prohibited.

## Chapter IX. Repression of Abuses and Infractions

**Art. 49.** The High Contracting Parties undertake to enact any legislation necessary to provide effective penal sanctions for persons committing, or ordering to be committed, any of the grave breaches of the present Convention defined in the following Article.

Each High Contracting Party shall be under the obligation to search for persons alleged to have committed, or to have ordered to be committed, such grave breaches, and shall bring such persons, regardless of their nationality, before its own courts. It may also, if it prefers, and in accordance with the provisions of its own legislation, hand such persons over for trial to another High Contracting Party concerned, provided such High Contracting Party has made out a prima facie case.

Each High Contracting Party shall take measures necessary for the suppression of all acts contrary to the provisions of the present Convention other than the grave breaches defined in the following Article.

In all circumstances, the accused persons shall benefit by safeguards of proper trial and defence, which shall not be less favourable than those provided by Article 105 and those following, of the Geneva Convention relative to the Treatment of Prisoners of War of 12 August 1949.

**Art. 50.** Grave breaches to which the preceding Article relates shall be those involving any of the following acts, if committed against persons or property protected by the Convention: wilful killing, torture or inhuman treatment, including biological experiments, wilfully causing great suffering or serious injury to body or health, and extensive destruction and appropriation of property, not justified by military necessity and carried out unlawfully and wantonly.

**Art. 51.** No High Contracting Party shall be allowed to absolve itself or any other High Contracting Party of any liability incurred by itself or by another High Contracting Party in respect of breaches referred to in the preceding Article.

**Art. 52.** At the request of a Party to the conflict, an enquiry shall be instituted, in a manner to be decided between the interested Parties, concerning any alleged violation of the Convention. If agreement has not been reached concerning the procedure for the enquiry, the Parties should agree on the choice of an umpire who will decide upon the procedure to be followed.

Once the violation has been established, the Parties to the conflict shall put an end to it and shall repress it with the least possible delay.

**Art. 63.** Each of the High Contracting Parties shall be at liberty to denounce the present Convention.

The denunciation shall be notified in writing to the Swiss Federal Council, which shall transmit it to the Governments of all the High Contracting Parties.

The denunciation shall take effect one year after the notification thereof has been made to the Swiss Federal Council. However, a denunciation of which notification has been made at a time when the denouncing Power is involved in a conflict shall not take effect until peace has been concluded, and until after operations connected with release and repatriation of the persons protected by the present Convention have been terminated.

The denunciation shall have effect only in respect of the denouncing Power. It shall in no way impair the obligations which the Parties to the conflict shall remain bound to fulfil by virtue of the principles of the law of nations, as they result from the usages established among civilized peoples, from the laws of humanity and the dictates of the public conscience.

## The Helsinki Accords

The participating States will respect human rights and fundamental freedoms, including the freedom of thought, conscience, religion or belief, for all without distinction as to race, sex, language, or religion.

They will promote and encourage the effective exercise of civil, political, economic, social, cultural, and other rights and freedoms all of which derive from the inherent dignity of the human person and are essential for his free and full development.

Within this framework the participating States will recognize and respect the freedom of the individual to profess and practise, alone or in community with others, religion or belief acting in accordance with the dictates of his own conscience.

The participating States on whose territory national minorities exist will respect the right of persons belonging to such minorities to equality before the law, will afford them the full opportunity for the actual enjoyment of human rights and fundamental freedoms and will, in this manner, protect their legitimate interests in this sphere.

The participating States recognize the universal significance of human rights and fundamental freedoms, respect for which is an essential factor for the peace, justice and well-being necessary to ensure the development of friendly relations and co-operation among themselves as among all States.

## The United Nations Universal Declaration of Human Rights

*Adopted by U.N. General Assembly Resolution 217A (III) of 10 December 1948.*
Whereas recognition of the inherent dignity and of the equal and inalienable rights of all members of the human family is the foundation of freedom, justice and peace in the world,

Whereas disregard and contempt for human rights have resulted in barbarous acts which have outraged the conscience of mankind, and the advent of a world in which human beings shall enjoy freedom of speech and belief and freedom from fear and want has been proclaimed as the highest aspiration of the common people,

Whereas it is essential, if man is not to be compelled to have recourse, as a last resort, to rebellion against tyranny and oppression, that human rights should be protected by the rule of law,

Whereas it is essential to promote the development of friendly relations between nations,

Whereas the peoples of the United Nations have in the Charter reaffirmed their faith in fundamental human rights, in the dignity and worth of the human person and in the equal rights of men and women and have determined to promote social progress and better standards of life in larger freedom,

Whereas Member States have pledged themselves to achieve, in cooperation with the United Nations, the promotion of universal respect for and observance of human rights and fundamental freedoms,

Whereas a common understanding of these rights and freedoms is of the greatest importance for the full realization of this pledge,

Now, therefore,

The General Assembly Proclaims this Universal Declaration of Human Rights as a common standard of achievement for all peoples and all nations, to the end that every individual and every organ of society, keeping this Declaration constantly in mind, shall strive by teaching and education to promote respect for these rights and freedoms and by progressive measures, national and international, to secure their universal and effective recognition and observance, both among the peoples of Member States themselves and among the peoples of territories under their jurisdiction.

## Article 1

All human beings are born free and equal in dignity and rights. They are endowed with reason and conscience and should act towards one another in a spirit of brotherhood.

## Article 2

Everyone is entitled to all the rights and freedoms set forth in this Declaration, without distinction of any kind, such as race, color, sex, language, religion, political or other opinion, national or social origin, property, birth or other status. Furthermore, no distinction shall be made on the basis of the political, jurisdictional or international status of the country or territory to which a person belongs, whether it be independent, trust, non-self-governing or under any other limitation of sovereignty.

## Article 3

Everyone has the right to life, liberty and security of person.

## Article 4

No one shall be held in slavery or servitude; slavery and the slave trade shall be prohibited in all their forms.

## Article 5

No one shall be subjected to torture or to cruel, inhuman or degrading treatment or punishment.

## Article 6

Everyone has the right to recognition everywhere as a person before the law.

## Article 7

All are equal before the law and are entitled without any discrimination to equal protection of the law. All are entitled to equal protection against any discrimination in violation of the Declaration and against any incitement to such discrimination.

## Article 8

Everyone has the right to an effective remedy by the competent national tribunals for acts violating the fundamental rights granted him by the constitution or by law.

## Article 9

No one shall be subjected to arbitrary arrest, detention or exile.

## Article 10

Everyone is entitled in full equality to a fair and public hearing by an independent and impartial tribunal, in the determination of his rights and obligations and of any criminal charge against him.

## Article 11

1. Everyone charged with a penal offence has the right to be presumed innocent until proved guilty according to law in a public trial at which he has had all the guarantees necessary for his defence.
2. No one shall be held guilty of any penal offence on account of any act or omission which did not constitute a penal offence, under national or international law, at the time it was committed. Nor shall a heavier penalty be imposed than the one that was applicable at the time the penal offence was committed.

## Article 12

No one shall be subjected to arbitrary interference with his privacy, family, home or correspondence, nor to attacks upon his honour and reputation. Everyone has the right to the protection of the law against such interference or attacks.

## Article 13

1. Everyone has the right to freedom of movement and residence within the borders of each state.
2. Everyone has the right to leave any country, including his own, and to return to his country.

## Article 14

1. Everyone has the right to seek and to enjoy in other countries asylum from persecution.
2. This right may not be invoked in the case of prosecutions genuinely arising from non-political crimes or from acts contrary to the purposes and principles of the United Nations.

## Article 15

1. Everyone has the right to a nationality.
2. No one shall be arbitrarily deprived of his nationality nor denied the right to change his nationality.

## Article 16

1. Men and women of full age, without any limitation due to race, nationality or religion, have the right to marry and to found a family. They are entitled to equal rights as to marriage, during marriage and at its dissolution.
2. Marriage shall be entered into only with the free and full consent of the intending spouses.
3. The family is the natural and fundamental group unit of society and is entitled to protection by society and the State.

## Article 17

1. Everyone has the right to own property alone as well as in association with others.
2. No one shall be arbitrarily deprived of his property.

## Article 18

Everyone has the right to freedom of thought, conscience and religion; this right includes freedom to change his religion or belief, and freedom, either alone or in community with others and in public or private, to manifest his religion or belief in teaching, practice, worship and observance.

## Article 19

Everyone has the right to freedom of opinion and expression: this right includes freedom to hold opinions without interference and to seek, receive and impart information and ideas through any media and regardless of frontiers. `

## Article 20

1. Everyone has the right to freedom of peaceful assembly and association.
2. No one may be compelled to belong to an association.

## Article 21

1. Everyone has the right to take part in the government of his country, directly or through freely chosen representatives.
2. Everyone has the right of equal access to public service in his country.
3. The will of the people shall be the basis of the authority of government; this will shall be expressed in periodic and genuine elections which shall be by universal and equal suffrage and shall be held by secret vote or by equivalent free voting procedures.

## Article 22

Everyone, as a member of society, has the right to social security and is entitled to realization, through national effort and international co-operation and in accordance with the organization and resources of each State, of the economic, social and cultural rights indispensable for his dignity and the free development of his personality.

## Article 23

1. Everyone has the right to work, to free choice of employment, to just and favourable conditions of work and to protection against unemployment.
2. Everyone, without any discrimination, has the right to equal pay for equal work.
3. Everyone who works has the right to just and favourable remuneration ensuring for himself and his family an existence worthy of human dignity, and supplemented, if necessary, by other means of social protection.
4. Everyone has the right to form and to join trade unions for the protection of his interests.

## Article 24

Everyone has the right to rest and leisure, including reasonable limitation of working hours and periodic holidays with pay.

## Article 25

1. Everyone has the right to a standard of living adequate for the health and well-being of himself and of his family, including food, clothing, housing and medical care and necessary social services, and the right to security in the event of unemployment, sickness, disability, widowhood, old age or other lack of livelihood in circumstances beyond his control.

2. Motherhood and childhood are entitled to special care and assistance. All children, whether born in or out of wedlock, shall enjoy the same social protection.

## Article 26

1. Everyone has the right to education. Education shall be free, at least in the elementary and fundamental stages. Elementary education shall be compulsory. Technical and professional education shall be made generally available and higher education shall be equally accessible to all on the basis of merit.
2. Education shall be directed to the full development of the human personality and to the strengthening of respect for human rights and fundamental freedoms. It shall promote understanding, tolerance and friendship among all nations, racial or religious groups, and shall further the activities of the United Nations for the maintenance of peace.
3. Parents have a prior right to choose the kind of education that shall be given to their children.

## Article 27

1. Everyone has the right freely to participate in the cultural life of the community, to enjoy the arts and to share in scientific advancement and its benefits.
2. Everyone has the right to the protection of the moral and material interests resulting from any scientific, literary or artistic production of which he is the author.

## Article 28

Everyone is entitled to a social and international order in which the rights and freedoms set forth in this Declaration can be fully realized.

## Article 29

1. Everyone has duties to the community in which alone the free and full development of his personality is possible.
2. In the exercise of his rights and freedoms, everyone shall be subject only to such limitations as are determined by law solely for the purpose of securing due recognition and respect for the rights and freedoms of others and of meeting the just requirements of morality, public order and the general welfare in a democratic society.
3. These rights and freedoms may in no case be exercised contrary to the purposes and principles of the United Nations.

## Article 30

Nothing in this Declaration may be interpreted as implying for any State, group or person any right to engage in any activity or to perform any act aimed at the destruction of any of the rights and freedoms set forth herein.

**Source:** © 1997 by the Office of the United Nations High Commissioner for Human Rights. Reprinted by permission.

# Vienna Declaration and Programme of Action

*The following excerpts are from the full Vienna Declaration and Programme of Action, adopted by the World Conference on Human Rights on 25 June 1993.*

The World Conference on Human Rights,

Considering that the promotion and protection of human rights is a matter of priority for the international community, and that the Conference affords a unique opportunity to carry out a comprehensive analysis of the international human rights system and of the machinery for the protection of human rights, in order to enhance and thus promote a fuller observance of those rights, in a just and balanced manner,

Recognizing and affirming that all human rights derive from the dignity and worth inherent in the human person, and that the human person is the central subject of human rights and fundamental freedoms, and consequently should be the principal beneficiary and should participate actively in the realization of these rights and freedoms,

Determined to take new steps forward in the commitment of the international community with a view to achieving substantial progress in human rights endeavours by an increased and sustained effort of international cooperation and solidarity,

Solemnly adopts the Vienna Declaration and Programme of Action.

**I**

1. The World Conference on Human Rights reaffirms the solemn commitment of all States to fulfil their obligations to promote universal respect for, and observance and protection of, all human rights and fundamental freedoms for all in accordance with the Charter of the United Nations, other instruments relating to human rights, and international law. The universal nature of these rights and freedoms is beyond question.

   In this framework, enhancement of international cooperation in the field of human rights is essential for the full achievement of the purposes of the United Nations.

Human rights and fundamental freedoms are the birthright of all human beings; their protection and promotion is the first responsibility of Governments.

2. All peoples have the right of self-determination. By virtue of that right they freely determine their political status, and freely pursue their economic, social and cultural development.

4. The promotion and protection of all human rights and fundamental freedoms must be considered as a priority objective of the United Nations in accordance with its purposes and principles, in particular the purpose of international cooperation. In the framework of these purposes and principles, the promotion and protection of all human rights is a legitimate concern of the international community. The organs and specialized agencies related to human rights should therefore further enhance the coordination of their activities based on the consistent and objective application of international human rights instruments.

5. All human rights are universal, indivisible and interdependent and interrelated. The international community must treat human rights globally in a fair and equal manner, on the same footing, and with the same emphasis. While the significance of national and regional particularities and various historical, cultural and religious backgrounds must be borne in mind, it is the duty of States, regardless of their political, economic and cultural systems, to promote and protect all human rights and fundamental freedoms.

7. The processes of promoting and protecting human rights should be conducted in conformity with the purposes and principles of the Charter of the United Nations, and international law.

8. Democracy, development and respect for human rights and fundamental freedoms are interdependent and mutually reinforcing. Democracy is based on the freely expressed will of the people to determine their own political, economic, social and cultural systems and their full participation in all aspects of their lives. In the context of the above, the promotion and protection of human rights and fundamental freedoms at the national and international levels should be universal and conducted without conditions attached. The international community should support the strengthening and promoting of democracy, development and respect for human rights and fundamental freedoms in the entire world.

9. The World Conference on Human Rights reaffirms that least developed countries committed to the process of democratization and economic reforms, many of which are in Africa, should be supported by the international community in order to succeed in their transition to democracy and economic development.

11. The right to development should be fulfilled so as to meet equi-

tably the developmental and environmental needs of present and future generations. The World Conference on Human Rights recognizes that illicit dumping of toxic and dangerous substances and waste potentially constitutes a serious threat to the human rights to life and health of everyone.

12. The World Conference on Human Rights calls upon the international community to make all efforts to help alleviate the external debt burden of developing countries, in order to supplement the efforts of the Governments of such countries to attain the full realization of the economic, social and cultural rights of their people.

17. The acts, methods and practices of terrorism in all its forms and manifestations as well as linkage in some countries to drug trafficking are activities aimed at the destruction of human rights, fundamental freedoms and democracy, threatening territorial integrity, security of States and destabilizing legitimately constituted Governments. The international community should take the necessary steps to enhance cooperation to prevent and combat terrorism.

18. The human rights of women and of the girl-child are an inalienable, integral and indivisible part of universal human rights. The full and equal participation of women in political, civil, economic, social and cultural life, at the national, regional and international levels, and the eradication of all forms of discrimination on grounds of sex are priority objectives of the international community.

19. Considering the importance of the promotion and protection of the rights of persons belonging to minorities and the contribution of such promotion and protection to the political and social stability of the States in which such persons live,

20. The World Conference on Human Rights recognizes the inherent dignity and the unique contribution of indigenous people to the development and plurality of society and strongly reaffirms the commitment of the international community to their economic, social and cultural well-being and their enjoyment of the fruits of sustainable development. States should ensure the full and free participation of indigenous people in all aspects of society, in particular in matters of concern to them.

21. The World Conference on Human Rights, welcoming the early ratification of the Convention on the Rights of the Child by a large number of States and noting the recognition of the human rights of children in the World Declaration on the Survival, Protection and Development of Children and Plan of Action adopted by the World Summit for Children, urges universal ratification of the Convention by 1995 and its effective implementation by States

parties through the adoption of all the necessary legislative, administrative and other measures and the allocation to the maximum extent of the available resources.

22. Special attention needs to be paid to ensuring non-discrimination, and the equal enjoyment of all human rights and fundamental freedoms by disabled persons, including their active participation in all aspects of society.

23. The World Conference on Human Rights reaffirms that everyone, without distinction of any kind, is entitled to the right to seek and to enjoy in other countries asylum from persecution, as well as the right to return to one's own country. In this respect it stresses the importance of the Universal Declaration of Human Rights, the 1951 Convention relating to the Status of Refugees, its 1967 Protocol and regional instruments.

24. Great importance must be given to the promotion and protection of the human rights of persons belonging to groups which have been rendered vulnerable, including migrant workers, the elimination of all forms of discrimination against them, and the strengthening and more effective implementation of existing human rights instruments.

25. The World Conference on Human Rights affirms that extreme poverty and social exclusion constitute a violation of human dignity and that urgent steps are necessary to achieve better knowledge of extreme poverty and its causes, including those related to the problem of development, in order to promote the human rights of the poorest, and to put an end to extreme poverty and social exclusion and to promote the enjoyment of the fruits of social progress. It is essential for States to foster participation by the poorest people in the decision-making process by the community in which they live, the promotion of human rights and efforts to combat extreme poverty.

26. The World Conference on Human Rights welcomes the progress made in the codification of human rights instruments, which is a dynamic and evolving process, and urges the universal ratification of human rights treaties. All States are encouraged to accede to these international instruments; all States are encouraged to avoid, as far as possible, the resort to reservations.

27. Every State should provide an effective framework of remedies to redress human rights grievances or violations. The administration of justice, including law enforcement and prosecutorial agencies and, especially, an independent judiciary and legal profession in full conformity with applicable standards contained in international human rights instruments, are essential to the full and non-discriminatory realization of human rights and indispensable to the processes of democracy and sustainable development.

28. The World Conference on Human Rights expresses its dismay at massive violations of human rights especially in the form of genocide, "ethnic cleansing" and systematic rape of women in war situations, creating mass exodus of refugees and displaced persons.

29. The World Conference on Human Rights expresses grave concern about continuing human rights violations in all parts of the world in disregard of standards as contained in international human rights instruments and international humanitarian law and about the lack of sufficient and effective remedies for the victims.

32. The World Conference on Human Rights reaffirms the importance of ensuring the universality, objectivity and non-selectivity of the consideration of human rights issues.

34. Increased efforts should be made to assist countries which so request to create the conditions whereby each individual can enjoy universal human rights and fundamental freedoms. Governments, the United Nations system as well as other multilateral organizations are urged to increase considerably the resources allocated to programmes aiming at the establishment and strengthening of national legislation, national institutions and related infrastructures which uphold the rule of law and democracy, electoral assistance, human rights awareness through training, teaching and education, popular participation and civil society.

35. The full and effective implementation of United Nations activities to promote and protect human rights must reflect the high importance accorded to human rights by the Charter of the United Nations and the demands of the United Nations human rights activities, as mandated by Member States. To this end, United Nations human rights activities should be provided with increased resources.

36. The World Conference on Human Rights reaffirms the important and constructive role played by national institutions for the promotion and protection of human rights, in particular in their advisory capacity to the competent authorities, their role in remedying human rights violations, in the dissemination of human rights information, and education in human rights.

38. The World Conference on Human Rights recognizes the important role of non-governmental organizations in the promotion of all human rights and in humanitarian activities at national, regional and international levels.

39. Underlining the importance of objective, responsible and impartial information about human rights and humanitarian issues, the World Conference on Human Rights encourages the increased involvement of the media, for whom freedom and protection should be guaranteed within the framework of national law.

## II

## A. Increased coordination on human rights within the United Nations system

1. The World Conference on Human Rights recommends increased coordination in support of human rights and fundamental freedoms within the United Nations system.
2. Furthermore, the World Conference on Human Rights calls on regional organizations and prominent international and regional finance and development institutions to assess also the impact of their policies and programmes on the enjoyment of human rights.
4. The World Conference on Human Rights strongly recommends that a concerted effort be made to encourage and facilitate the ratification of and accession or succession to international human rights treaties and protocols adopted within the framework of the United Nations system with the aim of universal acceptance.

### Resources

9. The World Conference on Human Rights, concerned by the growing disparity between the activities of the Centre for Human Rights and the human, financial and other resources available to carry them out, and bearing in mind the resources needed for other important United Nations programmes, requests the Secretary-General and the General Assembly to take immediate steps to increase substantially the resources for the human rights programme from within the existing and future regular budgets of the United Nations, and to take urgent steps to seek increased extrabudgetary resources.

## B. Equality, dignity and tolerance

### 1. Racism, racial discrimination, xenophobia and other forms of intolerance

19. The World Conference on Human Rights considers the elimination of racism and racial discrimination, in particular in their institutionalized forms such as apartheid or resulting from doctrines of racial superiority or exclusivity or contemporary forms and manifestations of racism, as a primary objective for the international community and a worldwide promotion programme in the field of human rights. United Nations organs and agencies should strengthen their efforts to implement such a programme of action related to the third decade to combat racism and racial discrimination as well as subsequent mandates to the same end. The World Conference on Human Rights strongly appeals to the international community to contribute generously to the Trust Fund for

the Programme for the Decade for Action to Combat Racism and Racial Discrimination.

23. The World Conference on Human Rights stresses that all persons who perpetrate or authorize criminal acts associated with ethnic cleansing are individually responsible and accountable for such human rights violations, and that the international community should exert every effort to bring those legally responsible for such violations to justice.

### Indigenous people

28. The World Conference on Human Rights calls on the Working Group on Indigenous Populations of the Sub-Commission on Prevention of Discrimination and Protection of Minorities to complete the drafting of a declaration on the rights of indigenous people at its eleventh session.

### Migrant workers

33. The World Conference on Human Rights urges all States to guarantee the protection of the human rights of all migrant workers and their families.

## A. The equal status and human rights of women

36. The World Conference on Human Rights urges the full and equal enjoyment by women of all human rights and that this be a priority for Governments and for the United Nations. The World Conference on Human Rights also underlines the importance of the integration and full participation of women as both agents and beneficiaries in the development process, and reiterates the objectives established on global action for women towards sustainable and equitable development set forth in the Rio Declaration on Environment and Development and chapter 24 of Agenda 21, adopted by the United Nations Conference on Environment and Development (Rio de Janeiro, Brazil, June 1992).

39. The World Conference on Human Rights urges the eradication of all forms of discrimination against women, both hidden and overt. The United Nations should encourage the goal of universal ratification by all States of the Convention on the Elimination of All Forms of Discrimination against Women by the year 2000. Ways and means of addressing the particularly large number of reservations to the Convention should be encouraged. Inter alia, the Committee on the Elimination of Discrimination against Women should continue its review of reservations to the Convention. States are urged to withdraw reservations that are contrary to the object and purpose of the Convention or which are otherwise incompatible with international treaty law.

### 4. The rights of the child

45. The World Conference on Human Rights reiterates the principle of "First Call for Children" and, in this respect, underlines the importance of major national and international efforts, especially those of the United Nations Children's Fund, for promoting respect for the rights of the child to survival, protection, development and participation.

### 5. Freedom from torture

54. The World Conference on Human Rights welcomes the ratification by many Member States of the Convention against Torture and Other Cruel, Inhuman or Degrading Treatment or Punishment and encourages its speedy ratification by all other Member States.

### Enforced disappearances

62. The World Conference on Human Rights, welcoming the adoption by the General Assembly of the Declaration on the Protection of All Persons from Enforced Disappearance, calls upon all States to take effective legislative, administrative, judicial or other measures to prevent, terminate and punish acts of enforced disappearances.

### 6. The rights of the disabled person

63. The World Conference on Human Rights reaffirms that all human rights and fundamental freedoms are universal and thus unreservedly include persons with disabilities. Every person is born equal and has the same rights to life and welfare, education and work, living independently and active participation in all aspects of society.

## C. Cooperation, development and strengthening of human rights

66. The World Conference on Human Rights recommends that priority be given to national and international action to promote democracy, development and human rights.

67. Special emphasis should be given to measures to assist in the strengthening and building of institutions relating to human rights, strengthening of a pluralistic civil society and the protection of groups which have been rendered vulnerable. In this context, assistance provided upon the request of Governments for the conduct of free and fair elections, including assistance in the human rights aspects of elections and public information about elections, is of particular importance.

70. The World Conference on Human Rights requests the Secretary-General of the United Nations to submit proposals to the United

Nations General Assembly, containing alternatives for the establishment, structure, operational modalities and funding of the proposed programme.

## D. Human rights education

78. The World Conference on Human Rights considers human rights education, training and public information essential for the promotion and achievement of stable and harmonious relations among communities and for fostering mutual understanding, tolerance and peace.

## E. Implementation and monitoring methods

83. The World Conference on Human Rights urges Governments to incorporate standards as contained in international human rights instruments in domestic legislation and to strengthen national structures, institutions and organs of society which play a role in promoting and safeguarding human rights.

84. The World Conference on Human Rights recommends the strengthening of United Nations activities and programmes to meet requests for assistance by States which want to establish or strengthen their own national institutions for the promotion and protection of human rights.

85. The World Conference on Human Rights also encourages the strengthening of cooperation between national institutions for the promotion and protection of human rights, particularly through exchanges of information and experience, as well as cooperation with regional organizations and the United Nations.

89. The World Conference on Human Rights recommends continued work on the improvement of the functioning, including the monitoring tasks, of the treaty bodies, taking into account multiple proposals made in this respect, in particular those made by the treaty bodies themselves and by the meetings of the chairpersons of the treaty bodies. The comprehensive national approach taken by the Committee on the Rights of the Child should also be encouraged.

92. The World Conference on Human Rights recommends that the Commission on Human Rights examine the possibility for better implementation of existing human rights instruments at the international and regional levels and encourages the International Law Commission to continue its work on an international criminal court.

96. The World Conference on Human Rights recommends that the United Nations assume a more active role in the promotion and protection of human rights in ensuring full respect for international humanitarian law in all situations of armed conflict, in accordance with the purposes and principles of the Charter of the United Nations.

## F. Follow-up to the World Conference on Human Rights

99. The World Conference on Human Rights recommends that the General Assembly, the Commission on Human Rights and other organs and agencies of the United Nations system related to human rights consider ways and means for the full implementation, without delay, of the recommendations contained in the present Declaration, including the possibility of proclaiming a United Nations decade for human rights. The World Conference on Human Rights further recommends that the Commission on Human Rights annually review the progress towards this end.

100. The World Conference on Human Rights requests the Secretary-General of the United Nations to invite on the occasion of the fiftieth anniversary of the Universal Declaration of Human Rights all States, all organs and agencies of the United Nations system related to human rights, to report to him on the progress made in the implementation of the present Declaration and to submit a report to the General Assembly at its fifty-third session, through the Commission on Human Rights and the Economic and Social Council.

**Source:** © 1997 by the Office of the United Nations High Commissioner for Human Rights. Reprinted by permission.

# CONTEMPORARY ETHICAL ISSUES

## Chapter 6:
## Selected Print
## Resources

A vast array of material is available that is useful in considering questions of international ethics. This chapter provides an annotated list of particularly helpful journals, books, and reference works.

## Books

Baer, M. Delal, et al., editors. 1996. *NAFTA and Sovereignty: Trade-Offs for Canada, Mexico, and the United States.* Washington, DC: Center for Strategic and International Studies. 176 pp. ISBN 0-8920-6322-X.

In this anthology, two authors from each nation that is a party to the North American Free Trade Agreement express their nation's concerns about the treaty. One author from each nation discusses the economic concerns, while the other examines the political issues.

Baer, M. Delal, and Sidney Weintraub, editors. 1994. *The NAFTA Debate: Grappling with Un-conventional Trade Issues.* Boulder, CO: Lynne Rienner Publishers. 211 pp. ISBN 1-55587-464-9.

This anthology of essays by specialists examines the national debates about the North American Free Trade Agreement rather than the agreement itself. In particular, the authors analyze concerns about the environment, workers' rights, human rights, health, and national sovereignty sparked by the NAFTA treaty.

Bailey, Kathleen. 1991. *Doomsday Weapons in the Hands of the Many: The Arms Control Challenge of the '90s.* Urbana: University of Illinois Press. 158 pp. ISBN 0-25201-826-5.

Bailey develops the argument that materials and expertise to construct devastating nuclear or chemical weapons are available to many terrorist or criminal groups and that current international mechanisms are inadequate to address this threat.

Bauer, P. T. 1981. *Equality, the Third World, and Economic Delusion.* Cambridge, MA: Harvard University Press. 293 pp. ISBN 0-67425-985-8.

This work is an extensive critical analysis of the assumptions underlying the aid policies of developed nations and of their intellectual justification.

Beitz, Charles. 1979. *Political Theory and International Relations.* Princeton, NJ: Princeton University Press. 212 pp. ISBN 0-69107-614-6.

This is a philosophical study of the question of whether nation-states are morally obligated to employ moral principles to guide their dealings with other nation-states and human beings in other parts of the world. Beitz develops a conception of human rights and applies it to questions of the moral constraints on national foreign policy, principles guiding intervention in the affairs of other nations, and the evaluation of democratic processes.

Benko, Robert B. 1984. *Protecting Intellectual Property Rights: Issues and Controversies.* Washington, DC: American Enterprise Institute for Public Policy Research. 62 pp. ISBN 0-84473-617-1.

This is a concise examination of the present state of legal protection of intellectual property rights on the national and international levels and a discussion of the controversies that they arouse.

Bossard, Andrâe. 1990. *Transnational Crime and Criminal Law.* Chicago: University of Illinois, Office of International Criminal Justice. 155 pp. ISBN 0-94251-134-4.

Bossard is a former secretary-general of Interpol, the international association of police organizations. He examines the varied aspects of international crime at the present time and offers suggestions for improving the world's response.

Bozeman, Adda. 1971. *The Future of Law in a Multicultural World.* Princeton, NJ: Princeton University Press. 229 pp. ISBN 0-691-05643-9.

A helpful study of the relationship between politics and law in various world cultures, this book analyzes the Islamic Middle East and Chinese cultures, among others. The book also discusses the implications of cultural diversity for the globalization of law.

Brown, Lester R., and Hal Kane. 1994. *Full House: Reassessing the Earth's Population Carrying Capacity.* New York: W. W. Norton. 261 pp. ISBN 0-393-03713-4.

Part of the Worldwatch Environmental Alert series, this book develops the argument that the world's farmers will soon be unable to produce sufficient food to feed the world's growing population and that greater efforts at population control are the only feasible way to address the problem.

Bull, Hedley. 1995. *The Anarchical Society: A Study of Order in World Politics.* 2nd ed. New York: Columbia University Press. 329 pp. ISBN 0-23110-297-6.

A multifaceted study of the conception of an order of world politics. It considers the relation of this conception to justice, the balance of power, international law, and war. It also has extensive discussion of the present system of order founded on nation-states and examines the question of whether nation-states have become obsolete or are in decline.

Castles, Stephen. 1993. *The Age of Migration: International Population Movements in the Modern World.* New York: Guilford Press. 307 pp. ISBN 0-89862-249-2.

This book examines international migration trends in this century. It compares the migration of the past 50 years with that prior to World War II and employs case studies of Austria and Germany to compare two nations' responses to migration. It also discusses the features migration is likely to have in the near future and its likely consequences for the nations where migrants alight.

The Center for Strategic and International Studies. 1996. *The Nuclear Black Market: An Assessment of the CSIS Task Force on the Nuclear Black Market.* Washington, DC: Center for Strategic and International Studies. 49 pp. ISBN 0-89206-287-8.

This report details the supply of, illegal trade in, and demand for nuclear weapons and nuclear material from the former Soviet Union. It includes recommendations for addressing this threat.

Chichilnisky, Graciela. 1982. *Basic Needs and the North/South Debate.* New York: World Order Models Project. 36 pp. ISBN 0-91164-611-7.

This is a very brief discussion of basic human needs and their relevance to the debate of the late 1970s and early 1980s between wealthy and poor nations on issues of international distributive justice.

Clark, Roger Stenson. 1994. *The United Nations Crime Prevention and Criminal Justice Program: Formulation of Standards and Efforts at Their Implementation.* Philadelphia: University of Pennsylvania Press. 331 pp. ISBN 0-81223-269-0.

This study analyzes the United Nations' efforts to combat crime dating from 1945. The book includes an assessment of the organizational structure of the United Nations in the area of crime and the success of its efforts to devise standards for combating crime. It also discusses important international documents and treaties related to crime, such as the Torture Declaration.

Clark, William, Jr., and Ryukichi Imani. 1996. *Next Steps in Arms Control and Non-Proliferation: Report of the U.S.-Japan Study Group on Arms Control and Non-Proliferation after the Cold War.* Washington, DC: Carnegie Endowment for International Peace. 196 pp. ISBN 0-87003-150-8.

A collection of essays by experts in the field, this book examines 13 issues in arms control and weapons nonproliferation, including the dangers posed by civilian nuclear power programs. The authors address questions of how to reduce the number of weapons and what policies governments should pursue toward this goal.

Claude, Innis L. 1988. *States and the Global System: Politics, Law, and Organization.* New York: St. Martin's Press. 205 pp. ISBN 0-31201-249-7.

This work discusses the relations and controversies between individual nation-states, generally from the perspective of the United States, and the emerging international order.

Claude, Richard Pierre, and Burns Weston. 1992. *Human Rights and the World Community: Issues and Action.* 2d ed. Philadelphia: University of Pennsylvania Press. 463 pp. ISBN 0-81223-154-6.

This broad-ranging anthology examines the nature of human rights, their importance for humanity, ways to implement them, and the role of national governments and nongovernmental organizations in the process of implementation.

Collins, Charles. 1994. *Management and Organization of Developing Health Systems.* Oxford and New York: Oxford University Press. 285 pp. ISBN 0-19262-423-7.

The author discusses the challenges of establishing effective public health systems in developing nations. He addresses problems of the role of national governments, the effects of decentralization, the difficulties of organization, and the benefits of district control.

Commoner, Barry. 1971. *The Closing Circle*. New York: Bantam Books. 326 pp. ISBN 0-39442-350-X.

A pioneering work on ecology, this was an early presentation of the argument that humanity is obligated to take rigorous measures to protect the environment.

Crawford, James. 1994. *Democracy and International Law*. Cambridge, England: Cambridge University Press. 43 pp. ISBN 0-52146-835-3.

The text of a lecture by a professor of international law at Cambridge University, this work discusses the relation between democratic governments and the development of a system of international law.

Damrosch, Lori. 1993. *Enforcing Restraint: Collective Intervention in International Conflicts*. New York: Council on Foreign Relations Press. 403 pp. ISBN 0-87609-155-9.

A collection of studies of intervention by the international community for the purposes of ending violence, restoring order, and giving humanitarian assistance, this work includes examinations of intervention in Haiti, Somalia, Liberia, and Cambodia, among other cases.

DeGeorge, Richard T. 1993. *Competing with Integrity in International Business*. New York: Oxford University Press. 233 pp. ISBN 0-19508-225-7.

DeGeorge has written an essay showing how ethical principles can be applied to the international conduct of business. He discusses the context of international business transactions, lays down a number of guidelines for morally responsible conduct, and discusses ways in which morally responsible conduct can be undertaken in differing business contexts, ranging from developing nations to the states of the former Soviet Union and the more advanced industrialized nations.

Deng, Francis Mading. 1993. *Protecting the Dispossessed: A Challenge for the International Community*. Washington, DC: Brookings Institution. 175 pp. ISBN 0-81571-825-X.

This is an examination of the ways in which the international community is addressing the problems of refugees at the present time. It contains studies of refugees from or in Russia, El Salvador, Sudan, and other countries.

Doctors without Borders (Médecins sans Frontières). 1996. *World in Crisis: The Politics of Survival at the End of the Twentieth Century*. New York: Routledge. 224 pp. ISBN 0-41515-378-6.

This collection of articles by the humanitarian aid group Doctors without Borders provides an analysis of the difficulties facing humanitarian organizations working to give aid in difficult and volatile circumstances, such as those found in Rwanda, Chechnya, and Bosnia. It examines a number of questions, including that of when humanitarian organizations should speak out against human rights abuses and how to address the needs of civilian populations in cases where control of aid distribution has become a center of political controversy.

Donaldsen, Thomas. 1989. *The Ethics of International Business.* New York: Oxford University Press. 196 pp. ISBN 0-19505-874-7.

This is a study of the nature and circumstances of multinational corporations and an attempt to construct a practical set of guidelines for them, based on a theory of human rights.

Donnelly, Jack. 1993. *International Human Rights.* Boulder, CO: Westview Press. 205 pp. ISBN 0-8133-8182-7.

A comprehensive analysis of various topics of international human rights, this book discusses various theories of human rights, the role of human rights issues in global politics, the relation between human rights and national foreign policies, the relation between human rights and international organizations, and the relation of human rights to other political conceptions.

Elfstrom, Gerard. 1990. *Ethics for a Shrinking World.* London and New York: Macmillan/St. Martin's Press. 232 pp. ISBN 0-31203-204-8.

This book provides an analysis of the context of international ethical issues, devises a moral perspective from which these issues may be analyzed, and then examines several different classes of international ethical issues, such as those of national sovereignty, national borders, and violence in international relations.

———. 1991. *Moral Issues and Multinational Corporations.* London and New York: Macmillan/St. Martin's Press. 144 pp. ISBN 0-33352-690-2.

This essay examines several aspects of the moral issues that face multinational corporations. It discusses the questions of whether multinational corporations can be held morally accountable for their activity and examines the particular features of the context of moral agency of multinational corporations. It then examines several domains of moral difficulty, such as those related to corporate size and power, cultural and economic diversity, and corporate mobility.

Elsom, Derek M. 1992. *Atmospheric Pollution: A Global Problem.* Oxford: Blackwell Publishing. 319 pp. ISBN 0-63117-308-0.

This extraordinarily comprehensive study of atmospheric pollution offers a scientific analysis of its generation and transmission and also discusses the differing contexts of atmospheric pollution as well as efforts to address it in developing and industrialized nations. The book also assesses the success of these efforts.

Falk, Richard. 1981. *Human Rights and State Sovereignty.* New York: Holmes & Meier Publishers. 251 pp. ISBN 0-84190-619-X.

A dedicated partisan of the role of international law and of international human rights, Falk examines U.S. policy regarding the violations of human rights in other nations and proposes modifications to this policy to enhance its effectiveness.

————. 1992. *Explorations at the Edge of Time: The Prospects of World Order.* Philadelphia: Temple University Press. 255 pp. ISBN 0-87722-860-4.

An impassioned work by a veteran campaigner for world order, this book discusses the controversies regarding the prospect of a world order, ways of addressing these issues, and prospects for the future.

Falk, Richard, et al. 1985. *International Law: A Contemporary Perspective.* Boulder, CO: Westview Press. 702 pp. ISBN 0-86531-241-9.

This is a broad-ranging collection of essays by a number of authors that addresses various aspects of international law, ranging from enforcement to conflict resolution and the relation of international law to conflicts between the individual and the state.

Fitzpatrick, Joan. 1994. *Human Rights in Crisis: The International Systems for Protecting Human Rights during Time of Emergency.* Philadelphia: University of Pennsylvania Press. 260 pp. ISBN 0-81223-238-0.

This book discusses the difficulties related to efforts to protect human rights during times of crisis, the U.N. institutions and mechanisms for responding to these difficulties, and the role of regional organizations and nongovernmental organizations.

Fooner, Michael. 1989. *Interpol: Issues in World Crime and International Criminal Justice.* New York: Plenum Press. 244 pp. ISBN 0-30643-135-1.

Fooner is a research scientist who examines the structure, function, and inner workings of Interpol, the global association of national police forces organized to combat international crime and conspiracies.

Foster, Bruce A. 1993. *The Acid Rain Debate: Science and Special Interests in Policy Formation.* Ames: Iowa State University Press. 166 pp. ISBN 0-81381-684-X.

This wide-ranging book presents the scientific background for the discussion of acid rain and the claimed environmental and economic effects of its presence in the environment. The book also discusses arguments regarding the quality of scientific validity of assertions regarding acid rain and the options for addressing the problems associated with it and its effects.

Gadbaw, R. Michael, and Timothy J. Richards. 1988. *Intellectual Property Rights: Global Consensus, Global Conflict?* Boulder, CO: Westview Press. 412 pp. ISBN 0-81337-550-9.

An exhaustive survey of the present circumstances of intellectual property rights and controversies about them, this work offers an examination of these issues in the context of the GATT (Global Agreement on Tariffs and Trade) negotiations and from the perspective of several individual nations, including Argentina, Mexico, and South Korea.

Garrett, Laurie. 1994. *The Coming Plague.* New York: Farrar, Straus & Giroux. 750 pp. ISBN 0-37412-646-1.

The author provides information on a number of newly discovered viruses, new versions of old viruses, and old viruses found in new locations and explores the implications of these developments for public health. She also offers her recommendations of what should be done to mitigate a possible future global plague.

Gibney, Mark, editor. 1988. *Open Borders? Closed Societies?: The Ethical and Political Questions.* Westport, CT: Greenwood Press. 199 pp. ISBN 0-31325-578-4.

This book is a collection of essays by several authors on the ethical and legal issues pertaining to refugees and immigration.

Gill, Terry. 1989. *Litigation Strategy at the International Court: A Case Study of the Nicaragua v. United States Dispute.* Dordrecht and Boston: M. Nijhoff. 362 pp. ISBN 0-79230-332-6.

Gill offers an in-depth examination of the history and structure of the International Court of Justice in The Hague and the nature of the system of international law that it employs. The work illustrates the working of this system by examining the court case in which Nicaragua charged that the United States had violated international law by mining one of its harbors even though the two nations were not at war with one another.

Ginsberg, Faye, and Rayna Rapp, editors. 1995. *Conceiving the New World Order: The Global Politics of Reproduction.* Berkeley: University of California Press. 450 pp. ISBN 0-52008-913-8.

This is an anthology of articles by a wide variety of authors who discuss reproduction and the efforts to control reproduction in various areas of the globe. The authors are particularly interested in relating these issues to the social status and political activity of women.

Goodwin-Gill, Guy. 1983. *The Refugee in International Law.* Oxford: Clarendon Press. 317 pp. ISBN 0-19825-518-7.

A comprehensive examination of international laws concerning refugees, this book examines treaties as well as national and international policies.

Gorman, Robert F., et al. 1993. *Refugee Aid and Development: Theory and Practice.* Westport, CT: Greenwood Press. 229 pp. ISBN 0-31328-580-2.

A collection of essays by a number of authors, this work examines various aspects of refugee aid programs and policies and evaluates their effectiveness.

Gray, Colin. 1992. *House of Cards: Why Arms Control Must Fail.* Ithaca, NY: Cornell University Press. 242 pp. ISBN 0-80142-703-7.

Gray argues that arms control strategies are inherently flawed because they ignore central political realities—namely, that the more motivated nations are to go to war, the less they will be motivated to accept the constraints of arms control agreements. He supports his assertion with an analysis of various arms control agreements and the contexts in which they were created.

Green, Leslie. 1988. *The Authority of the State.* Oxford: Oxford University Press. 273 pp. ISBN 0-19824-926-8.

This is a respected examination of the moral and political foundations of the state's authority over citizens, the limits to this authority, and the circumstances under which it is no longer valid.

Greenfeld, Liah. 1992. *Nationalism: Five Roads to Modernity.* Cambridge, MA: Harvard University Press. 581 pp. ISBN 0-67460-318-4.

This is a historical and comparative study of five nations and the process by which they developed a sense of national identity and national unity.

Gronlund, Lisabeth, and David Wright. 1994. *Beyond Safeguards: A Program for More Comprehensive Control of Weapons-Usable Fissile Material.* Cambridge: Union of Concerned Scientists. 86 pp.

A survey of efforts to control access to highly enriched uranium and plutonium, this work analyzes the adequacy of present measures of control and suggests improvements.

Grotius, Hugo. 1962. *The Law of War and Peace.* Tr. Francis Willey Kelsey. Indianapolis: Bobbs-Merrill. 946 pp.

This is a modern translation of the first definitive statement of international law, written by the Dutch jurist Hugo Grotius in 1625.

Haass, Richard N. 1994. *Intervention: The Use of American Military Force in the Post–Cold War Era.* Washington, DC: Carnegie Endowment for International Peace. 258 pp. ISBN 0-87003-056-6.

The author provides 12 case studies of instances where the United States has employed military force in recent years to intervene in other nations. The examples range from Bosnia to the Gulf War and include a variety of military operations, from peacekeeping or humanitarian assistance to all-out war. The author suggests guidelines that should govern military intervention and discusses why particular instances of intervention might have turned out differently if his guidelines had been followed.

Halpern, Morton H., and David Scheffer, with Patricia Small. 1992. *Self-Determination in the New World Order.* Washington, DC: Carnegie Endowment for International Peace. 178 pp. ISBN 0-87003-018-3.

The authors discuss the number of groups recently seeking political self-determination around the world, the state of international law regarding political self-determination, and the policies that the United States should adopt in addressing these movements. In particular, the authors examine the question of how self-determination pertains to efforts at intervention.

Hannum, Hurst. 1987. *The Right to Leave and Return in International Law.* Leyden, The Netherlands: M. Nijhoff. 189 pp. ISBN 9-02473-445-2.

This is a comprehensive examination of the history and operation of international law governing leaving and returning to a nation.

Hardin, Garrett. 1993. *Living within Limits: Ecology, Economics, and Population Taboos.* New York: Oxford University Press. 339 pp. ISBN 0-19507-811-X.

In this recent restatement of the author's argument in favor of rigorous population control policies based on a comparison of the earth with a lifeboat, Hardin claims that the earth is like a lifeboat in possessing strictly limited resources to sustain human life. An attempt to support a larger number of human beings than the earth's resources allow will result in disaster for all.

Harkavy, Oscar. 1995. *Curbing Population Growth: An Insider's Perspective on the Population Movement.* New York: Plenum Press. 274 pp. ISBN 0-30645-050-X.

Harkavy has 35 years' experience working in the population control movement. He traces the history of the movement from its origins in the 1950s to the present and discusses the contemporary divide separating those in the movement who are most concerned with the welfare of poor women and their children and who fear that population control efforts can coerce them from those who believe that population control initiatives should be given highest priority.

Harris, Marvin. 1987. *Death, Sex, and Fertility: Population Regulation in Preindustrial and Developing Societies.* New York: Columbia University Press. 227 pp. ISBN 0-23106-270-0.

Harris's useful study examines the state of population regulation in differing cultures and at various stages in human history. It concludes with some general observations on the relation between population regulation and economic development.

Harris, Nigel. 1995. *The New Untouchables: Immigration and the New World Order.* London: I. B. Tauris. 272 pp. ISBN 0-14014-689-X.

Harris offers evidence and arguments to support his belief that the advanced, industrialized nations of the world must open their borders to the free movement of people if they are to avoid economic decline. He believes this is necessary because these nations have populations that are declining and aging, and they must replenish their labor supply. He also asserts that freedom of movement is necessary to provide economic opportunity for people from poor, undeveloped nations.

Harrison, Selig S., and Masashi Nishihara, editors. 1995. *U.N. Peacekeeping: Japanese and American Perspectives.* Washington, DC: Carnegie Endowment for International Peace. 178 pp. ISBN 0-87003-066-3.

This volume contains the views of eight Japanese and American specialists on the domestic political controversies within Japan and the United States over U.N. peacekeeping efforts and whether and how nations should support U.N. peacekeeping. They also examine the record of U.N. peacekeeping operations and discuss the criteria that should govern U.N. intervention.

Hartmann, Betsy. 1995. *Reproductive Rights and Wrongs: The Global Politics of Population Control.* Boston: South End Press. 388 pp. ISBN 0-89608-491-4.

An analysis of global patterns of population and reproduction control, this work includes case studies of successful and unsuccessful population and reproduction control programs, linking population growth and reproduction to economic and social pressures.

Heyzer, Noeleen, et al., editors. 1995. *A Commitment to the World's Women: Perspectives on Development for Beijing and Beyond.* New York: UNIFEM. 269 pp. ISBN 0-91291-738-5.

This anthology features articles by a number of authors from quite varied backgrounds. The articles examine the economic conditions of women, their political status, the role of the United Nations in advancing the cause of women, prospects for the future, and reports on various U.N. conferences on women.

Hobsbawm, Eric. 1990. *Nations and Nationalism since 1780.* Cambridge, England: Cambridge University Press. 206 pp. ISBN 0-52143-961-2.

Hobsbawm presents a shrewd historical analysis of the conditions under which the concept of nationalism originally developed, its development and permutations in past centuries, the ways in which politicians and monarchs have employed it to manipulate citizens and maintain power, and the role it has played in international policies and in warfare.

Hoffmann, Stanley. 1984. *Duties beyond Borders: On the Limits and Possibilities of Ethical International Politics.* Syracuse, NY: Syracuse University Press. 252 pp. ISBN 0-81560-168-9.

The author, currently a professor at Harvard University, addresses the questions of whether international political relations allow ethical action and what sort of difficulties confront efforts to act in morally upright fashion in the domain of international political relations. He then devises a course of ethical political activity and suggests relevant applications to the domains of human rights, warfare, and international distributive justice.

Holmes, Robert. 1989. *On War and Morality.* Princeton, NJ: Princeton University Press. 310 pp. ISBN 0-69107-794-0.

In a careful and thoughtful examination of the moral arguments purportedly justifying war, Holmes concludes that none succeed and that restraint from violence is the only morally viable option.

Horseman, Matthew. 1994. *After the Nation-State: Citizens, Tribalism, and the New World.* London: HarperCollins. 298 pp. ISBN 0-00255-145-4.

This is a study of the contemporary processes that are undermining the powers and predominance of the nation-state, the institutions that are emerging to take its place, and the consequences of these developments for human order and stability.

Houck, John, and Oliver Williams, editors. 1996. *Is the Good Corporation Dead?: Social Responsibility in a Global Economy.* Lanham, MD: Rowman & Littlefield. 318 pp. ISBN 0-87468-208-0.

This wide-ranging anthology offers essays by authors from diverse backgrounds. Several of the essays develop varying points of view on the question of whether it is possible for corporations to be morally upright in present circumstances. Other essays discuss ways of improving corporate moral accountability, and others examine concrete cases to illustrate various aspects of corporate moral accountability.

Hout, Wil. 1993. *Capitalism and the Third World: Development, Depen-*

*dence, and the World System.* Aldershot, Hants, England: E. Elgon. 227 pp. ISBN 1-85278-785-6.

Hout presents a comparative analysis of the views of several scholars on the relationship between the present global economy and the less developed nations.

Hurrelmann, Klaus, and Ulrich Laaser. 1996. *International Handbook of Public Health.* Westport, CT: Greenwood Press. 470 pp. ISBN 0-31329-500-X.

A synopsis of the state of public health in different nations, this work contains an overview of advances and developments in the science of public health as well as case studies of the public health systems of 20 nations.

International Labor Organization. 1996. *World Employment 1996/1997.* Geneva, Switzerland: International Labor Organization. 212 pp. ISBN 9-22110-326-9.

This global review of current employment trends offers data to support the argument that full employment is both feasible and desirable under present economic conditions. It contains labor policy recommendations for industrialized nations, developing nations, and nations with transitional economies, as well as information designed to set national policies in a global context.

International Women's Leadership Forum. 1997. *Leadership—Is Gender an Issue?: Women's Leadership in the 21st Century.* Washington, DC: Center for Strategic and International Studies. 30 pp. ISBN 0-89206-290-8.

This report of the International Women's Leadership Forum, which met in Stockholm in May 1996, examines the varied leadership roles of women in the current era and discusses prospects for the future.

Jacobson, David. 1996. *Rights across Borders: Immigration and the Decline of Citizenship.* Baltimore, MD: Johns Hopkins University Press. 181 pp. ISBN 0-80185-150-5.

The author believes that international migration since World War II has had a significant impact on our ideas about citizenship and the state. He asserts that international human rights are now gaining importance for individuals and that citizenship is declining in importance.

Johnson, James T. 1982. *Just War Traditions and the Restraint of War.* Princeton, NJ: Princeton University Press. 380 pp. ISBN 0-69107-263-9.

Johnson presents a careful and intelligent analysis of the historical development of the moral principles governing war and their application to the conditions of the present era.

Kagan, Donald. 1995. *On the Origins of War.* New York: Doubleday. 606 pp. ISBN 0-38542-375-6.

Kagan, a noted historian, examines two ancient wars, two others that took place in the twentieth century, and the Cuban Missile Crisis in an attempt to identify the causes of war. Based on his findings, he makes several recommendations that he believes might prove useful in maintaining peace.

Katzenstein, Peter, editor. 1996. *The Cultures of National Security: Norms and Identity in World Politics.* New York: Columbia University Press. 562 pp. ISBN 0-23110-468-5.

This anthology presents articles by a number of specialists examining various facets of national security in light of the end of the cold war and the present currents of globalism.

Kemf, Elizabeth, editor. 1993. *The Law of the Mother: Protecting Indigenous People in Protected Areas.* San Francisco: Sierra Club Books. 296 pp. ISBN 0-87156-451-3.

In this large and wide-ranging collection of essays, a variety of authors discuss the lives and circumstances of indigenous groups around the world and present arguments to support the view that steps should be taken to protect them.

Kennedy, Paul. 1993. *Preparing for the Twenty-first Century.* New York: Random House. 428 pp. ISBN 0-67974-705-2.

Kennedy's widely discussed book focuses on global population growth, the development of new technology, and the emerging global economy, exploring the likely long-term consequences of current trends for the environment, use of natural resources, social stability, and national security.

Kommers, Donald, and Gilbert Loescher, editors. 1979. *Human Rights and American Foreign Policy.* Notre Dame, IN: University of Notre Dame Press. 333 pp. ISBN 0-26801-071-4.

Various authors examine facets of the relationship between human rights and foreign policy. This anthology covers the state of respect for human rights in different parts of the world, examines the role of international bodies in protecting human rights, the activity of international human rights monitoring agencies, and the implications of international human rights for U.S. foreign policy.

Kosta, Tsipia. 1989. *New Technologies: Defense Policy and Arms Control.* New York: Harper & Row. 138 pp. ISBN 0-88730-382-X.

Kosta examines the development of technologies that will allow the creation of new generations of more potent and effective weapons and discusses the ways in which political and military policies should be revised to take account of them.

Lee, Dixie Ray. 1993. *Environmental Overkill: Whatever Happened to Common Sense?* Washington, DC: Regnery Gateway. 260 pp. ISBN 0-89526-512-5.

The author is a scientist and former chairman of the U.S. Atomic Energy Commission and the former governor of the state of Washington. In this book, she argues that many assertions made in behalf of more aggressive efforts to preserve the environment are based on inaccurate data or faulty reasoning, or both. She asserts that many environmental policies are scientifically unjustified and harmful to society.

Leeman, Richard. 1991. *The Rhetoric of Terrorism and Counter-Terrorism.* New York: Greenwood Press. 217 pp. ISBN 0-31327-587-4.

This useful book examines the nature of terrorism and the major arguments used to justify it or to marshal opposition to it.

Levi, Werner. 1991. *Contemporary International Law: A Concise Introduction.* 2d ed. Boulder, CO: Westview Press. 365 pp. ISBN 0-81331-094-6.

This broad-ranging study addresses the role and place of individuals, states, and international bodies in international law and explores the use of that law in resolving conflicts and guiding the use of force.

Levin, Michael David, editor. 1993. *Ethnicity and Aboriginality: Case Studies in Ethnonationalism.* Toronto: University of Toronto Press. ISBN 0-80202-918-3.

In this anthology, eight specialists discuss the claims of particular aboriginal peoples to nationhood based on their ethnicity. The authors examine a variety of cases, ranging from French Canadians to Australian aborigines and to the indigenous people of Kenya.

Liemt, Gijsbert van. 1988. *Bridging the Gap: Four Newly Industrializing Countries and the Changing International Division of Labor.* Geneva: International Labor Organization. 123 pp. ISBN 9-22105-556-6.

This study was commissioned by the International Labor Organization to compare the experience of four nations—Brazil, Mexico, South Korea, and Singapore. It examines the role of governments in these countries' economic development, the structures of their economies, and the status and conditions of their laborers.

Loescher, Gil. 1993. *Beyond Charity: International Cooperation and the*

*Global Refugee Crisis.* New York: Oxford University Press. 260 pp. ISBN 0-19508-183-8.

Loescher, who has written extensively on refugees, presents an overview of the refugee problem and the circumstances of refugees in the post–cold war era. He discusses the work of international agencies in addressing refugees' problems and presents both short-term and long-term recommendations for increasing the effectiveness of those efforts.

Loescher, Gil, and Laila Monahan, editors. 1989. *Refugees and International Relations.* Oxford: Oxford University Press. 430 pp. ISBN 0-19827-564-1.

In this volume of essays, the authors discuss various aspects of the problems facing refugees and the international community in meeting their needs.

Lury, Celia. 1993. *Cultural Rights: Technology, Legality, and Personality.* London and New York: Routledge. 239 pp. ISBN 0-41503-155-9.

Lury examines several important modes of reproducing and transmitting cultural property, such as television, print media, and computers, and their relation to law and to culture as well as their implications for gender.

Lusztig, Michael. 1996. *Risking Free Trade: The Politics of Trade in Britain, Canada, Mexico, and the United States.* Pittsburgh, PA: University of Pittsburgh Press. 180 pp. ISBN 0-88293-932-0.

Lusztig examines the issues of free trade in several different nations and in various eras. He discusses the motives that impel politicians to support free trade and the possible consequences of these policies.

Mann, Jonathan, et al. 1992. *AIDS in the World.* Cambridge, MA: Harvard University Press. 1037 pp. ISBN 0-67401-265-8.

The primary author of this study is director of the World Health Organization's Global Program on AIDS. He has assembled a group of specialists to assess the evolution of the global AIDS plague, its effects on humanity, and the worldwide response. The book also makes recommendations for providing a more effective global response to the AIDS challenge.

McMichael, A. J., et al. 1996. *Climate Change and Human Health.* Geneva: World Health Organization, Division of Publication. 305 pp.

This is an assessment of the effect that global climate change may have on the world's population, prepared by a task force on behalf of the World Health Organization, the World Meteorological Organization, and the U.N. Environment Programme.

McWhinney, Edward. 1987. *The International Court of Justice and the Western Traditions of International Law.* Dordrecht and Boston: M. Nijhoff. 158 pp. ISBN 9-02473-524-6.

This work examines contemporary international law and its relation to the U.N. International Court of Justice. It examines the operations of the Court, discusses several cases presented to it, and analyzes controversies about it.

Meadows, Donnella, et al. 1974. *The Limits to Growth: A Report for the Club of Rome on the Predicament of Mankind.* 2d ed. New York: Universe Books. 205 pp. ISBN 0-87763-165-0.

An alarming study, this work concludes that contemporary trends in population, pollution, and exploitation of natural resources will soon result in global catastrophe.

Mies, Maria. 1986. *Patriarchy and Accumulation on a World Scale: Women in the International Division of Labor.* London: Zed Books. 251 pp. ISBN 0-86232-341-X.

The author examines the position of women around the world from a Marxist perspective. She argues that the present capitalist system necessarily results in violence to women and that the only way to remedy this abuse is to dismantle the system.

Miller, Henri. 1996. *Free Trade versus Protectionism.* New York: H. W. Wilson. 128 pp. ISBN 0-82420-889-7.

A recent anthology of articles, essays, and speeches, this helpful work presents arguments for and against free trade and policies of protectionism, culled from an array of sources.

Miller, Marc. 1993. *State of the Peoples: A Global Human Rights Report on Societies in Danger.* Boston: Beacon Press. 262 pp. ISBN 0-80700-220-8.

This book discusses the difficulties of seven native societies that face extinction. The seven range from a North American Indian tribe to African bushmen to Malaysian forest nomads. The work also examines the condition of a variety of aboriginal peoples in various parts of the world and lists resources available to assist them.

Minear, Larry. 1993. *Humanitarian Action in Times of War.* Boulder, CO: Lynne Rienner Publishers. 107 pp. ISBN 1-55587-437-1.

This work is designed to serve as a reference for those working to provide humanitarian assistance under conditions of violence.

Moffett, George. 1994. *Critical Masses: The Global Population Challenge.* New York: Viking Press. 353 pp. ISBN 0-67085-235-X.

Moffett is a journalist who presents an extended analysis of population control issues in various parts of the world, including Mexico, Kenya, and Egypt. Using information gained in interviews with people in the areas he analyzes, he addresses the complexity inherent in the pressures affecting population. He also recommends particular control measures that he believes are apt to be successful because they take account of the specific circumstances of the areas where they are to be applied.

————. 1994. *Global Population Growth: 21st Century Challenges.* Ithaca, NY: Cornell University Press. 72 pp. ISBN 0-87124-158-7.

In this brief work, the author discusses the nature of global population growth, its likely consequences for humanity, various possible responses to it, and the role of the United States in addressing it.

Mueller, John E. 1989. *Retreat from Doomsday: The Obsolescence of Major War.* New York: Basic Books. 327 pp. ISBN 0-46506-939-8.

Mueller offers a broad treatment of the nature and circumstances of war in this century, particularly those of the cold war and the advent of nuclear weapons. He concludes that the present conditions of the world have made war between the major powers an obsolete instrument for achieving national interests.

Nadelmann, Ethan Avram. 1993. *Cops across Borders: The Internationalization of U.S. Criminal Law Enforcement.* University Park: Pennsylvania State University Press. 524 pp. ISBN 0-27101-094-0.

This is a useful recent study of the ways in which U.S. police organizations have come to operate on a transnational scale.

Nader, Ralph, editor. 1993. *The Case against Free Trade: GATT, NAFTA, and the Globalization of Corporate Power.* San Francisco: Earth Island Press. 230 pp. ISBN 1-55643-169-4.

In this anthology, authors from a variety of backgrounds develop arguments that free trade agreements have negative consequences for the environment, biodiversity, the consumer, developing nations, and national sovereignty. The authors also commonly contend that the most significant consequence of this activity is to increase the power of multinational corporations.

Nardin, Terry, and David Mapel, editors. 1992. *Traditions of International Ethics.* Cambridge, England: Cambridge University Press. 326 pp. ISBN 0-52140-458-4.

This anthology examines issues of international law and international ethics from a variety of theoretical perspectives, including those of Marxism, Christianity, liberalism, and utilitarianism.

National Geographic Society. 1995. *The Emerald Realm: Earth's Precious Rainforests.* Washington, DC: National Geographic Society. 196 pp. ISBN 0-87044-790-4.

This beautifully illustrated book explains the nature and ecology of rain forests, the threat to their existence and to that of the indigenous tribes inhabiting them, the obstacles to saving them, and ways of overcoming those obstacles.

Natsios, Andrew S. 1997. *U.S. Foreign Policy and the Four Horsemen of the Apocalypse: Humanitarian Relief in Complex Emergencies.* Westport, CT: Praeger. 192 pp. ISBN 0-2759-5920-1.

The author notes that U.S. aid in response to foreign crises increased from $300 million in 1989 to $1.3 billion in 1994, demonstrating that the United States has become far more active in providing humanitarian aid in difficult and violent settings like Bosnia, Haiti, or Rwanda than in past years. He discusses what leadership role the United States should play in responding to these emergencies and what guidelines should direct U.S. intervention.

Netanyahu, Benjamin. 1995. *Fighting Terrorism: How Democracies Can Defeat Domestic and International Terrorists.* New York: Farrar, Straus & Giroux. 151 pp. ISBN 0-37415-492-9.

The author, former Israeli soldier and current prime minister of Israel, canvasses the current state of terrorism across the world and offers a ten-point program that he believes will assist democratic nations in defending themselves against terrorism.

Organization for Economic Cooperation and Development. 1993. *The Changing Course of International Migration.* Paris: OECD. 263 pp. ISBN 9-26413-827-2.

This compendium of articles examines various aspects of the current state of transnational migration and considers its consequences for a variety of matters, such as employment, the transfer of technological expertise, and economic development. It also contains discussions of national policies regulating migration.

Orme, William. 1993. *Continental Shift: Free Trade and the New North America.* Washington, DC: Washington Post Company. 235 pp. ISBN 0-96259-712-0.

Orme, a strong proponent of the North American Free Trade Agreement, presents various arguments supporting ratification of the treaty and attacking those opposed to it. The book includes a discussion of the historical and economic background to the agreement.

Papademetriou, Demetrios. 1996. *Coming Together or Pulling Apart?: The European Union's Struggle with Immigration and Asylum.* Washington, DC: Carnegie Endowment for International Peace. 133 pp. ISBN 0-87003-116-3.

The author examines the problems of immigration that the 15 member nations of the European Union are facing. In particular, he analyzes the difficulty that each nation wishes to act independently in dealing with immigration while at the same time maintaining a union without internal borders.

Papademetriou, Demetrios, and Kimberly Hamilton. 1995. *Managing Uncertainty: Regulating Immigration Flows in Advanced Industrial Countries.* Washington, DC: Carnegie Endowment for International Peace. 36 pp. ISBN 0-87003-069-8.

The authors examine the contemporary state of immigration in advanced industrialized nations and discuss the issues that immigration policies must address in order to be effective.

Partridge, Ernst, editor. 1981. *Responsibilities to Future Generations.* Buffalo, NY: Prometheus Press. 319 pp. ISBN 0-87975-142-8.

A number of authors discuss the philosophical question of whether people living today have moral obligations to generations that do not yet exist. They explore the implications of this issue for ecology, nuclear weapons, and genetic engineering.

Raine, Linnea, and Frank Cillufo, editors. 1994. *Global Organized Crime: The New Empire of Evil.* Washington, DC: Center for Strategic and International Studies. 185 pp. ISBN 0-89206-312-2.

This anthology contains articles by a variety of specialists who examine the facets of contemporary international crime. They discuss the links between international crime and national and economic security, corporate security, national intelligence, and law enforcement. There are special studies of credit cards, the Internet, drugs, money laundering, terrorism, Russian organized crime, and fissionable material.

Rieff, David. 1995. *Slaughterhouse: Bosnia and the Failure of the West.* New York: Simon & Schuster. 240 pp. ISBN 0-67188-118-3.

Rieff offers a chilling firsthand account of the atrocities of the civil war in Bosnia and of the failure of the international community to adequately respond.

Roberts, Brad. 1996. *Weapons Proliferation and World Order: After the Cold War.* The Hague and Boston: Kluwer Law International. 398 pp. ISBN 9-04110-205-1.

This is a study of current views of nuclear proliferation, changes in the forces affecting proliferation, and the implications for world stability.

Rothkopf, David J. 1977. *The Ultimate Peacekeeper: Economic Intervention and U.S. Foreign Policy.* Washington, DC: Carnegie Endowment for International Peace. 108 pp. ISBN 0-87003-150-3.

The author discusses the ways in which the United States could promote increased economic opportunities and improved living conditions, taking as examples U.S. intervention in Bosnia, the Palestinian territories, and Haiti. He suggests that economic outcomes will have a great effect on the peace and stability of such areas and, ultimately, will determine the success of U.S. efforts.

Sassen, Saskia. 1996. *Losing Control? Sovereignty in an Age of Globalization.* New York: Columbia University Press. 148 pp. ISBN 0-2311-0608-4.

The author argues that there are good reasons to believe that nation-states are losing sovereignty over their territory. She believes this process is being driven by multinational agreements to increase trade, the pressures of global financial markets, and the increasing influence of international human rights movements.

Sebenius, James. 1984. *Negotiating the Law of the Sea.* Cambridge, MA: Harvard University Press. 251 pp. ISBN 0-67460-686-8.

This is a comprehensive examination of the issues, arguments, and interests involved in negotiating a multinational agreement to establish an international law on exploitation of the wealth of the world's seabeds.

Sen, Amartya. 1981. *Poverty and Famine.* Oxford: Clarendon Press. 257 pp. ISBN 0-19828-426-8.

In this highly influential book, Amartya Sen develops the argument that famine does not result simply from natural processes. He asserts that there is often food available in nations beset by famine. Starvation does not occur because no food is available but because poor people lack money to buy it. Hence, Sen believes that famine results from economic and political factors as much as from natural disaster. He recommends that governments change their policies to make money available to people so that they can buy food rather than simply giving them food.

Serra, Jamie, et al. 1997. *Reflections on Regionalism: Report of the Study Group on International Trade.* Washington, DC: Carnegie Endowment for International Peace. 73 pp. ISBN 0-87003-076-0.

This report by a study group of the Carnegie Endowment for International Peace examines the interrelation of regional trade agreements and global free trade. The authors, all well-recognized authorities on the subject, offer their proposals for addressing the difficulties besetting this relationship.

Shawcross, William. 1984. *The Quality of Mercy: Cambodia, Holocaust and Modern Conscience.* New York: Simon & Schuster. 464 pp. ISBN 0-67144-022-5.

This is a classic study of the activity and difficulties facing the various aid and relief agencies and national governments in providing aid and reconstruction to war-torn Cambodia in the 1970s and early 1980s.

Sherwood, Robert. 1990. *Intellectual Property and Economic Development.* Boulder, CO: Westview Press. 226 pp. ISBN 0-81338-019-7.

This book provides general discussions of the nature of intellectual property and its economic significance. It also presents case studies of the economic impact of intellectual property and its regulation by governments in Brazil, Mexico, Japan, and South Korea.

Shiller, Nina Glick, et al. 1992. *Towards a Transnational Perspective on Migration: Race, Class, Ethnicity, and Nationalism Reconsidered.* New York: New York Academy of Sciences. 259 pp. ISBN 0-89766-704-2.

This anthology employs the concept of transnationalism in analyses of contemporary patterns and problems of migration.

Shue, Henry. 1996. *Basic Rights: Subsistence, Affluence, and U.S. Foreign Policy.* 2d ed. Princeton, NJ: Princeton University Press. 248 pp. ISBN 0-69102-929-6.

The author develops a conception of the requirements of human rights that he then employs to make the argument that the United States has the moral obligation to withhold aid from governments that do not work to ensure that their citizens have access to the basic requirements of a decent human life. He argues, in addition, that the wealthy nations of the world have a moral obligation, based on human rights, to share some of their riches with the impoverished people of the world.

Siddiqi, Javed. 1995. *World Health and World Politics: The World Health Organization and the U.N. System.* Columbia: University of South Carolina Press. 272 pp. ISBN 1-57003-038-3.

Siddiqi offers an evaluation of the World Health Organization's (WHO) achievements from 1948 to 1985 and an examination of the role of politics in its operations. The book discusses the problems of the WHO, offers an analysis of its mandate, includes a case study of its efforts to eradicate malaria, and concludes with an overall assessment of its success.

Silver, Cheryl Simon, et al. 1990. *One Earth, One Future: Our Changing Global Environment.* Washington, DC: National Academy Press. 196 pp. ISBN 0-30904-141-4.

A general overview of the facets of global pollution, this work emphasizes acid rain and ozone depletion and the role that human beings play in these processes.

Snider, Don M., and Stuart J. D. Schwartzstein, editors. 1995. *The United Nations at Fifty: Sovereignty, Peacekeeping, and Human Rights.* Washington, DC: Center for Strategic and International Studies. 74 pp. ISBN 0-89206-268-1.

A group of U.N. officials, members of the U.S. government, and specialists from around the world examine the United Nations' increased role and responsibilities in the period following the end of the cold war. They address the questions of what the organization's role should be and the conditions most likely to affect U.S. support for the United Nations in the future.

Soroos, Marvin. 1986. *Beyond Sovereignty: The Challenge of Global Policy.* Columbia: University of South Carolina Press. 388 pp. ISBN 0-87249-474-8.

Soroos catalogs and discusses the various problems he believes confront humanity as a whole, such as nuclear proliferation, pollution, human rights, and managing ocean resources. He then develops arguments to support the claim that the nations must address these problems as a world community, even at the cost of yielding portions of their national sovereignty.

———. 1997. *The Endangered Atmosphere: Preserving a Global Commons.* Columbia: University of South Carolina Press. 339 pp. ISBN 1-57003-160-6.

In this broad-scale study of global atmospheric pollution, the mechanisms causing it, and the efforts being made to combat it, Soroos asserts that present efforts to combat atmospheric pollution are inadequate. He contends that only vastly greater cooperation and coordination among nation-states will suffice to adequately address the challenge of global pollution.

Stahl, Shelly A., and Geoffrey Kemp. 1990. *Arms Control and Weapons Proliferation in the Middle East and South Asia.* New York: St. Martin's Press/Carnegie Endowment for International Peace. 248 pp. ISBN 0-87003-070-X.

In this anthology, a group of experts on the Middle East and South Asia examine the flow of advanced weapons systems to these areas and the difficulties such weapons cause. The essays also discuss ways in which arms control can work to improve regional security.

Stewart, George R., et al. 1994. *International Trade and Intellectual Property: The Search for a Balanced System.* Boulder, CO: Westview Press. 195 pp. ISBN 0-81332-160-3.

This collection of articles by a number of scholars examines the implications of intellectual property rights on international trade, taking account of major free trade agreements such as GATT and NAFTA.

Tamir, Yael. 1993. *Liberal Nationalism.* Princeton, NJ: Princeton University Press. 194 pp. ISBN 0-69107-893-9.

In this book, Tamir develops an argument in which she claims that nationalism, with its values of communalism, tradition, and personal bonds, can be made compatible with the salient values of liberalism—autonomy, freedom of expression, and freedom of choice.

Tarimo, E., and E. B. Webster. 1997. *Primary Health Care Concepts and Challenges in a Changing World: Alma-Ata Revisited.* Geneva: World Health Organization, Department of Publication. 118 pp.

This book reviews the conclusions of the Alma-Ata Conference, held in 1978, assessing the success of the primary health care approach and suggesting how it might be improved to better meet the world's health needs.

Trice, Robert, et al. 1995. *Corporate Diplomacy: Principled Leadership for the Global Community.* Washington, DC: Center for Strategic and International Studies. 51 pp. ISBN 0-89206-282-7.

A group of experts on the subject discuss ways in which corporations can play more active roles in building the global community, in light of the diminishing role of governments.

Turco, Richard P. 1996. *Earth under Siege: Air Pollution and Global Change.* New York: Oxford University Press. ISBN 0-19507-287-1.

This recent study of air pollution and acid rain, with a foreword by Carl Sagan, presents the basic scientific principles underlying the study of these pollutants. It discusses the mechanisms by which pollutants are produced and dispersed, and their likely consequences for the global climate.

Turshen, Meredith, and Briavel Holcomb. 1993. *Women's Lives and Public Policy: The International Experience.* Westport, CT: Greenwood Press. 217 pp. ISBN 0-31327-354-5.

This diverse collection of essays by various authors addresses a number of aspects of women's political and social status. Topics include economic policies, migration, sex and marriage, and violence, with emphasis on their consequences for women's lives.

Tussie, Diana, and David Glover, editors. 1993. *The Developing Countries in World Trade: Policies and Bargaining Strategies.* Boulder, CO: Lynne Rienner Publishers. 267 pp. ISBN 1-55587-384-7.

In this anthology, chapter authors examine the recent Global Agreement on Trade and Tariffs (GATT) negotiations from the perspective of several developing nations, including Mexico, Argentina, India, and Brazil.

UNESCO. 1996. *UNESCO Statistical Yearbook 1996.* Paris: UNESCO Publications. 900 pp. ISBN 9-23003-344-8.

An annual reference book, this work is designed to provide statistical information on education, science, technology, culture, and communications in 200 nations.

United Nations. 1996. *The Path to The Hague.* New York: United Nations Publications. 84 pp. ISBN 92-1-056702-1.

This publication contains major speeches, documents, and texts relevant to the International Criminal Tribunal for the former Yugoslavia.

Urquhart, Brian. 1989. *Decolonization and World Peace.* Austin: University of Texas Press. 121 pp. ISBN 0-29273-853-6.

Urquhart, with many years of experience as a U.N. official, examines the nature of the contemporary process of decolonization, the responsibility of the world community to respond to turmoil in recently decolonized nations, and the role that the United Nations can play in this effort.

Vernon, Raymond. 1977. *Storm over the Multinationals: The Real Issues.* Cambridge, MA: Harvard University Press. 260 pp. ISBN 0-67483-875-0.

This is an older but still helpful study of the multifaceted character of multinational corporations, their activities in developed and developing nations, and the controversies about their activities.

Vincent, R. J. 1974. *Nonintervention and International Order.* Princeton, NJ: Princeton University Press. 457 pp. ISBN 0-69105-652-8.

This is an exhaustive study of the principle of nonintervention, its history, its role in contemporary international politics, and its relevance to the achievement of international order.

Walker, Barbara, Norman Cousins, and the World Federalist Association. 1991. *The World Federalist Bicentennial Reader and Study Guide.* Washington, DC: World Federalist Association. 217 pp.

An anthology of essays commissioned by the World Federalist Association that examine the U.S. federal system, this work discusses a possible world federation and the relationship between the two federal systems.

Wallerstein, Michael, et al. 1993. *The Global Dimension of Intellectual Property Rights in Science and Technology.* Washington, DC: National Academy Press. 442 pp. ISBN 0-30904-833-8.

This broad-ranging collection of essays by a variety of authors examines aspects of intellectual property rights in the context of international relations and discusses how recent scientific and technological advances have brought these issues to the center of attention.

Walzer, Michael. 1977. *Just and Unjust Wars.* New York: Basic Books. 361 pp. ISBN 0-46503-704-6.

Walzer's widely read and influential book lays out the theoretical foundations for determining under what circumstances war is justified. It also examines the principles that guide the conduct of combatants within wars and presents a useful discussion of the issues involved in deciding responsibility for violation of the moral standards governing the conduct and initiation of war.

———. 1983. *Spheres of Justice.* New York: Basic Books. 345 pp. ISBN 0-46508-190-8.

Walzer's influential book develops the argument that genuinely effective moral bonds and constraints can only emerge within groups of people who share communal ties and have a common history. He is sharply critical of attempts to construct moral points of view that are global in scope and do not take account of personal and communal bonds and traditions.

Wardlaw, Grant. 1989. *Political Terrorism: Theory, Tactics, and Counter-Measures.* 2d ed. Cambridge, England: Cambridge University Press. 248 pp. ISBN 0-52136-296-2.

A useful analysis of the nature and types of terrorism and the motives that drive it, this study also has a lengthy examination of the various possible responses.

Weatherford, J. McIver. 1994. *Savages and Civilization: Who Will Survive?* New York: Crown. 310 pp. ISBN 0-5175886-09.

In this book, anthropologist Weatherford seeks to demonstrate the validity and worth of the values held by indigenous peoples, their contributions to modern culture, and their importance for addressing several of the problems currently facing humanity, such as ecology and the exploitation of natural resources.

Weatherford, Roy. 1993. *World Peace and the Human Family.* London and New York: Routledge. 172 pp. ISBN 0-41506-302-7.

The author examines the ideals of world peace and the global human family and discusses the feasibility of attaining and sustaining them by appropriate institutions.

Weintraub, Sidney. 1997. *NAFTA at Three: A Progress Report.* Washington, DC: Center for Strategic and International Studies. 120 pp. ISBN 0-89206-298-3.

Weintraub seeks to address concerns about the impact the North American Free Trade Agreement has had on the United States by examining data that reveal its consequences for the U.S. economy. He presents criteria by which he believes the agreement should be assessed and concludes that NAFTA has performed reasonably well.

Weisband, Edward, editor. 1989. *Poverty amidst Plenty: World Political Economy and Distributive Justice.* Boulder, CO: Westview Press. 270 pp. ISBN 0-81330-523-3.

The essays in this volume, by various authors, examine various aspects of the world economy and offer a variety of theoretical perspectives on its workings and on issues of global distributive justice.

Werther, Guntram F. A. 1992. *Self-Determination in Western Democracies: Aboriginal Politics in a Comparative Perspective.* Westport, CT: Greenwood Press. 113 pp. ISBN 0-31328-432-6.

This book is an analysis of various efforts by aboriginal peoples to gain a measure of self-determination in the nations where they reside and the responses of the national governments to their claims.

Wilkinson, Paul. 1986. *Terrorism and the Liberal State.* 2d ed. London: Macmillan. 322 pp. ISBN 0-33339-490-9.

Wilkinson explores the nature and justification of violent acts in general, the particular threat that terrorism poses to liberal states, and the responses that liberal states may make to terrorism without compromising the principles on which they stand.

Wolf, Aaron. 1995. *Hydropolitics along the Jordan River: Scarce Water and Its Impact on the Arab-Israeli Conflict.* Tokyo and New York: United Nations University Press. 251 pp. ISBN 9-2808-0859-1.

This book is a study of the conflict over access to the water of the Jordan River and the ways in which this conflict is likely to shape relations between Israel and its Arab neighbors in future years. It is an illuminating discussion of the crucial role that control of natural resources is likely to have in the future and its consequences for the security of nations.

Wongaman, J. Philip, editor. 1973. *The Population Crisis and Moral Responsibility.* Washington, DC: Public Affairs Press. 340 pp.

This anthology by various authors examines the relationship between ethical concerns and public policy formation in the area of population control.

World Health Organization. 1996. ***Biodiversity, Biotechnology, and Sustainable Development in Health and Agriculture: Emerging Connections.*** Geneva: World Health Organization, Division of Publication. 229 pp. ISBN 9-27511-560-5.

This collection of essays by specialists examines the extent to which the biodiversity of Latin America and the Caribbean may be utilized for economic benefit and the improvement of human health.

———. 1997. ***The World Health Report 1997: Conquering Suffering, Enriching Humanity.*** Geneva: World Health Organization, Division of Publication. 162 pp. ISBN 9-24156-185-8.

The latest of the annual WHO reports, this work assesses the current state of world health. It includes statistical analyses of world health problems, discussions of health trends, and analysis of prospects for the future.

Wriston, Walter. 1992. ***The Twilight of Sovereignty.*** New York: Charles Scribner's Sons. 192 pp. ISBN 0-68419-454-6.

The author, a noted executive and former U.S. presidential cabinet member, argues that worldwide computer linkages, advances in transportation, and the emerging global economy are conspiring to erode the sovereign powers of nation-states.

Yunker, James. 1993. ***World Union on the Horizon: The Case for Supernational Federation.*** Lanham, MD: University Press of America. 332 pp. ISBN 0-81919-037-3.

Yunker develops a proposal for creating a worldwide supernational federation, discusses the advantages of a system of this sort, and provides an assessment of the feasibility of such a system and the likelihood that it can be established.

Zuijdwijk, Ton J. M. 1982. ***Petitioning the United Nations.*** Hampshire, England: Gower. 397 pp. ISBN 0-55600-463-1.

Zuijdwijk offers a careful and thorough examination of efforts to provide avenues that would allow individuals to seek U.N. assistance in protecting human rights and the ways in which particular national governments have worked to short-circuit these endeavors.

# Reports

A number of agencies and organizations offer periodic reports on matters pertinent to international ethics.

Amnesty International. *Amnesty International Report 1997.* London: Amnesty International.

This is the annual report of an organization that has been very active in monitoring human rights violations across the globe. The 1997 report has information on violations of legal and human rights in 151 nations.

International Committee of the Red Cross. 1996. *Annual Report 1996.* Geneva: International Committee of the Red Cross.

Provides a narrative of the difficulties in various troubled parts of the globe, an account of ICRC activities in those locations, discussions of developments relevant to international humanitarian law, and discussion of prospects for the future.

Transparency International. 1996. *Transparency International Annual Report 1996.* Berlin: Transparency International.

This report presents an overview of progress in fighting corrupt business practices around the world.

U.S. Department of State. Bureau of Democracy, Human Rights, and Labor. 1996. *1996 Human Rights Reports.* Washington, DC: U.S. Department of State.

As a result of legislation passed in the U.S. Congress in 1974, the U.S. Department of State reports to Congress each year on the status of internationally recognized human rights in all nations receiving foreign aid from the United States and all nations that are members of the United Nations but do not receive foreign aid from the United States. The report is compiled from data received from U.S. embassies around the world.

World Bank. 1997. *World Development Report 1997: The State in a Changing World.* Oxford: Oxford University Press.

This is the annual World Bank report. The 1997 issue focuses on the nation-state and its evolving role in response to contemporary international trends.

Worldwatch Institute. 1997. *State of the World 1997: A Worldwatch Institute Report on Progress toward a Sustainable Society.* Washington, DC: Worldwatch Institute.

This is the annual Worldwatch Institute report on the world's progress toward addressing its environmental problems.

————. 1997. *Vital Signs 1997: The Environmental Trends That Are Shaping Our Future.* New York: W. W. Norton & Company.

This is the most recent of a series of annual reports from the Worldwatch Institute. Its researchers have gathered information on conditions around the world and have drawn conclusions regarding trends in the global environment, economy, and social stability.

# Journals

The following selected and annotated list includes journals published by organizations, governments, international bodies, and academic institutions that contain material pertinent to international ethics. A web address is included for journals that are available on the Internet.

### The Bulletin of the Atomic Scientists
6042 Kimbark Avenue
Chicago, IL 60637
Web site: http://www.bullatomsci.org

This is a journal that reports on issues of international security, military matters, and nuclear matters. It is supported by the Educational Foundation for Nuclear Science and traces its history to a plea made by Albert Einstein in 1946 for public education regarding the dangers of atomic weapons.

### The Bulletin of the World Health Organization
World Health Organization Headquarters
CH-1211 Geneva 27
Switzerland
Web site: http://www_pll.who.ch/programmes/pll/pll_index_frames.html

This is a bimonthly publication that has appeared since 1947. It publishes research findings that are relevant to human health.

### Environmental Matters
Environmental Department Publications
The World Bank
1818 H Street NW, Room S-5057
Washington, DC 20433
Web site: http://www-esd.worldbank.org/envmat

This publication of the World Bank is issued three times a year in both print and electronic media. It contains articles addressing issues such as biodiversity, water management, climate change, and pollution management.

### Foreign Policy
The Carnegie Endowment for International Peace
1779 Massachusetts Avenue NW
Washington, DC 20036
Web site: http://www.foreignpolicy.com

This journal has been published since 1970 by the Carnegie Endowment for International Peace. It appears four times a year and is devoted to discussing the issues that face U.S. foreign policy makers.

### Fourth World Journal
Center for World Indigenous Studies
1001 Cooper Point Road SW, Suite 140-214
Olympia, WA 98502
E-mail: FWJ@speakeasy.org
Web site: http://www.halcyon.com/FWDP

This is an on-line quarterly journal that publishes articles on politics, culture, society, economics, and science as they pertain to indigenous peoples.

### The Human Rights Brief
The Center for Human Rights and Humanitarian Law
Washington College of Law, American University
4801 Massachusetts Avenue NW
Washington, DC 20016-8084

This journal is a publication of the Center for Human Rights and Humanitarian Law. It appears three times a year and reports on contemporary human rights and humanitarian law issues.

### Human Rights Quarterly
The Johns Hopkins University Press
701 West 40th Street, Suite 275
Baltimore, MD 21211-2190

This journal is published four times per year and carries articles addressing various aspects of human rights.

### Human Rights Research and Education Bulletin
Human Rights Research and Education Centre
University of Ottawa
67 Louis-Pasteur Street, P.O. Box 450, Station A
Ottawa, Ontario, Canada K1N 6N5

This bulletin generally appears two or three times a year and has articles addressing various human rights issues.

### International Migration
International Organization for Migration
P.O. Box 71
CH-1211 Geneva 19
Switzerland

This periodical is published four times a year and contains important documents pertaining to migration as well as articles and reports of relevant conferences.

### International Peacekeeping News
Editor
53 Campus Road
Bradford DB7 1HR
England (UK)
Web site: http://csf.colorado.edu/dfax/ipn/ipnblrb.htm

This is a bimonthly journal published jointly by the University of Bradford, School of Peace Studies, and the Farndon House Information Trust. It has been in publication since 1994, providing updates on peacekeeping activities around the world. It contains commentary on theoretical issues of peacekeeping as well as examination of the practical aspects of peacekeeping, such as training and logistics.

### International Review of the Red Cross
International Committee of the Red Cross
17, avenue de la Paix
CH-1211 Geneva
Switzerland
Web site: http://www.icrc.ch/unicc/icrcnews.nsf/

This journal is published six times per year and offers articles on international law as it pertains to humanitarian aid.

### Journal of International Refugee Law
Oxford University Press
Walton Street
Oxford OX2 6DP
England (UK)

It appears four times a year and contains articles on refugee law and policies.

*Transition*
Macroeconomics and Growth Division
The World Bank
1818 H Street NW, Room N11-025
Washington, DC 20433

This is a bimonthly newsletter published by the World Bank that examines the economic and social difficulties faced by postsocialist and socialist economies undergoing market-oriented reform.

*UNESCO Courier*
31, rue François Bonvin
757321 Paris Cédex 15
France
Web site: http://www.unesco.org/general/eng/publish/courier/index.html

This UNESCO monthly is published in 30 languages. It is designed to serve as a cultural magazine, an international forum, and a champion of human rights.

*World Health Forum*
World Health Organization Headquarters
CH-1211 Geneva 27
Switzerland
Web site: http://www_pll.who.ch/programmes/pll/pll_index_frames.html

This journal has been published four times per year, since 1980, by the World Health Organization. It is a forum for discussion of public health policies, reasons for policy failure or success, and ways in which policies can be improved.

*World Health Statistics Quarterly*
World Health Organization Headquarters
CH-1211 Geneva 27
Switzerland
Web site: http://www_pll.who.ch/programmes/pll/pll_index_frames.html

This journal of the WHO provides statistical data and analysis based on information collected in 190 nations with the purpose of identifying health problems and trends, monitoring the success of therapies, and forecasting future trends.

*World Watch*
Worldwatch Institute
1776 Massachusetts Avenue NW
Washington, DC 20036
Web site: http://www.worldwatch.org/mag/index.html

This magazine is published by the Worldwatch Institute six times a year. It is devoted to covering issues that have an impact on the earth's long-term health. These range from problems of global warming and threats to biodiversity to the ecological consequences of the consumer culture.

# CONTEMPORARY ETHICAL ISSUES

## Chapter 7:
## Selected Nonprint
## Resources

M any sources offer videotapes and CD-ROMs
with presentations pertinent to international
ethics. This chapter lists a sample of visual materials in those formats. Because the Internet is an increasingly necessary research tool, an array of
helpful web sites is also included.

## Videotapes

**Ambassador of Goodwill**
*Length:*    14 min.
*Date:*    1991
*Source:*    UNHCHR
    United Nations Plaza
    New York, NY 10017

This brief film outlines the activities of the U.N.
High Commissioner for Human Rights.

**Development and the Environment:**
**A New Partnership**
*Length:*    26 min.
*Date:*    1992
*Source:*    The World Bank
    1818 H Street NW
    Washington, DC 20433

This film offers a broad overview of the relation between economic development and environmental protection.

**Greenhouse Crisis: The American Response**
*Length:*      11 min.
*Date:*        1989
*Source:*      The Union of Concerned Scientists
               2 Brattle Square
               Cambridge, MA 02238–9105

A video that discusses the relation between energy use in the United States and global warming.

**Panorama 1996**
*Length:*      13.5 min.
*Date:*        1996
*Source:*      International Committee of the Red Cross
               19, avenue de la Paix
               CH-1202 Geneva
               Switzerland

This film gives a broad overview of humanitarian concerns in 1996. It portrays the horrors of war and reminds nations of their obligation, based on international law, to make efforts to ensure that the rights of victims of war are respected. The film also provides an overview of ICRC activities during the year, with an emphasis on its effort to achieve a global ban on the use of antipersonnel land mines.

# CD-ROMs

Amnesty International. **Amnesty Interactive Human Rights Education CD-ROM.** Distributed by The Voyager Company.

This interactive presentation covers the history of human rights and examines matters that influence human freedom around the globe.

International Committee of the Red Cross. **International Humanitarian Law.** Geneva: International Committee of the Red Cross.

This CD-ROM has information on 89 treaties and other documents of international humanitarian law, commentaries on the Geneva Conventions, and lists of nations that have signed international humanitarian law treaties.

———. **Random Ambush.** Geneva: International Committee of the Red Cross.

A multimedia presentation designed to enhance awareness of the dangers posed by land mines.

Organization for Economic Cooperation and Development. **OECD Health Data 97 Edition.** Paris: OECD.

This CD-ROM provides data on significant health indicators for 27 nations for the period from 1960 to 1994.

————. **The OECD Statistical Compendium.** Paris: OECD.

This is a compendium of 280,000 monthly, quarterly, and annual data series from OECD resources. The data series includes agriculture and food; development aid; economic and financial indicators; energy; and industry, science, and technology.

World Bank. **Toward Gender Equality.** Washington, DC: World Bank.

A report that relies on case studies to examine ways in which public policy can be employed to enhance social and economic opportunities for women.

# Internet Resources

The Internet is an enormously useful source of information on issues of international ethics. The following annotated list includes electronic archives and links to various other Internet sources.

### AAAS Directory of Human Rights Resources on the Internet
http://shr.aaas.org/dhr.htm

This site is maintained by the Science and Human Rights Committee of the American Association for the Advancement of Science. It offers an archive, a bulletin board, a search facility, and links to other sites.

### Amazing Environmental Organization WebDirectory
http://www.webdirectory.com

A web directory and search facility designed to give quick access to the major topics in ecology.

### ConflictNet
http://www.igc.org/igc/conflictnet/index.html

This site was established as a forum for dialogue and transfer of information between groups and individuals working to establish ways to resolve conflicts in an appropriate, nonviolent fashion. It has links to other sites, archives, bulletins, action alerts, and a search facility.

### EcoNet
http://www.igc.org/igc/econet

A site maintained by EcoNet/IGC. It is an archive of information on major topics in ecology.

### EnviroLink Library
http://www.envirolink.org/envirogov.html

This site is maintained by EnviroLink, a nonprofit, grassroots organization dedicated to providing information on environmental issues. The site offers an on-line newsletter, an archive of documents, links to other sites, and a search facility.

### Environmental Links Page of the Environment and Natural Resources Information Center (ENRIC)
http://www.info.usaid.gov/environment/enric/cities.htm

A site maintained by the U.S. Agency for International Development that has links to other sites containing information about environmental issues.

### The Foreign and International Law Web
http://www.wuacc.edu/forint/forintmain.html

This is a site maintained by the Washburn University School of Law Library. It provides links to foreign and international law resources, research aids, and web sites.

### ILOEX
http://www.unirc.org/ilo/public/english/50normes/infleg/iloeng/index.htm

This site is maintained by the International Labor Organization. It contains an extensive archive of documents, legislation, and reports related to international labor standards.

### The Indigenous Peoples Page
http://www.igc.org/igc/issues/ip/index.html

This page contains links to the web sites of organizations related to the culture and interests of indigenous peoples.

### Institute for Global Communications
http://www.igc.org/igc

This site was established to link social activist groups and organizations, including those concerned with women's issues, ecology, and world peace.

### International Trade Law Monitor
http://ra,irv.uit.no/trade_law/itlp.html

This site contains an archive of documents relevant to issues of international trade law and provides links to other servers with information on international trade law. It is currently hosted by the law faculty at the University of Tronso, Norway.

## LaborNet
http://www.igc.org/igc/labornet/index.html

This site was established to support human rights and to encourage economic justice for laborers by providing news, information, and training for labor groups and unions. It has links to other sites, news bulletins, action alerts, archives, and a search facility.

## Natural Resources Research Information Pages
http://sfbox.vt.edu:10021/Y/yfleung/forestry.html

This site is maintained at the Department of Forestry at Virginia Tech and is designed to serve as a guide to Internet sources with information on natural resources and the environment.

## PeaceNet
http://www.igc.org/igc/peacenet/index.html

This site is devoted to transmitting information relevant to efforts to achieve peace, social and economic justice, racial harmony, and human rights. It contains bulletins, action alerts, links to other sites, archives, and a search facility.

## ReliefWeb
http://www.reliefweb.int

This is an electronic archive maintained by the U.N. Department of Humanitarian Affairs that offers practical information to those engaged in humanitarian assistance.

## Rule of Law Online
http://www.rol.org

This site was founded in 1994 with a grant from the U.S. Agency for International Development and is sponsored by the U.S. National Institute of Justice in the U.S. Department of Justice. Its mission is to provide a multilingual World Wide Web–based information server that will facilitate the transfer of U.S. democratic experience to those in the states of the former Soviet Union who are laboring to construct democratically based systems of law.

## United Nations International Criminal Tribunal for the Former Yugoslavia (UNICTY) Page
http://www.un.org/icty/index.html

A web site maintained by the United Nations that offers documents, press releases, and case records relevant to the International Criminal Tribunal for the former Yugoslavia.

## University of Minnesota Human Rights Library
http://www.umn.edu/humanrts

An ample archive of documents pertaining to human rights. It also has links to other servers with human rights documents.

## WomensNet
http://www.igc.org/igc/womensnet/index.html

This site was designed to support the activities of women's organizations by facilitating the transmission of information. It has links to other sites, archives, news releases, action alerts, and a search facility.

## WWW Virtual Library: Demography and Population Studies (CERN/ANU)
http://coombs.anu.au/ResFacilities/DemographyPage.html

A site maintained at Australian National University to provide information on demography. It currently has links to 155 other sites.

# CONTEMPORARY ETHICAL ISSUES

## Chapter 8:
## Directory of
## Organizations

The following list includes selected international, governmental, and private organizations that are active in matters of international ethics. A number of the organizations listed here offer publications useful for the study of issues of international ethics. They are included under the headings "Reports" and "Journals" in Chapter 6.

**American Red Cross**
780 Third Avenue, 28th Floor
New York, NY 10017
Phone: (212) 371-0770
Fax: (212) 838-5397
E-mail: info@usa.redcross.org
Web site: http://www.redcross.org

The American Red Cross is a volunteer organization with chapters in all states. At present, it has 1.5 million volunteers assisting in its programs. It is devoted to providing disaster relief, helping people prepare for and respond to disasters, collecting and distributing blood, and providing assistance to the members of the U.S. armed forces and their families. *See also* International Committee of the Red Cross.

**Amnesty International**
322 Eighth Avenue
New York, NY 10001
Phone: (598) 242-8848
Fax: (598) 242-8849
E-mail: aimember@aiusa.org
Web site: http://www.amnesty.org

Amnesty International's history began in 1961. Early that year, London attorney Peter Berenson began a campaign for the release of prisoners of conscience. His campaign spread to other nations, and Amnesty International was founded later in the year. At present, it has more than 1 million members active in more than 150 nations. It seeks fair trials, an end to abuse and torture of prisoners, and the release of prisoners of conscience. Its members pursue these ends by collecting reports of human rights abuses and working to verify them, initiating campaigns of letter writing on behalf of prisoners, and taking other action on behalf of individual prisoners.

**The Arms Control Association (ACA)**
1726 M Street NW, Suite 201
Washington, DC 20036
Phone: (202) 463-8270
Fax: (202) 463-8273
E-mail: aca@armscontrol.org
Web site: http://www.armscontrol.org

The ACA was founded in 1971 as a nonpartisan organization devoted to promoting public understanding of and support for arms control.

**CARE**
151 Ellis Street NE
Atlanta, GA 30303-2439
Phone: (404) 681-2552
Fax: (404) 577-5761
E-mail: info@care.org
Web site: http://www.care.org

CARE began in 1945, when a group of U.S. citizens joined together to send relief supplies to the survivors of World War II. It now has a staff of 9,000 and manages more than 340 relief programs in 63 nations. Its primary concern is to provide assistance in the areas of emergency relief and rehabilitation, education, and health.

**The Carnegie Endowment for International Peace**
2400 N Street NW
Washington, DC 20037-1153
Phone: (202) 862-7900

Fax: (202) 862-2610
E-mail: info@ceip.org
Web site: http://ceip.org

Established in 1910 with funds donated by Andrew Carnegie, the Carnegie Endowment supports research, discussion, and education in international affairs and U.S. foreign policy.

### The Carter Center
453 Freedom Parkway
Atlanta, GA 30307
Phone: (404) 331-3900
E-mail: carterweb@emory.edu
Web site: http://www.emory.edu/CARTER_CENTER

The Carter Center, founded by U.S. President Jimmy Carter and his wife Rosalynn in 1982, is funded primarily by private donations. It is devoted to fighting disease, hunger, poverty, conflict, and oppression by supporting programs in the areas of democratization and development, global health, and urban revitalization. It has 13 core programs that affect people in 65 countries around the world.

### The Center for Human Rights and Humanitarian Law
Washington College of Law
American University
4810 Massachusetts Avenue NW
Washington, DC 20016-8084
Phone: (202) 274-4180
Fax: (202) 274-4130
E-mail: humlaw@wcl.american.edu
Web site: http://www.wci.american.edu/pub/humright/home.htm

This program at the Washington College of Law of American University works to promote human rights and the advancement of humanitarian law by offering training programs for jurists and helping emerging nations develop laws and institutions to protect human rights.

### Center for World Indigenous Studies
1001 Cooper Point Road SW, Suite 140-214
Olympia, WA 98502
Phone: (888) 286-2947
E-mail: jburrows@halcyon.com
Web site: http://www.halycon.com/FWDP

This independent, nonprofit organization conducts research and education promoting the understanding and appreciation of indigenous peoples.

## Centers for Disease Control and Prevention (CDC)
1600 Clifton Road NE
Atlanta, GA 30333
Phone: (404) 639-3311
E-mail: netinfo@cdc.gov
Web site: http://www.cdc.gov

The CDC is an agency of the U.S. government, the primary mission of which is to promote health and improve the quality of human life by preventing disease, injury, and disability. It serves this mission by monitoring public health, detecting and investigating health problems, conducting research to improve prevention of disease, and devising public health strategies. It has 11 centers and offices scattered across the United States and sends teams around the world to investigate outbreaks of disease.

## Chemical and Biological Arms Control Institute (CBACI)
2111 Eisenhower Avenue, Suite 302
Washington, DC 22314
Phone: (703) 739-1538
Fax: (703) 739-1525
E-mail: cbaci@capitol.net
Web site: http://www.capitol.net/~cbaci

CBACI is a nonprofit organization created to promote arms control and nonproliferation, with special emphasis on chemical and biological weapons. It pursues these goals by employing an international network to support a program of research, analysis, and education.

## The Coalition for International Justice
American Bar Association
740 Fifteenth Street NW, Eighth Floor
Washington, DC 20005-1009
Phone: (202) 662-1595
Fax: (202) 662-1597
E-mail: jheffernan@cij.org
Web site: http://www.cij.org/cij

This international, nongovernmental support network was created under the auspices of the American Bar Association to provide the International War Crimes Tribunal with technical assistance and support. The Tribunal was established to try those accused of war crimes in the former Yugoslavia and in Rwanda.

## Doctors without Borders USA, Inc.
11 East 26th Street, Suite 1904
New York, NY 10010
Phone: (212) 679-6800

Fax: (212) 679-7016
E-mail: dwh@newyork.msf.org
Web site: http://www.dwb.org/index.htm
*See* Médecins sans Frontières.

## Friends of the Earth–United States (FOE)
1025 Vermont Avenue NW
Washington, DC 20005-6303
Phone: (202) 783-7400
Fax: (202) 783-0444
E-mail: FOE@foe.org
Web site: http://www.foe.org

FOE–United States, active since 1969, is one of 54 FOE advocacy groups scattered around the world. The organization is devoted to protecting the planet from environmental degradation; preserving biological, cultural, and ethnic diversity; and empowering citizens to give input to decisions that affect their lives. FOE–United States has three main program areas: lobbying governments to change economic policies that harm the environment; encouraging citizen initiation of global action projects to promote sustainable development and work for environmental justice; and helping communities to address their environmental problems.

## The Global Warming International Center
22W381 75th Street
Naperville, IL 60565-9245
Phone: (630) 910-1551
Fax: (630) 910-1561
E-mail: krreddy@csrumsu.ars.ag.gov
Web site: http://www.www2.msstate.edu/~krreddy/glowar

This international body sponsors research and disseminates information on global warming.

## Human Rights Watch
485 Fifth Avenue
New York, NY 10017-6104
Phone: (212) 972-8400
Fax: (212) 972-0905
E-mail: hrwnyc@hrw.org
Web site: http://www.hrw.org

Founded in 1978 as the Helsinki Watch, this group was formed in response to calls for assistance from several officials in Eastern Europe who desired help in monitoring their nations' compliance with the Helsinki Accords. By 1987, the organization had developed techniques for monitoring human rights abuses all over the world and had established a network of regional human rights watch centers. It currently works to combat abuses of human rights by gathering information on violations of human rights through investigations in nations where abuses are reported. It then makes use of the information gathered to publicize human rights violations and to enlist the support of other agencies in putting pressure on rights violators.

### International Alliance of Women (IAW)
1 Lycavittou Street
GR-10672 Athens
Greece
Phone: 30-1-362-6111
Fax: 30-1-362-2454

The IAW was originally founded in Berlin, Germany, in 1904, as the International Women Suffrage Alliance. It now has 80 affiliate groups as well as individual and honorary members scattered across the globe. Its goals are to work for reforms necessary to achieve equality of "liberty, status, and opportunity" between women and men in all aspects of human life.

### International Business Ethics Institute
1129 20th Street NW, Suite 400
Washington, DC 20036
Phone: (202) 296-6938
Fax: (202) 296-5897
E-mail: INFO@BUSINESS-ETHICS.ORG

Web site: http://www.business-ethics.org
A nonprofit educational organization, the International Business Ethics Institute is dedicated to the mission of encouraging business practices that promote equitable economic development, resource stability, and democratic governmental practices.

### International Committee of the Red Cross (ICRC)
19, avenue de la Paix
CH-1202 Geneva
Switzerland
Phone: (41-22) 734-6001
Fax: (41-22) 733-2057
E-mail: webmaster.gva@icrc.org
Web site: http://www.icrc.ch
Contact: Public Information Division

Founded in 1863 by Jean-Henri Dunant, a Swiss citizen, the International Committee of the Red Cross has received a mandate from the international community to assist victims of war and violence within nations, and to help nations and people apply humanitarian standards restraining the use of armed violence. The ICRC is currently active helping victims of violence in 50 nations around the world. *See also* American Red Cross.

## International Labor Organization (ILO)

CH-1211 Geneva 22
Switzerland
Phone: (41-22) 799-7940
Fax: (41-22) 788-3894
Web site: http://www.ilo.org/public/english/index.htm
Contact: Bureau of Public Information

The International Labor Organization was created in 1919, following World War I. It subsequently became a part of the League of Nations, and it is the only part of the League of Nations that survived to become part of the United Nations. It became the first specialized agency of the United Nations in 1946. Its broad mandate is to work to achieve social justice and the advancement of recognized human rights and laborers' rights.

## International Monetary Fund (IMF)

700 19th Street NW
Washington, DC 20431
Phone: (202) 623-7300
Fax: (202) 623-2728
E-mail: webmaster@imf.org
Web site: http://www.imf.org
Contact: IMF External Relations Department

The International Monetary Fund was established at a conference in Bretton Woods, New Hampshire, in 1944, and began operations in 1947. Its primary purposes are to nurture monetary cooperation among the world's nations, encourage the expansion of international trade, and assist member nations that are having difficulty meeting their external balance-of-payments obligations. It works to achieve these goals by preserving a stable system for the sale of currency among its members and providing loans to members who are temporarily having difficulty meeting their balance-of-payments obligations. At present, it counts 181 nations among its members. It has current loan projects with 60 nations, and made loans totaling more than $40 billion in 1996.

## International Organization for Migration (IOM International)

17, route des Morillons, P.O. Box 71
CH-1211 Geneva 19
Switzerland
Phone: (41-22) 717-9111
Fax: (41-22) 798-6150
E-mail: telex@geneva.iom.ch
Web site: http://www.iom.ch

IOM is an intergovernmental body devoted to working with governments and other agencies to assure orderly migration processes. Its goals include advancing the understanding of migration, encouraging social and economic development through migration, assisting in improving the systems controlling migration, and supporting the well-being of migrants. It has been in existence since 1951 and has assisted more than 9 million people.

### International Rescue Committee (IRC)
122 East 42nd Street
New York, NY 10165
Phone: (212) 551-3000
Fax: (212) 551-3180
E-mail: bode@intrescom.org
Web site: http://www.intrescom.org

The IRC was founded in 1933 at the request of Albert Einstein to assist those fleeing the Nazis. At present, it is at work in 23 nations and is providing assistance to more than 25 million refugees. It provides assistance of several types: For refugees in emergency situations, it works to provide the necessities of life, such as food, water, sanitation, shelter, and health care. In stable situations where refugees are unable to return to their homelands, the IRC helps them to adjust to their lives in exile. Finally, for some of those unable to return to their homelands, the IRC works to help them gain residence in the United States.

### International Society of Business, Economics and Ethics (ISBEE)
Department of Philosophy
University of Kansas
Lawrence, KS 66045
Phone: (913) 864-3976
E-mail: georges.enderle.1@nd.edu
Web site: http://www.nd.edu/~isbee

This society was organized to promote discussion and exchange of information among academics, businesses, and professional societies on ethical issues pertinent to international business and economics.

### Médecins sans Frontières (Doctors without Borders)
MSF-International
Rue de la Tourelle 39
1040 Brussels
Belgium
Phone: (322) 280-1881
Fax: (322) 280-0173
E-mail: office-intnl@brussels.msf.org
Web site: http://www.msf.org

This private, nonprofit humanitarian organization was founded by physicians in 1971. Its mission is to provide humanitarian aid to populations in crisis in all parts of the world, and in some cases, to publicize violations of human rights. The organization relies on the voluntary service of health professionals and has local chapters in 19 countries. In 1995, it had 2,520 volunteers in association with 12,000 local staff in 70 nations of the world, ranging from Zaire and Rwanda to the former Yugoslavia and the Caucasus region.

## Open Society Institute–New York

888 Seventh Avenue
New York, NY 10106
Phone: (212) 757-2323
Fax: (212) 974-0367
E-mail: osnews@sorosny.org
Web site: http://www.soros.org

The Open Society Institute–New York is one of more than 24 autonomous organizations around the world supported by the Soros Foundations. It works to promote open societies in all parts of the world, both by awarding grants to others and by operating its own programs. It works to create open societies by operating or supporting programs in areas such as education; communications; human rights; and social, legal, and economic reform.

## Organization for Economic Cooperation and Development (OECD)

2, rue André-Pascal
75775 Paris Cédex 16, France
Phone: (33-01) 4524-8200
Fax: (33-01) 4524-8500
E-mail: news.contact@oecd.org
Web site: http://www.oecd.org

The OECD, founded in 1961, is the descendant of an international organization formed to coordinate reconstruction in the aftermath of World War II. Today's organization has 29 members from among the industrialized democracies and provides a forum for the examination and construction of optimal social and economic policies. Its goals include high rates of sustainable growth for its members and other nations, sound policies of economic expansion, and the promotion of global free trade.

## Oxfam America

26 West Street
Boston, MA 02111-1206
Phone: (617) 482-1211
Fax: (617) 728-2596
E-mail: oxfamusa@igc.apc.org
Web site: http://www.interaction.org/ia/mb/oxfam.html

Oxfam America has been operating since 1970. Since then, it has provided more than $100 million in financial aid and technical support for community-based organizations in all parts of the world. At present, it makes more than 250 grants each year to individuals and organizations around the world that are working to improve the lives of the poor. Its goals are to increase food security, improve health and education, protect the rights of women and indigenous peoples, and encourage public awareness and discussion of issues related to poverty. Its policy is to seek small projects where modest amounts of money can make a significant difference in poor people's lives. *See also* Oxfam International.

## Oxfam International
274 Banbury Road
Oxford OX2 7DZ, England
Phone: (44-1865) 311-311
E-mail: oxfam@glastonbury
Web site: http://www.oneworld.org/oxfam

Oxfam International has its roots in the Oxford Committee for Famine Relief, which was founded in Oxford in 1942 with the purpose of assisting refugees and providing emergency help to those in need. Currently, there are 12 regional Oxfam organizations across the world, and Oxfam International was created in 1995 as a partnership of the individual groups. The Oxfam International partnership now operates in more than 120 nations and raises about $350 million each year to carry out its activities. The partnership is dedicated to relieving poverty and suffering in all corners of the globe and to educating the public about poverty. *See also* Oxfam America.

## PEN American Center
568 Broadway
New York, NY 10012
Phone: (212) 334-1660
Fax: (212) 334-2181
E-mail: pen@echonyc.com
Internet site: gopher://gopher.igc.apc.org5000/11/int/pen

PEN was founded in 1921 in London by John Galsworthy to nurture understanding among men and women of letters across the globe. At present, it has more than 120 centers in the nations of the world and a total membership of more than 10,000. Members are selected by the PEN Membership Committee. PEN's membership includes authors of literary works as well as those who have been active in literature in some other fashion, such as by working as editors. PEN supports human rights generally, but it is particularly dedicated to supporting freedom of expression. Its primary mode of action is waging campaigns of letters and faxes in behalf of individuals and groups whose freedom of expression is imperiled.

**PEN International.**

*See* PEN American Center.

**Physicians for Human Rights**
110 Boylston Street
Suite 702
Boston, MA 02116
Phone: (617) 695-0041
Fax: (617) 695-0307
E-mail: phrusa@igc.apc.org
Internet site: gopher://gopher.igc.org5000/00/int/phr

Physicians for Human Rights is an organization of health professionals, scientists, and concerned citizens dedicated to employing the knowledge and skills of forensic science and medicine in investigating violations of humanitarian law and human rights. It has existed since 1986 and has sent teams to several different nations, including Bosnia, Turkey, and El Salvador, to gather information on possible violations of human rights.

**The Population Institute**
107 Second Street NE
Washington, DC 20002
Phone: (202) 544-3300
Fax: (202) 544-0068
E-mail: web@populationinstitute.org
Web site: http://www.populationinstitute.org

The Population Institute is dedicated to achieving global population stability and encouraging future generations of population activists. Its activities are focused in three areas: advocating policy initiatives to the U.S. government, recruiting and encouraging future leaders in population control activism, and providing public information on issues of population control. It has members in 160 nations.

**Project HOPE**
P.O. Box 250
Millwood, VA 22646-0250
Phone: (800) 544-4673
Fax: (540) 837-1813
Web site: http://www.projhope.org

This project began in 1960 with the SS *HOPE*, a nonmilitary hospital ship, which provided medical services to people in the South Pacific. The ship was retired in 1974, and the organization evolved into Project HOPE (Health Opportunity for People Everywhere), dedicated to offering medical training and health care assistance. At present, it has 45 health care and assistance programs in 20 nations across the world. It aids an estimated 1 million people each year and distributes more than $80 million in aid.

## Stockholm International Peace Research Institute (SIPRI)
Frösunda
S-169-70 Solna
Sweden
Phone: (46-8) 655-9700
Fax: (46-8) 655-9733
E-mail: sipri@sipri.se
Web site: http://www.sipri.se

SIPRI was established by the Swedish Parliament, at the request of Prime Minister Tage Erlander, in 1966. It is an independent organization funded by the Swedish government and other sources. Its mission is to seek to understand the conditions for achieving stable peace and peaceful resolutions to international conflicts. It serves these ends by conducting research focused on armaments, the limitation and reduction of arms, and the control of arms.

## Transparency International (TI)
Otto-Suhr-Allee 97-99
D-10585 Berlin
Germany
Phone: 49-30-343-820-0
Fax: 49-30-347-039-12
E-mail: webmaster@transparency.de
Web site: http://www.transparency.de

This nonprofit, nongovernmental organization is devoted to combating corruption in international business transactions and transactions within nations. It pursues these goals by working to establish national and international coalitions to urge governments to establish and implement effective laws to prohibit corruption, by building public support for anticorruption legislation, and by gathering information related to issues of corruption.

## Union of Concerned Scientists
2 Brattle Square
Cambridge, MA 02238-9105
Phone: (617) 547-5552
Fax: (617) 864-9405
E-mail: ucs@ucsusa.org
Web site: http://www.ucsusa.org

The Union of Concerned Scientists was founded at the Massachusetts Institute of Technology in 1969 by faculty and students concerned about the misuse of science and technology. At present, it receives support from more than

70,000 people across the globe. The group's primary goals are the achievement of global security and the global sustainability of natural resources. It conducts technical studies, carries out public education, and attempts to influence governmental policy in the areas of global warming, transportation, natural resources, energy, agriculture, and arms control.

## United Nations Children's Fund (UNICEF)
UNICEF House
3 United Nations Plaza
New York, NY 10017
Phone: (212) 326-7000
Fax: (212) 888-7465
E-mail: netmaster@unicef.org
Web site: http://www.unicef.org

UNICEF was founded in 1946 and is dedicated to seeking the protection of children's rights and to helping them achieve their full potential. It sponsors activities to help children in more than 140 nations, particularly in the areas of health, education, and sanitation.

## United Nations Development Fund for Women (UNIFEM)
304 East 45th Street, Sixth Floor
New York, NY 10017
Phone: (212) 906-6400
Fax: (212) 906-6705
E-mail: unifem@undp.org
Web site: http://www.unifem.undp.org

UNIFEM's mandate is to support the economic and political empowerment of women in developing nations and to serve as a catalyst for issues of concern to women within the United Nations. It is based in New York but has regional advisers in other parts of the world. It was created in 1976 and became an autonomous agency in 1985.

## United Nations Educational, Scientific, and Cultural Organization (UNESCO)
7, place de Fontenoy
75352 Paris 07 SP
France
Phone: (33-1) 45-68-1000
Fax: (33-1) 45-67-1690
Web site: http://www.unesco.org

The constitution of UNESCO came into force in 1946. It currently has 185 member nations, and its mandate is to promote human peace and security by encouraging collaboration among nations in education, science, and culture. It serves this mandate by means of five major functions: producing studies of the future state of education, science, and culture in the world; advancing and transferring knowledge through research and training; setting international standards; providing expertise for its member states; and encouraging the exchange of specialized information.

## United Nations High Commissioner for Human Rights/ Centre for Human Rights (UNHCHR)

Palais des Nations, 8-14, Avenue de la Paix
CH-1211 Geneva 10, Switzerland
Phone: (41-22) 917-3456
Fax: (41-22) 917-0213
E-mail: webadmin.hchr@unorg.ch
Web site: http://www.unhchr.ch/

This post was created in 1993 by the General Assembly of the United Nations. The high commissioner is appointed by the U.N. secretary-general with the approval of the General Assembly. Its function is to promote and protect all human rights. It is composed of three branches. The Research and Right to Development Branch has the mandate of gathering and analyzing information pertinent to the support and protection of human rights. The Support Services Branch has the task of assisting other U.N. human rights bodies. The Activities and Programmes Branch is devoted to providing assistance to nations and regions suffering from protracted violence and human rights violations, such as the former Yugoslavia and Rwanda.

## United Nations High Commissioner for Refugees (UNHCR)

UNHCR Public Information
P.O. Box 2500
1211 Geneva 2, Switzerland
Phone: (41-22) 739-8502
Fax: (41-22) 739-7314/15/16
E-mail: HQPI00@UNHCR.CR
Web site: http://unhcr.ch//

The office of the U.N. High Commissioner for Refugees was created by the General Assembly of the United Nations in 1951 to carry out the task of resettling 1.2 million refugees created by World War II. At present, it is assisting approximately 26 million people in 140 nations. It has offices in 115 nations and a staff of 5,000. Its mandate is to protect refugees from physical harm; to assist them by providing food, shelter, health care, and sanitation; and to seek permanent settlement for them.

## United States Agency for International Development (USAID)

320 21st Street NW
Washington, DC 20253-0016
Phone: (202) 647-1850

Fax: (202) 647-8321
E-mail: pinquiries@usaid.gov
Web site: http://www.info.usaid.gov

USAID is a governmental agency established in 1961 by President John Kennedy with the goal of providing economic and humanitarian assistance to nations around the world in order to advance U.S. political and economic interests. Its activities are varied and include supporting immunization and family planning programs in developing nations and assisting governments in transition to democracy.

**United States Peace Corps**
1990 K Street NW
Washington, DC 20526
Phone: (202) 606-3360
Fax: (202) 606-1371
E-mail: blonardo@peacecorps.gov
Web site: http://www.peacecorps.gov/

The U.S. Peace Corps began with an Executive Order signed by President John Kennedy on 1 March 1961. Its task is to promote world peace and understanding by sending skilled volunteers to nations that request assistance. Volunteers are U.S. citizens who serve a two-year term and receive special training from the Peace Corps for the activities they will perform. There are 6,500 volunteers serving at present in more than 90 nations around the world.

**U.S. Arms Control and Disarmament Agency (ACDA)**
320 21st Street
Washington, DC 20451
Phone: (800) 581-2232
Fax: (202) 647-6928
E-mail: webmaster@acda.org
Web site: http://www.acda.org

The ACDA's mission is to strengthen U.S. security by developing, advocating, negotiating, and implementing arms control, weapons nonproliferation, and disarmament policies, strategies, and agreements among nations. At present, its goals include the implementation of the Chemical Weapons Convention, ratification and implementation of the Comprehensive Test Ban Treaty, strengthening of the Nuclear Nonproliferation Treaty, and negotiation of an antipersonnel land mines agreement.

**World Bank**
1818 H Street NW
Washington, DC 20433
Phone: (202) 473-3798
Fax: (202) 522-2632/3

Web site: http://www.worldbank.org
Contact: Chief of Media Relations

The World Bank began operations in spring 1946. Its initial purpose was to help finance the reconstruction of the war-devastated economies of Western Europe and Japan. Today, it is a group of five separate institutions, all dedicated to providing loans for projects in developing nations around the world. It works to promote growth in these nations by supporting projects to improve infrastructure, undertake economic reform, and gain technical assistance. In 1996, these organizations were able to provide well over $20 billion in loans to support more than 250 projects.

### World Health Organization (WHO)
CH-1211 Geneva 27
Switzerland
Phone: (41-22) 791-2111
Fax: (41-22) 791-0746
E-mail: inf@who.ch
Web site: http://www.who.ch

The constitution of the WHO was adopted by its members in 1946 and became effective in 1948. It currently has 190 nation-states as members. The WHO's constitution is based on the principle that the attainment of the highest possible level of health is the right of each human being. To serve this principle, the WHO performs two functions. It coordinates the worldwide health network, and it nurtures technical cooperation among the health care systems of the world. Among its achievements are the global eradication of smallpox and the imminent global eradication of several other infectious diseases.

### World Trade Organisation (WTO)
154, rue de Lausanne
1211 Geneva 21
Switzerland
Phone: (022) 739-5208
Fax: (41-22) 739-5458
E-mail: webmaster@wto.org
Web site: http://www.wto.org

This is currently the only international organization whose function is to deal with trade between nations. It was created in 1995, and its functioning is directed by an array of international trade agreements that establish the ground rules of trade between member nations. It has three major goals: to encourage free trade between its members, to achieve further liberalization of trade through negotiation and treaty, and to provide an impartial means of settling trade disputes. The WTO is operated by the governments of its member nations. At present it has 131 members and an additional 29 observer nations. Decisions are made by the members as a whole.

**World Wildlife Fund International (WWF)**
CH-1196 Gland
Switzerland
Phone: (41-22) 364-9111
Fax: (41-22) 364-0074
E-mail: ddenhardt@wwfine.org
Web site: http://www.newmedium.com/wwf

The World Wildlife Fund traces its history to 1961, when it was established by a group of British citizens in Switzerland. Its goal is to halt and eventually reverse the degradation of the earth's natural environment. It is now a global network of 24 national organizations, five associates, and 26 program offices. In 1995, it had over 3,500 employees and invested over $252 million in programs in 96 countries.

**Worldwatch Institute**
1776 Massachusetts Avenue NW
Washington, DC 20036-1904
Phone: (202) 452-1999
Fax: (202) 296-7365
E-mail: webmaster@worldwatch.org
Web site: http://www.worldwatch.org/index.htm

The Worldwatch Institute was founded in 1974 with the aid of a grant from the Rockefeller Brothers Foundation. It is a nonprofit research institute dedicated to the cause of creating an environmentally sustainable society able to meet human needs in ways that do not harm the environment or threaten the needs of future generations. It pursues this goal by conducting research into environmental and population issues and disseminating the results of this research across the world. The Worldwatch Institute publishes *World Watch* magazine, the annual *State of the World* reports, and other publications.

# CONTEMPORARY ETHICAL ISSUES

## Glossary

**apartheid** The policy once employed by the South African government to keep blacks and whites separated. The policy granted essentially no civil rights to blacks and also ensured that they would remain economically dependent on whites.

**citizenship** The legal status under which an individual is a member of a particular nation. Often citizenship is gained by birth in a nation, but it may also be granted by national governments to those not citizens by birth.

**distributive justice** This concept is concerned with issues of how the world's goods, whether social or material, are to be allocated to people and institutions. In the international context, it includes issues of whether wealthy nations have a moral obligation to assist the economic development of, or transfer some of their wealth to, underdeveloped nations.

**economic refugees**   People who are unable to make a living in their homelands and travel elsewhere in search of employment and economic opportunity.

**emigration**   A person's departure from a nation to take up residence in another.

**environmental pollution**   The loss of purity and value of the earth's resources of air, water, and land resulting from human activity, including human release of harmful substances into the environment.

**environmental refugee**   A person displaced from his or her home by natural disaster, such as flood, drought, or storm, or by environmental degradation caused either by pollution or abuse of land.

**ethics**   The discipline that examines questions of what is morally right, what is morally wrong, and how human beings should behave.

**free trade agreements**   Treaties or covenants established by nations to eliminate or reduce barriers impeding the flow of goods and services across international boundaries.

**genocide**   The deliberate mass killing of a particular ethnic or religious group, with the intent of eliminating the victim group.

**global pandemic**   An epidemic disease affecting people in all the major population centers of the world.

**global warming**   A sustained increase in the average temperature of the earth. Scientists are concerned that an increase of even a few degrees in the world's temperature might result in changes in climate, which might, in turn, cause economic and political upheaval.

**globalization**   The process of knitting the people, nations, and corporations of the world more tightly together. Globalization has resulted from developments in communication, technology, and commerce.

**human rights**   Moral rights that are enjoyed by all human beings simply in virtue of their status as human. Many in the Western European intellectual tradition believe human rights are strong moral entitlements that all humans may claim at present. Others, particularly those in developing or socialist nations, believe instead that rights are goals that societies should attempt to achieve for their people. The U.N. Universal Declaration of Human Rights is presently the most widely acknowledged and influential compendium of human rights. It contains both the rights viewed as entitlements and rights viewed as goals. Human rights are distinct from legal rights, which are rights granted by governments and therefore enjoyed only by people under the authority of those governments.

**immigration**   A person's act of entering a nation with the intention of establishing residence.

**indigenous peoples**   People, generally living in small tribes of hunters and gatherers, who follow the ways of life that were common before agricultural and industrialized societies emerged.

**intellectual property**   Inventions, ideas, books, computer software, music, movie films, and similar materials that are owned by particular people or organizations. This ownership is generally legally established by patents or copyright laws.

**international ethics**   The discipline that examines ethical issues and responsibilities that span international boundaries. The fundamental question of international ethics is whether human beings have the same moral obligations to, and responsibilities for, people in foreign lands as to people in their homeland.

**international humanitarian law**   The body of laws, treaties, and conventions that regulate the conduct of war and the treatment of prisoners of war, war causalities, civilians, and noncombatants.

**intervention**   In the sense of the term relevant for this work, intervention refers to the intrusion into the affairs of a sovereign nation by another nation or by the community of nations. Though the Charter of the United Nations stipulates that the United Nations is not entitled to intrude in the domestic affairs of a state, many now believe that intervention is justified when a national government is engaged in the wholesale violation of its citizens' rights or those of a minority group.

**multinational corporations**   Business enterprises that have significant portions of their organizations located in more than one nation. For example, a multinational corporation might have manufacturing plants, warehouses, or sales outlets in several nations. A business that simply exports goods to other nations is not a multinational corporation.

**national identification**  A person's sense of being part of a particular national or ethnic group.

**national sovereignty**  The legal authority that national governments have over their people, and the legal claim these governments have to be free from intrusion by other governments in their affairs.

**nationalism**  The view that a distinct people, with a distinct culture and language, is entitled to its own nation-state. It commonly includes the belief that the citizens of a given state are morally entitled to give greater weight to the needs and desires of their fellow citizens than to foreigners.

**natural law**  In the context of ethics, natural law is the view that there is a set of moral standards, binding on all human beings, which is independent of all human cultures and legal systems.

**nongovernmental organizations (NGOs)**  Private groups that work to address civic or political issues. Most focus on only one or a few areas, such as refugees, treatment of prisoners of war, or the conditions of women. The International Committee of the Red Cross, Amnesty International, and Transparency International are examples of prominent nongovernmental organizations.

**ozone depletion**  Ozone is a form of oxygen consisting of three atoms to the molecule $(O_3)$ rather than the more common two atoms to the molecule $(O_2)$. Ozone found in the earth's atmosphere collects in the higher altitudes and absorbs radiation from the sun. Gasses released into the atmosphere by human activity bind with ozone and transform it into other forms. Loss of this upper atmosphere ozone is believed to contribute to the process of global warming.

**population control**  An array of practices, both cultural and governmental, designed to regulate the rate of human reproduction. The programs can be voluntary, relying on incentives or moral appeals, or coercive, when legal or cultural sanctions are used to attempt to regulate birthrates. At present, most population control programs aim to slow or halt the rate of population increase. However, in some cases where a government or culture's concern is low rates of reproduction, population control programs seek to increase birthrates.

**refugees**  People who have been forced to leave their homes and abandon their means of gaining a livelihood by war, political upheaval, ethnic animosity, or natural disaster.

**resettlement**   The transfer of refugees from temporary camps to a nation where they can gain permanent residence and establish new lives for themselves. In some cases, refugees can be resettled in their homelands. In other cases, where their homelands are too devastated to receive them or are hostile to them, refugees may be resettled in Third World countries.

**resident alien**   A noncitizen who is permanently or semipermanently settled in a nation.

**terrorism**   Activity generally designed to achieve some political end by causing fear. It is most often associated with small political groups, but a number of states are also believed to employ terrorism to achieve their ends. Terrorism commonly relies on physical harm, or its threat, to achieve its purposes. However, it need not. For example, cutting off power supplies or disrupting computer communication might be employed to achieve political ends by causing fear.

**war**   Sustained violent conflict between organized bodies in which each participant seeks to cause the other to submit to its will.

**weapons control**   Various measures, usually established by treaties signed by groups of nations, designed to regulate the number and types of weapons nations employ. In some cases, such as the SALT treaties of the United States and Russia (and the Soviet Union before it collapsed), arms control measures set numerical limits to the number and types of weapons each party may possess. In other cases, such as the Chemical Warfare Convention, the intent is to ban the use and possession of certain types of weapons.

# Index

Gerard Elfstrom, Ph.D., is professor of philosophy at Auburn University, Auburn, Alabama. He is the author of *Moral Issues and Multinational Corporations* (1991) and *New Challenges for Political Philosophy* (1997).